One of Bud's
and
Carol's Kids

Valloyd Becker

NEWMAN SPRINGS PUBLISHING
320 Broad Street
Red Bank, NJ 07701

First originally published by Newman Springs Publishing 2022

Some names and characteristics have been changed.

ISBN 978-1-63881-411-5 (Paperback)
ISBN 978-1-63881-412-2 (Digital)

Printed in the United States of America

Preface

There is a book called *Fighters* by Pete Hamill and George Bennett. It is a black-and-white book of pictures with minimal writing. There is a description of the chapter ahead and a paragraph about a picture you might be looking at. Other than that, it is a book of pictures. Deep, intense pictures. It isn't about superstar fighters. It is about club fighters.

There is a quote in that book I have never forgotten. I got this book when I was about ten, eleven years old. This fighter was quoted as saying, as he looked down from the third floor gym on to the street, "They ain't got what we got." Meaning the average person who has never experienced the wonderful world of pugilism.

The older I get, the more sense that makes to me. From Bruce "The Mouse" Strauss to Artie Diamond to Walker Smith Jr. to the current journeyman who either works a real job or not, trains or not, really has heart or not, if you've never been involved in the circus of boxing, you ain't got what we got.

I am a heretic in a royal blue blood family. I do not matter. I do not count. I am the cum stains on Aunt Irene's blanket. I should not have been born. I am your retarded cousin Lenny who gets high on model glue and hitchhikes all over Lorain County, and the entire family, even Great-Gram, wishes I would just die. Yep. That's me.

People have been telling me my whole life I should write a book. Why, I haven't a clue. I mean, I have a sixth-grade education, I'm a convicted felon, I'm an alcoholic, I can't call myself a junkie, but some would, my own dogs can't stand me. As retarded as some

3

women are, I have yet to find one retarded enough to marry me, and I have accomplished not one single, solitary goddamn thing in life. Not one.

Sounds like the makings of a painted masterpiece, eh?

Ever heard of Keith Moon? If not, I feel so, so bad for you. He was the drummer for this band called The Who. Moony had this, in essence, babysitter named Dougal Butler. And Dougal wrote a book about his times and experiences with Moon the Loon. At the very end of the book, Dougal says something like, "The only thing Moony did, really did, is just up and fucking die."

I am at that age and have those health problems and live that lifestyle that I could just "up and fucking die." Maybe today. So I figured I'd give that book a whirl! Before I am in an iron lung or someone has to feed and change me again. Or I lose my mind.

Ever heard of a twelve-step program like Alcoholics Anonymous? They have these two steps, the fourth and fifth, where you write down every god-awful, mean, rotten, selfish, hateful, stingy, greedy thing you've ever done in your life, and you share it with another human being. That, in a nutshell, is the fourth and fifth steps of Alcoholics, and I'm certain many other, Anonymous groups.

I'm not saying I belong to Alcoholics Anonymous or any other anonymous group. If I did, and I was, I wouldn't be upholding the anonymity part of the program up very well, would I? I don't belong to any programs. The only program I belong to is the one that pays my bills and affords me the wants and needs I am able to indulge in. I have been to five rehabs throughout the years and am quite familiar with the linking of the words *anonymous* and *program* together.

The gist of these steps is to cleanse your mind, body, and spirit and become a more wholesome useful human being. It is not to show where others wronged you or fucked you or screwed you over. It is about you.

Ever heard of that book *A Million Tiny Pieces*, something like that? Guy was the biggest crackhead Christ ever saw, lost everything, disowned by everyone, homeless, the whole ensemble?

Guy cleaned up, wrote a book, Oprah had him on. His book flew off the shelves faster than shit out of a bird's ass; guy got everything back, it's a great fucking story, really!

Ah, that's what it was, a story. A made-up, fake, fictional story. Ever heard of that used condom, cum dumpster, sack of monkey shit, liar, liar, pants on fuckin' fire retard that wrote that book? I took it real personal when it came out this sack of shit is a fraud.

Either way, I am not that smegma pie piece of shit. This is my life. Anything I say can be proved through court records, newscasts, newspaper articles, witnesses, and however else people prove shit nowadays.

Yes, witnesses can lie. First of all, people are too goddamn dumb to lie. Second, there are people on this planet who hate me so much they wouldn't lie for me if it benefited them a billion fold. I promise.

People like Jennifer Smith Niskey. Jennifer Smith Niskey, to this day, has got to be one of the most stinky, fake, plastic, gross, ovulating pig cunt I have ever met. She wouldn't lie for me if it turned her into a human being. Really.

J Dub, you didn't always hate me. Actually once the stinky cunt showed up, all things in your life went south quick, brah, so I was told. Let's just say, I heard you weren't happy at all with your choice in life partners. Got yourself a stinky sack of shit, J Dub. Sorry, pal.

Let's not talk about the stenchy cunt you married right now. Let's talk about being kids. Remember 1975 through, like, '80? How old was I, seven or eight? How old were you, guys, fifteen, sixteen, seventeen? Remember the whiffle ball games in your backyard?

Remember the hardball games at the Legion? There was you, Donny Hause, Mark Mahar, Tommy Dunlap, Rat, Brian, Mark's older brother played with us and bought us beer, those guys come to mind quickly. Remember those days?

You guys were driving there, and I rode my sister's pink Huffy every day to play baseball with you guys. You remember that?

First time you and Mark Mahar took me up there to play, everyone laughed at you guys, remember? Then they hit me flies and grounders and made me bat, remember that?

I do. Like it was yesterday. Seven-year-old kid playing baseball with high schoolers and not only hanging in but doing well. Remember, J Dub? Played every day after that, shortstop.

Two infielders, two outfielders, a pitcher, a catcher, and pitchers were out for first. Hit to right field was an out. And I batted left-handed! That was how I learned to place a hit, playing with you guys, and hit fast pitches that weren't controlled by the Bud Man.

Remember guys getting pissed because a seven-year-old was hitting their curveball? I do. Remember them hitting me the next time up 'cause I got a hit the time before? I remember you beating someone's ass for nailing me with a pitch. Can't remember who it was, but you had my back.

Remember when I brought Scott Silvasi with me? He was the second-best player on my Rainbow League team, the Purples; he was nine, I was eight, and you guys hit him some grounders and flies and said he couldn't play, not to bring anyone else my age anymore. Remember that, J Dub?

Who lived in that blue-and-white house on the corner of Elyria Avenue and Shupe Avenue? You and Tommy Dunlap used to get me stoned in that garage before we'd go to the Legion to play ball, remember that? Remember your mom busting us smoking weed in your garage? No more weight room in the garage after that! I was nine. You were a freshman or sophomore.

Remember the basketball games at Central, Donny's dad, Mr. Hause, used to let us in Saturday mornings? If he wasn't there, we went straight to Marble Manor to get the keys. Again, how old was I? Oh yeah, seven, eight, nine.

Same thing there, J Dub, remember? A grade-schooler not only playing with high school kids but playing well, no?

There was a time, J Dub, when you would have bet the farm I was going to be a pro ball player or world champion. I'm not sure if you've been informed, but it is still in the works.

Don't worry, J Dub, I'm going to do my best to relive all those years, even the California years.

I blame no one for my life. As I get older, I realize by the time Jack Wayne Niskey befriended little Brucey, he was already not damaged but ruined, worthless, beyond repair, destroyed goods.

By the time I was seven, it was over. Doesn't make any sense, does it?

I mention those fourth and fifth steps of the Anonymous program because they can be some pretty deep shit, as deep as you care to get honest and put some time in delving into your life. That's been my experience anyhow.

You learn a lot of shit in these rehabs. The second time I was in rehab is my all-time favorite. I was nineteen. Place was called Lakeland Institute. After a couple weeks in detox at the hospital, they took me over to the institute part of the property.

I was standing in the cafeteria, and this Jewish girl came up to me and went, "I have an oral infatuation, and my last name really is Seaman."

Needless to say, we found a stairwell, pronto! We spent as much goddamn time in that stairwell those twenty-eight days as humanly possible, no shit!

I only saw Julie a couple of times after rehab. I'm not sure if she was able to get her horrendous pot addiction under control, but I sure hope so.

I recall getting drunker than a motherfucker the night I got out of that rehab. Woke up on Radar's couch the next morning. It was Christmastime. He came out of his bedroom with a young white kid, who he was on his way to New York with, and was surprised as hell to see me there!

I have Radar stories. They aren't really all that interesting. He was a black guy living in an all-white town. He was from Long Island—Sag Harbor to be exact—and he was an air traffic controller. His door was never locked, he always had plenty of beer in the fridge, good shit, St. Pauli Girl, Heineken, the good stuff. He always had Green Label Jack Daniels and Cognac buds hidden in the cupboard or behind the couch.

The cliques of kids that hung out there were infinite. From the hippy Martin twins, Jim and Joe, to the hipster preppy crowd of some Brad kid, and a bunch of people I can't remember the names of.

Ray tried to kiss me on the cheek once, and I was like, "What the fuck was that?"

He went, "Nothin'."

Right. Right. Nothin'!

Other than getting fucked up nine zillion times at Ray's house, that's about the only Radar story I have. Was he a pedophile? You tell me.

My objective in writing this isn't to tell stories about what a badass I am or what a survivor I am, not even sure what a fuckin' survivor is, none of that monkey shit. Not sure what my objective is. Having a sixth-grade education has led to a solid career with a hustle on a street corner. That only works when it's warm. Maybe I'm doing this because I have time on my hands. Maybe because I have questions to be answered, maybe I'm scorned and hurt, maybe I'm a vindictive prick, maybe—just maybe—I hate being lied to, and this is my way of seeking truth. Maybe this is the only way I can say my side of things that have happened in my life. Maybe I'm bored.

Any way you slice it, I did it. Here it is.

The only source I've used in the writing of this broken-down palace is my mind. I'm certain to get years, dates, states, people I was with and where, and all sorts of other stuff mixed up. Oh well. I invite you to correct me.

I invite you, Aunt Sue, to prove to me that you and that fat sissy fuck sack of shit you were married to, Uncle Charlie "Sissy Pants" Hammond, who did the entire world a favor and died, aren't the biggest worst liars ever put on earth.

Shall we?

Chapter 1

I was three years and one day old when Howard Duane Allman lost his life. I do not recall Walter Cronkite's broadcast of that horrific tragedy the day it happened, but I do have a memory that goes back that far. A little furthr (intended).

I know we lived in Wellington, Ohio, when Howard Duane died, and I know my dad had just gotten back from Vietnam. We lived in Union Street.

One night, my dad was lying on the couch, kicking his legs and arms, wailing and screaming at the top of his lungs. He had a shotgun barrel up to his chin.

I knelt down in the catcher's position with my poodle, Fluffy, next to me, and I went, "Dad, are you okay?" Every time I'd ask that, he'd scream and wail louder and harder!

What the fuck does a two-year-old kid do? My mom was on the front porch, so I went out there and had an asthma attack. She went in the house and told my dad I was having an asthma attack. He jumped off the couch and got me to the hospital immediately like nothing was going on at all. It was like he was woken up from a dream.

I was born a sickly little prick. Asthma, pneumonia a lot when young, you know, sickly little prick. Almost died more than once, I've been told.

For a lot of years after that, I wondered if me having that attack saved my dad from blowing his brains out that night, and I'd look back on that moment in my life for years and wish it would have killed me then.

From Wellington, we moved to Amherst. Oberlin Road in Amherst, Ohio. I was three. That was the first time I ever saw my Spirit Guide; his name is John, and to this point, it has been the only time.

I was sitting at this little table I had, eating cookies and drinking coffee, and this guy showed up out of nowhere in the chair next to me! He went, "Hi! I'm John!"

I told him I was Bruce, and he said he knew.

This table was for small people like me, and John was sitting in one of those chairs with his legs crossed. He didn't look or ever appear to be uncomfortable, but he sure did look funny. He was a normal-sized guy with long black hair.

I asked him if he wanted some cookies and coffee, but he said he didn't eat much.

I have no idea what we talked about, but we talked. After a long silence, John looked at me, with his elbow on the table, and his head resting against his chin, and he went, "I'll be seeing you." And he was gone.

I have yet to see him again to this day.

I have to say here, by the time I was fifteen, we had lived in thirteen different houses and apartments. My mom did always keep us in Amherst schools, even if we weren't living in Amherst. So shit gets hazy. Bear with me. However, by six, I learned not to unpack everything. I still don't.

Funny, those early years. I have an uncle say he can't remember dick about his childhood. I'd give my nut sack to be him!

I can remember being young, still in diapers, and playing catch with my dad. Every time he threw the ball to me—didn't matter what kind, baseball, basketball, football—it would knock me on my ass! I'd get up and throw it back.

One time, we were playing catch, and the baseball busted me in the face. I had a bloody nose, lip, swelling; I started crying like a bitch, and my dad went, "That's it! No more baseball!" And he went in the house. Didn't even check me out, see if I was really hurt.

What? What the fuck do you mean no more baseball? I'm two, for fuck's sake! I went in the house and asked my dad why I can't ever play baseball again. And here's the reason, as it was explained to me. "Son, you know all those great ball players you admire, Joe DiMaggio, Pete Rose, Roy Campanella, Roberto Clemente? Those guys aren't sissies, son. They don't cry when they get hit with the ball, they pick it up and throw it back. Even if they're bleeding, even if someone shoots them. Those guys are men, and when they were your age, they got hit with hammers, and men punched them, stuff like that, and they never cried. They just wanted to play baseball.

"You can't play baseball because you cry when you get hit with the ball, son. I'm not calling you a sissy, but you aren't tough enough to play ball. Didn't your mom buy you some kind of boy doll?"

We were back out in the yard in no time, and I can assure you, I took a few of Bud's changeups in the chest just to prove I was no fucking sissy!

One day, he was pitching to me, and I was bailing out 'cause he was throwing me fucking Nolan Ryan fastballs. Mind you, I'm in fucking diapers yet. How did he fix me bailing out? Nailed a pair of tennis shoes to a board and made me stand in them while he pitched his heat everywhere but the strike zone. Over my head, behind me, right above my head. Bet your ass I didn't bail out or fall down. Didn't even cry when he hit me on purpose either. I'm not fucking stupid!

The first time I ever drank alcohol, we lived on Oberlin Road. My mom's real dad (turns out he isn't; Dick Ritter from Waverly, Ohio, is my mom's real dad, so she's been told by her aunt Nellie), Charles Jones, and his son, Bubby, were visiting us from Mansfield.

My dad came home in the middle of the night with a bottle of Crown Royal still in the bag, a six-pack of Pabst, and a box of Dutch Master cigars.

My dad went in the kitchen and called me in. He poured a shot of Crown and downed it, then took a drink of Pabst and went, "That's how you do it. Now it's your turn." And he poured me a shot.

I sniffed it, took a sip, and ran and poured it down the sink! Shit was awful! My dad went, "I have a whole goddamn bottle here, and I'll pour it down your goddamn throat! Now come here!"

He proceeded to pour me another shot, and I drank it, then drank the beer, then puffed on the Dutch Masters. I never did get sick. I actually liked the Pabst. I just went in the family room and sat down on the floor.

That was my first drink. Don't worry, I didn't start drinking full-time after this. Not at all. Took five more years for that to kick in. Was it a full shot? Doubtful, but you didn't know, Bud.

Chapter 2

These early years are pretty fucked up, and they only get better, I promise. Around this time, I might have been three. We were living on Franklin Street in Amherst, and I walked in on my dad's sperm donor, Valloyd Deed Becker, raping my mom, his daughter-in-law.

Soon as I opened the door to my mom's screaming, he went, "If you don't get back outside and play, I'm going to kill you, just like your dad did all those little kids in Vietnam, now go!"

Yep. Those words came out of Grandpa's mouth, directly to me. I was fucking three. Cool grandpa, eh? Loved his son, eh? Great human being, eh?

The one thing I always had at this early age was sports. When I was still in diapers, you could throw a pop-up to the clouds, and I would catch it. The glove was as big as me, and I'd have to hold it with both hands, so if the ball wasn't real close to me, it would be hard to run and catch it. The fuckin' glove was bigger than me.

My dad's brother, Russ, and his friend Bobby Lesko used to have people over, and they'd bet them cash I could catch any pop-up they threw, and then they'd proceed to get their—turns out—beer money together because of me.

Aside from my dad going to blow his brains out on our couch, and my dad's sperm donor telling me he would kill me if I didn't get back outside and play while he raped my mom, I guess things were pretty normal for me at this age.

Chapter 3

I had an Aunt Lucille and Uncle Joe Szabo. They weren't really my aunt and uncle but family friends. I'm told Uncle Joe used to watch me often when I was an infant, and he'd put coffee in my bottle, and I'd drink it all gone.

I'm told people would get a kick out of me drinking coffee off of a spoon when I was an infant, thought it was cute and funny.

It is cute and funny. Real cute and funny. I have been drinking coffee my entire fucking life, literally.

My great-grandma on my dad's side, his cum dumpster mom's mom, Ma, was a great lady. No angel, mind you, but a great lady.

Ma dipped snuff. That powder shit you can sniff. H&B sweet snuff, some shit like that. She'd put a jaw full in and spit every now and then. I always wanted some, and she'd always let me pack my lip full. Trouble was, the shit would melt as fast as I put it in. The solution? Chewing tobacco, of course!

I spent a lot of time with that old woman when I was a young kid, and she made damn sure I always had a sack full of chew. I used to pick it out at the drugstore, Higgins. I'd decipher which pack looked the coolest and go from there. I can honestly say by five years old, I most certainly had a taste for Beechnut and Red Man.

This is like 1970, '71, '72, '73, when all this shit is taking place. My parents had a 1967 Chevrolet Impala that, when they'd be driving, I'd be in the back climbing up into the back window and rolling down into the seat.

Crazy? Bad parents? That's a great question. If I had bad parents, how did they get that way? Were their parents bad to them? Were they just bad seeds?

My mom was repeatedly raped and abused beyond comprehension when she was a kid by her stepdad, Leroy Collins, from Garrison, Kentucky. That's in Lewis County, heart of the empty belt. Her mom, Ruth, didn't care because Leroy had a good job at the mill in Lorain, Ohio, and took care of Ruth. So why would she care if her kids were getting abused? She was doing good. She and Leroy had their own kids to raise by now anyhow.

Valloyd Deed, what can I say? His wife, Dorothy, was a fuckin' beauty too. I remember being over their house at 909 Dodge Drive. Once when I was real young, and I was eating some cookies Dorothy had given me, I was already eating them over the sink, and the haggard old cunt still came over and put her fucking hands under my chin to catch the crumbs! I swear.

Valloyd Deed and Dorothy Becker, my dad's sperm donor and cum dumpster for parents, are both dead. Dot-head Dorothy had Alzheimer's for years before she signed off, and while I don't think he had a conscience, I did write Valloyd Deed about a ten-page letter and let that worthless piece of elephant shit know some things before he died. I also let him know I was available for discussion and included my phone number. I'm still waiting for him to call. Why? Because he was a gutless sack of shit with no balls and refused to accept his part in his actions. Most rapists don't. He is nastier than a pile of Don King's shit.

I've been told—not by my dad either—that by the time my dad was twelve, that piece of shit used to beat my dad with closed fists. And at twelve, my dad went to work full-time on a Pepsi truck so he could buy school clothes and things he needed. Valloyd Deed was too busy boozing, whoring, and raping women—when he wasn't abusing and bullying his kids and spineless wife.

By fifteen, my mom was working full-time at the Ohio turnpike, as a waitress, to buy everything she needed. School clothes, supplies, shoes, everything she needed or wanted, she was getting for herself by fifteen.

When I started school, we lived at Williamsburg Heights Apartments off Cooper Foster Park Road. Couple things stand out from living there. There was a cop that lived there, Lonnie Dillon, who eventually became chief of police in Amherst, Ohio. Lonnie had three stepkids: Danny, Deana, and Bobby.

I was kindergarten age, and Danny was in about third grade, fourth grade. One day we were playing outside, and Danny threw a rock through a picture window of an empty apartment, then he took off.

Later that day, Lonnie came by and picked me up in a cop car and rode me by the broken picture window and went, "See that, Bruce? Who did that?"

I told him Danny did it, and he went, "Danny's a good kid, Bruce. I think you did it."

Now at two, I saw my dad and the shotgun incident; at three, I got threatened with death by my dad's sperm donor if I didn't get out while he raped my mom, and had my first drink. Who the fuck knows what happened at four? And at five, I had a piece of shit maggot cop accusing me of breaking a fucking window his fucking step kid broke, and all I wanted to do was play fucking baseball!

Chapter 4

One really funny memory does stand out from living at Williamsburg Heights. There was this fat girl Michelle McGee, who would come over and play with me at our apartment, and the fat little bitch would steal something from me every time she came over.

I'd go to their apartment and steal my own shit back. One day, her dad asked me what I was taking, and I said it was my toy, I was taking it home. He asked me if I had a receipt. No shit, a five-year-old kid.

He proceeded to tell me that it was Michelle's toy if I didn't have a receipt, and that I had better take it back upstairs to her room before I leave. So I did.

Before I left, old man McGee told me I was lucky I put the toy back because he was strong enough to lift the entire apartment building up, and he could'a used that strength to hurt me for stealing my own toys back. I asked him to pick it up, and he said he didn't want to because there were people in it, and he could hurt them.

When my dad got home, I told him what had happened. He was working second shift at the turnpike, and he was drunk, so it had to be two, three o'clock in the morning when he came in.

He went down to McGee's apartment and started beating on the door and window, going, "Come out here, you fucker! Come pick the goddamn building up now, you fucker! There isn't anybody in it now, you prick!" Stuff like that.

Of course, that fat sack of shit didn't come out! The rest of the complex did, though!

Chapter 5

We moved to Pinecrest Apartments after I started school, so I went to South Amherst schools for first and second grade. It was during these two years I would roll paper cigarettes up and "smoke" them in class.

My teachers, both years, would give me clay to make ashtrays for my "butts." I had Mrs. Vanderwyden one year and Mrs. Can't Remember Her Name the other year. I think it was Mrs. Poplar. I might be wrong.

It is also during the time we lived at Pinecrest I discovered what alcohol can do for one's mind. There was a bottle of red Riunite in the refrigerator forever, and one day, I just opened it and took a big swig. Shit wasn't bad, so I took another. Next thing I knew, I had a pretty good alcohol buzz going!

I had never felt anything on earth so warm and all-encompassing.

It's during this time my parents got us a babysitter so they could go out. This bitch put us to bed at, like, six in the evening. She had people over, and they were partying. You know, smokin' reefers and stuff. I went out in the living room and demanded we be allowed up, and I get to hit that cigarette!

So the babysitter let me hit the joint, and we were allowed up. The next day, the shit hit the fan!

The old man came up to me and went, "They were smokin' fuckin' dope in here last night! Did you smoke any?"

"No, Dad! What's dope?"

"I'll beat your fuckin' ass I find out you did! I'll break your fuckin' neck, son! What happened to all the goddamn wine in the refrigerator?"

"I don't know, Dad. Did that babysitter drink it?"

I didn't get high when I smoked the weed. I didn't inhale it.

During this time in my life, things started going awry, and dreaming about being a pro baseball player didn't make the world go away anymore.

My dad's drinking and whoring around when I was this age was causing all kinds of problems at the homestead, if you could imagine.

At one point, my parents, my mom basically, sent my sister and brother, Sam and Aug, to live with these people from our church, Four Square. These people were named Dan and Shirley.

They lived about an hour south of Amherst, in a town called Sullivan. They didn't live in town. They lived where the mob buries people and never get found, the middle of fucking nowhere!

There were, and still are, a lot of Amish people there. I was supposed to stay with them, and I tried, but I threw fits—I mean, fucking fits to be tied!

I'd pick the phone up to call my mom, and someone else would be on it. It was a fucking party line! You were surrounded by woods and fields for miles. I was graced and allowed to stay with Mom and Dad, who now had a one-room shithole located in my Aunt Faye's building on Twenty-Eighth Street, in South Lorain, Ohio. The rationale being I was in school, and Sam and Aug weren't.

While we lived in Aunt Faye's building, my mom still took me to South Amherst schools. About a twenty, thirty-minute drive every morning. Needless to say, I missed a lot of school.

Aunt Faye "Flushie the Comody" was a real beaut as well.

Chapter 6

Here's where things get a little more interesting. While living in dear old Aunt Flushie's dump, we spent a lot of time at my Aunt Carol's house. She also lived in South Lorain, in a duplex by Southview High School, and she had four sons: Gary, Tony, Mike, and Mark.

Carol's husband at the time was a guy named Ernie Murray. She is Great-Grandma Ma's daughter. Ernie sure did like to drink and show the boys who the man was around the house. If I can't say I was fucked for life and already a toxic train wreck before, after spending time with these fuckers, I should'a killed myself then, no shit.

They were high school to middle-school aged. I was in second grade. These guys smoked dope, drank, did acid, basically, well, they are close with their Aunt Flushie, if that says anything!

I mean, my Aunt Flushie was amazing. At one point in her life, she was working at a whorehouse in Philadelphia, and she went back to Ohio to visit. She had her black pimp with her, and Pa, Ma's husband, Flushie's dad, told her to never go back there again. And she didn't till Pa died.

She ran this apartment building full of old people, drunks, drug addicts, and people of lesser abilities.

For quite a few of these people, Aunt Flushie "took care" of their money for them. That means she used to steal from them if you aren't hip to how life works. She used to steal from Ma a lot too. My mom too.

When my Aunt Flushie got pregnant with my Uncle Tyrone, out of wedlock, she said she was raped. Of course, everyone knew that was bullshit.

My Uncle Tyrone was a crazy motherfucker, and I loved him and I miss him. Owned a biker bar, loved his cocaine. He and David Alan Coe, the country singer, were good pals.

Aunt Flushie died some years ago, and I can't say anything good about her, other than she's dead. Uncle Tyrone hated her with all of his being, and he wasn't shy about letting her, or anyone else, know.

One day, we were in the Hondas, these trails by their duplex, and my cousins crushed up aspirin and rolled it in cigarette tobacco and smoked it. They said someone told them it would get you high. All it got me was a headache.

They used to let me smoke weed and drink. Taught me how to break in a car, start a car without keys, switch price tags on shit at the store—all kinds of neat stuff, these guys taught me.

Couple of them were fucking perverts too.

At six years old, my psychological makeup was shattered into fragments of complete fucking mush. And it has never returned.

How do you describe being sexually abused? I mean, is it like writing a *Penthouse Forum* letter? I don't know. I've never tried to write about it in a way for other people to hear it.

Here's a really good fucked-up knuckleball to throw in to the equation. While Tony and Mike were showing me things at their place, and we were living in Aunt Flushie's dump, we moved to Pinecrest. There was a fuckin' perv there, his name was Rick, and guess who liked to "play" sports with young boys? Yep! You guessed it, this sick fuck Rick!

As Ray Ray Gray used to say, "It's blerry, I can't see."

All I know is for two years of my life, weird shit happened, and I knew it wasn't right. I never told a single soul for twenty-seven years about this episode of my life.

I mean, I thought if I told my dad, he would beat the fuck out of me and possibly kill me. My dad had the power, with his voice alone, to make me piss my pants like a fuckin' garden hose, till I was ten. If he yelled my name a certain way, in a certain tone, the river started flowing! Instantly! And you didn't tell Bud if you were dying because you didn't want to hear how you fucked up, and "that's why you're dyin'! Now, get the fuck out of here and leave me alone, after you get me a cup of coffee! I have a goddamn headache!"

He was rarely around at this time, and when he was, I prayed and begged God—whoever that nonlistening fucker was—he'd leave real soon.

I never told my mom because, well, maybe I didn't want to hurt her; maybe I was afraid she'd tell my dad. Probably that right there. See, you didn't want Bud to find out any goddamn thing!

Finding the booze helped. I was just sitting here thinking about those days, and I smiled in my mind when I saw myself drinking that wine. Ah, childhood memories.

Chapter 7

Somewhere along the way, we had moved back to Amherst. I know I was in second grade because I went to Harris Elementary. This was 1975. Sara Smile.

My cousin Billy Collins also went to Harris. From birth, Billy and I were joined at the hip. Up till we hit junior high school, we were always together. He's my mom's brother, Bill's kid (Rumor I heard since I was a young kid on paper).

Funny thing, our birthdays are two weeks apart. He was born, I'm positive, on November 11, 1968.

As I said, I was three years and one day when Howard Duane was called to the great gig in the sky.

Raymond Berry Oakley III was called to the great gig in the sky on November 11, 1972.

I was a day over three when Howard Duane died, and Billy was born on the day Raymond Berry died, four years later.

If you don't know who Howard Duane and Raymond Berry Oakley III are, well, I have to say it, I feel for you, and I pray for people like you.

I remember when we lived on Franklin Street, Billy was spending the night with me, and I showed him how to throw your dirty cup up in the sink.

Keep in mind, we were little kids. I mean, *little*—two, three years old. I was born with multiple *abilities*. One of the abilities I was graced with is athletic ability. The second I was squeezed out, my brain said, "Let's play some goddamn baseball before we drink some beers, smoke some weed, and try to get some pussy! If not, let's fight! Fuck it! We'll fight, then fuck!"

So I was always throwing stuff, anything, garbage in a can was Lew Alcindor hitting a skyhook or Carl Yaz throwing someone out at home or Thurman Munson nailing a guy at second or Willie Pep knockin' a guy's head off with a well-placed right hand.

I was allowed to throw cups into the sink because I was too short to reach it, but they had to be plastic! Got that? Plastic cups only are allowed to be thrown in the sink, plastic! Again, plastic cups are allowed to be thrown into the sink only! *Plastic cups only!*

I got that. Had no problem understanding that. Never did throw a glass cup into the sink; to this day, I haven't. Billy, on the other hand, cannot say those words formed in that sentence.

One night, he threw a glass cup in the sink, and my mom stuck her hand in to wash the dishes, and she got a good ole gash on the side of her hand, and we all had to walk up to Amherst Hospital with my mom pouring blood out of her hand so she could get sewn up.

The shit he and I did was what normal kids that age did, I guess. They moved to West Thirty-Seventh Street in Lorain when were around this age. It was around third grade.

I remember one time, when they still lived on Oak Point Road, we were young, and I threw a cat up in the air, and my mom's mom yelled out the window, "How would you like me to throw you up in the air!" I never forgot that, and I have never harmed an animal since then.

All my life, I've never forgotten that, and every time that thought pops in my head, I always wonder why Ruth wasn't that way with her kids but she was animals? I mean, her husband was allowed to rape her daughter, but God (whoever that nonlistening motherfucker is) forbid, she let her grandkid hurt a cat. Maybe Leroy was fuckin' it too.

One time, Billy and I threw rocks at the neighbor's RV and broke the windows. We went in the garage and switched clothes, thinking they couldn't identify us, and went back out to look at our handiwork! Fucking geniuses, eh?

We were living somewhere in Amherst, and I ended up at Shupe school. Third grade. I had Mrs. Dickinson for English/history and Mrs. Games for math and science.

Up through seventh grade, I spent the night at Billy's a whole, whole bunch. I mean, I *loved* staying at my cousin Billy's house!

With my dad drinking and comin' home at whatever in the morning, wreaking complete havoc and chaos on us, who the fuck wanted to be there? Not me!

Staying at my Uncle Bill's and Aunt Irene's house was quite the education.

I mention all this shit from when I was really young. There are things I have been told about myself from multiple sources, so I know it isn't bullshit. I was speaking in full sentences with correct pronunciation of words before I was one year old, *ABCs*, shit like that? Yep, same thing. I was writing before I started school. In full sentences.

I mean, I have a recollection of the first dead body I ever saw. There was a car wreck on a curve not far from Ruth's and Leroy's on Route 58, just north of Webster Road. Everyone ran up there to see the wreck, maybe a quarter-mile.

My mom took me up there, and I remember seeing a body in a car. We were there before ambulance, fire, anything. Other people had stopped and were trying to get the people out of the car.

I just remember seeing that body lying there, and my mom went, "I hope they're okay. They look dead."

I have always wondered if that was John in that car. I was young, we had to have lived in Wellington when this transpired.

I was a vacuum for shit when I was young. I took everything in. The sad thing is, it all stuck. When everything sticks, the bad is certain to win over the good every time. It's an endurance thing.

I remember the first funeral I ever went to, my great-grandfather on my mom's side. In Lewis County, Kentucky. Christ! I was real young. I remember that old man lying in that casket, and I asked my mom, if I yelled in his ear, would he wake up?

These things that stick, some are good. I can count them on two fingers! Adults always think kids don't have a clue about what's going on. Adults are fucking retarded sacks of monkey shit. The ones I knew were, anyhow. And the ones still alive have only gotten more retarded as the years roll by. Adults fail to realize little kids are people too. And some us have a great idea about what is going on, even if we are two years old. Some of us don't forget shit, even if we were two years old when it happened.

Chapter 8

There were reprises in my young life. It wasn't all bad. One time, my mom and I went with Aunt Flushie to Toledo, Ohio, to see my Aunt Margarette; she was dying, though I didn't know it at the time. Hell, I didn't even know Aunt fuckin' Margarette! Again, I was young.

Aunt Margarette had a spider monkey named Charlie. That monkey went nuts when I'd talk to him! I'd go, "Eat your peas, Charlie!" And he'd throw them at me every time I said that! I had a ball with that little fucker that night.

The night, we headed back to Lorain. We were on I-90 eastbound, and a car came flying by us in the passing lane going west; they were on the wrong side of the road! Scared the fuck out of my mom and Aunt Flushie!

Aunt Flushie started praising Jesus, quoting the Bible, the whole ensemble! Lesson learned here I didn't know at the time was, anyone who constantly praises Jesus, carries and/or quotes the Bible constantly, and is always letting you know what a good Christian they are, well, that person, I'm betting my money, is a whore, scumbag, liar, liar, pants on fuckin' fire, cheating, lying, stealing, scumbag motherfucker, just like Aunt Flushie was.

Chapter 9

I gotta tell ya, brah, that fuckin' monkey, Charlie, was a riot! I learned some life lessons from that rambunctious maniacal maniac!

Not long after going to visit Aunt Margarette, she died. I remember we went up for the funeral, and there was this kid, probably about ten to thirteen years old, and we were talking, and he was crying. I asked him why he was crying, and he said because poor Aunt Margarette was dead and gone forever! Then he sobbed, and snot was getting all over his face, and he just cried and cried!

I never thought it was funny or comical. Actually I was sad because he was upset. I just remember thinking, *Why is he so upset?*

After Aunt Margarette died, all her stuff was divvied up, and guess who got to take Charlie home? You guessed it—dear old Aunt Faye "Flushie the Comody!"

Now at Aunt Margarette's, in the Glass City, Charlie had a house to roam. I remember it being a nice middle-class home. Charlie's cage was in the dining room, but they let him run amok in the house.

When Charlie got shipped to Aunt Flushie's in South Lorain, his cage took up the entire living room and part of the kitchen! You had to eke by that cage to get anywhere in her apartment!

One of the five senses is smell.

I haven't mentioned anything about smell in my life. Even though it all stinks, smell hasn't been mentioned up to this point. At this stage of my life, I can't smell shit. I've had my nose broken—I don't know how many times. And hopefully for the last time.

But I can still smelt this: When we were living in Flushie's building, our apartment was right next to hers. It should go without saying, I spent a lot of time with her at her apartment while my parents worked, and I missed school.

Aunt Flushie used to take the most rancid, putrid, grotesque, stomach-churning, vomit-inducing shits I have ever smelted! To this day, that dead haggard old cunt wins! This shit didn't smelt, it *smelted*! And smelted real fuckin' bad! The smelt of Aunt Flushie's shits matched her character makeup and personality.

Charlie, the monkey, living in this seven feet by thirteen feet box of an apartment, most certainly competed with Aunt Flushie in the smelly shit department! She didn't keep his cage cleaned either. Nor did she have him in diapers the way Aunt Margarette did.

I'm not sure to this day which smelt was worse, Aunt Flushie's shits or Charlie's shits. Or Charlie just being there after about a month and his cage not being cleaned, mingling with Aunt Flushie's shits and being—

Tell ya what, with Charlie and Aunt Flushie in that apartment together, it smelted worse than a decaying dead body that's been in a closet in the summer with no ventilation, for about five days in South Philly, no shit.

One day, Charlie was gone. Just gone. I hope that monkey had a good rest of his life.

Chapter 10

Around '77, '78, things are starting to become a little more vivid, a little more.

We lived on South Main Street, west side of the road, in Amherst. Mitchell's were to the south of us, Moss' were to the north.

Brad Moss. Hey, Brad, could I play ball? How's your brother, Doug? Is your dad still getting drunk and passing out in the car in the driveway the way he used to when I was eight, or did he grow out of that?

How old were you? You drove. Brad, I've never forgotten you. I mean, all you did was play sports with me. Every day. Never wanted to see my dick, never tried to get me high or drunk, taught me words like *hoo-ahh* and *doy*. I'd like to take this time to thank you, Brad Moss, for being a good dude to a troubled young soul. I hope your life has been, and continues to be, nothing but a big long float from titty cloud to titty cloud.

Old man Perv, on the other hand, used to stand in the windows, first and second floors, naked, and whack his pee-pee. No shit.

Now I only saw this a couple of times. Needless to say, I never stuck around to enjoy the show. After going through the shit I had, we just had to move next to another fucking pervert! I did say something to my mom, and it did stop. I'm not sure what was said, but it stopped. As I got older, I'm sure she told him if it happened again, she was going to tell the Bud Man. Looking back, I think old man Perv had it hot for my mom, not me.

My cousin Jimmy Melon and his older brother, John, lived on the same side of the road as us, about five, six houses up. Jeff Sang lived a couple of houses before them, same side of the street. Jeff is Jimmy's age. They were pals. They were in about seventh grade.

There was a big hill in their backyards. We used to sled down Jimmy's, but Jeff's had woods in it. This was 1977, '78. That song by Samantha Sang, "Emotion," was topping the charts, and Jeff's mom had the 45 spinning every goddamn time I went in that house! And I was in that house a lot!

She played that fuckin' song so much I asked Jeff if they were related to Samantha. He said, "No. My mom just loves the song!"

Couple things about Jeff when he was this age, thirteen, fifteen. The fucker ate sugar sandwiches. A piece of bread loaded—I mean an anthill full of pure fuckin' white sugar, folded over, no-second-piece-of-bread sandwiches!

I was eight. I had never even conceived this before! First time he did it in front of me, he asked me if I wanted one. Fuck! Yeah! I wanted one! Give me thirteen of those cocksuckers!

I bit into that sugar sandwich and couldn't wait to spit that nasty god-awful shit out of my mouth! As sweet as it was, it was as nasty as one of Aunt Flushie's shits!

Something else stands out in my mind about Mr. Jeff Sang. He is the first person to ever get me stoned on reefers and show me how to do it right.

It was summertime, and he took me in the woods behind his house and went, "Let's get high." And he pulled out a half of a joint.

I, being the experienced stoner I was, retorted, "That isn't going to be enough, do you have more?" Jeff said we would smoke that first, and if we needed more, he'd get it.

He lit that fucker and handed it to me, and he said, "Hold it in as long as you can after you hit it."

So I did, and I'll tell you what, after about two or three of those hold-it-in-as-long-as-you-cans, I was fuckin' stoned like I have never have been to this day! Holy fuckin' Christ!

What did we do after getting stoned in the sanctuary of the woods in Jeff's backyard? We walked to Keidrowski's bakery uptown, on the corner of Church Street and Park Avenue, and we each got a jelly donut.

Jeff made me pay for them. He said he supplied the weed, so I should buy the munchies. As soon as we walked out the door, he threw his half-eaten jelly donut on the windshield of a parked car, and I started laughing so hard I had to sit on the curb, and I was choking on my fucking donut! You'd have thought I was on acid.

Early memories of getting stoned. Once I was over my cousin Jimmy's, and he got me high, and he said to me, "You have to listen to this album!" And he put on ELO's *Out of the Blue*, and he said we had to listen to the entire album and not talk.

We were in this little room in his basement, smokin' weed and listenin' to this album, and I was seein' pink elephants and shit, and well, it was a pretty fuckin' trippy experience for an eight-year-old! A little prewall, I guess. The room was so full of dope smoke you couldn't see in front of you.

Jimmy's parents were devout Four Square Church members, as well. Most of the Becker clan were. How they didn't smell that weed, I'll never know.

Jeff Sang, I've been told, is an air traffic controller today. I hope he isn't smokin' anything more than reefers guiding those big birds across the sky! Jimmy is a union truck driver. Hasn't smoked in years and thinks Foreigner is a great band. I don't hold that against him.

Chapter 11

When I was in kindergarten, or first grade, my mom noticed I didn't like to go to school a certain day of the week, and she couldn't figure it out, so she went to the school with me to see what the problem was.

Turns out, they had me in a special class on this day of the week. It was a class for kids with coordination problems. They said I was uncoordinated because I couldn't color between the lines' worth a monkey shit.

My mom proceeded to tell them that I was far from uncoordinated, that I didn't color between the lines because I hated to color. Never liked it before I was in school, didn't like it after.

She told them to get me a basketball. So right there in Mr. Hooker's office, at Shupe Elementary School, they brought me a basketball.

I started spinning that ball on my finger and going through the entire Harlem Globetrotter bit. Dribbling between the legs, rolling it up one arm, down the other without fucking up, behind the back shit, the entire ensemble of tricks you could do with a basketball.

They took me out of that uncoordinated class immediately!

Once I was in third grade, it was a different kind of class for special kids.

One day, Mrs. Dickinson called some names out and said, "You boys and girls will be going with Ms. Whoever today! You are going to have fun! Fun! Fun!"

There were a bunch of us that went with a bunch of other kids, and we took these tests. Seems like it took all fuckin' day, and it seems like these tests were impossible. I mean, whatever it was, it was pig Latin to me!

Next thing you know, they sent a letter home to my parents saying something along the lines, "Your son is a bona fide goddamn genius! He scored whatever on this fucked-up test we gave him, and he is in excelled, advanced, microstudy college course future-world-leader classes."

I'll never forget when my dad read that letter that my mom handed him, he went, "Bruce, I sure am proud of you."

I remember thinking, *I am way, way too goddamn motherfuckin' stupid to be in classes with all those smart kids! Brian Affolder, that fuckin' doctor's kid, fuck! Me? Nah.*

For some reason, they kept me in them, though.

Chapter 12

Now during my time in Mrs. Dickinson's class, I met a friend, Bryce Rogers. Bryce was cool as fuck.

One day before venturing off to school, I smoked a joint and got stoned as fuck. I had never done this before, but I had a joint, and it seemed like a good idea. Had to be from Jimmy or Jeff. I still remember, it was rolled in a pink paper.

As I walked to school, across the creek in the woods and out the other side to the neighborhood where the school was and my cousin Danny lived, I was super paranoid! I just knew everyone was going to know I was high on dope!

I walked in the school and sat down in class, and Bryce and I were talkin' before bell, and I had to tell him.

I mean, it's like when you're on acid, and you're the only one on acid, and nobody knows you are wiggin' balls. Ya gotta let someone know where you're at so you have a copilot. Make sense? Not if you've never done acid, it doesn't.

Anyhow I told Bryce I was stoned as fuck on weed, and I didn't know what to do, and I knew everyone knew, and I was gonna get killed because they're gonna tell my dad, and they're gonna call the cops! All kinds of crazy shit, I told Bryce.

Bryce got in his backpack, pulled out his lunch bag, and gave me two cookies and went, "Eat these, Bruce, and you'll be fine. I get high. I get my weed from my sister, where do you get yours?"

I ate those cookies, and Bryce was right. All was well!

He and I got high together a couple times before school in third grade, but it was far from something we did regularly. Need I say, as we got older, we did more than smoke a joint or two together?

The first time I got caught with a pack of cigarettes, it was third grade. Had a pack of Kools in my locker, and someone ratted me out. I remember my cousins telling me menthol cigarettes got you higher after smokin' weed, so I lifted these Kools off the old man and got nailed with them, probably, that day.

Chapter 13

Now during these days of scholastic enlightenment at Shupe, and smokin' dope with Jimmy and Jeff, I was learning other things at night at Billy's house.

By this time, my dad had given up on selling mausoleums and was selling cars, which he would do, for the most part, the rest of his get-out-of-as-many-as-I-can working days. And he was living the Playboy life, and his family came in about fourth on the list, at best.

My mom was a waitress at Brown Derby eventually, and she did that, double shifts, every day till she was hired by Wrigley Chewing Gum Co., then Philip Morris Tobacco Company, as a sales rep.

The things that happened at, I believe, 2737 West Thirty-Seventh Street in Lorain, Ohio, were just, well, they were just my life.

Lynyrd Skynyrd's *Street Survivors* hit the shelves on October 17, 1977. It was on the shelves one week before it was pulled, and the album cover was replaced. I was almost nine.

The original had the band members standing in flames, and then a week later, the plane crash. The replacement cover was just a black cover with the same picture, if I'm not mistaken.

I bought a copy of the original right there at Discount Drug Mart on Route 58 in Amherst, Ohio! Sure did!

Maybe a year later, fourth grade, Billy and I went to an all-night skate at Skate World. You could skate from 8:00 p.m.–8:00 a.m.

After we got there, I hooked up with some guys, and I got drunker than fuck!

The next morning, after we had gotten picked up and taken back to Billy's, I passed out on a bed in Billy's room and woke up in his brother, Tommy's, room.

I was sleeping with an electric blanket, and it caught on fire, and I had no recollection of that at all, none. They told me I also puked my guts out on the floor. All over the albums I brought over. Guess which one was on top? It was ruined.

They took me outside and showed me the mattress and box spring, they were burnt toast. To this day, nobody has ever mentioned me drinking during this scene in my life.

There was Billy, Tommy, Michael, and Michelle, Uncle Bill and Aunt Irene's kids.

As I've said, Billy and I were inseparable. I spent the night there a lot.

Bill and Irene were always going out, so there was always a babysitter. Usually Irene's sister Brenda, or her other sister, Ruth Ann.

Billy would fall asleep like he was shot dead by eleven o'clock, every fucking night! I mean, we'd make a pack we were gonna stay up all night, and this fucker'd be out before the news was on!

Bill and Irene had a full-sized pool table in their basement. They also had a refrigerator down there full of beer and other goodies.

We spent a lot of time playing pool. I mean, ask Ken Barlow, they called him "Stick" at the Odyssey, in Amherst. It was a game room. He was in high school—again how old was I, J Dub? Oh yeah, eight, how good a pool player I was.

Now there's good and bad in everything. Pros and cons, this and that, the good side and the bad side of things. This here and that there, as haggard old cunt Aunt Flushie used to say.

Staying at uncle Bill and Aunt Irene's had its tradeoffs. I mean, at our place, we never had to ask for shit. If we had bags of candy or chips or a carton of soda (pop) or ice cream, or anything to eat or drink, we didn't have to ask, we just ate and drank the shit till it was gone.

At Bill and Irene's, you were allowed water. I mean, they always had cases of Pepsi (remember the eight-pack returnable bottles?) and tons of shit to snack on.

However, that was for the adults. Kids need water and dinner when it's cooked.

I'm not saying Uncle Bill and Aunt Irene malnourished their kids or me. I'm just sayin', it was different than wherever I was calling home at the time when it came to the goodies. They did have Kool-Aid, but you had to ask, and the answer was usually, "No, water is better for you, go get me a Pepsi."

Speakin' of askin' people for shit, do you have any idea what it's like getting a cup of coffee out of someone when you're two, three, four years old? You'd have thought I was askin' these fuckin' people for a gram of coke!

"Would you like something to drink, little Brucey?"

"I sure would! I'd love a cup of that coffee you just made!" In my mind, I'm thinkin', *That shit doesn't smell anywhere near as good as my mom's, and it looks weak as goat piss, but I sure would like a cup.*

The responses were always the same—"Coffee! You're way too young to drink coffee! How old are you, three? You must'a saw something on TV to want coffee!"

"Coffee? It's eight o'clock at night! You'll be up all night!"

"Are you crazy? Your parents will kill me if I give you coffee!"

If you can think of something to say to a young kid, two, three years old as to why they shouldn't drink coffee, I can assure you I have heard it.

I used to tell them to call my mom or dad, it was okay, I can drink coffee. I know by five, I made good and goddamn sure to have my mom tell whoever was watching us it was okay for me to drink coffee anytime I wanted it. I could make my own. Remember the percolator pots you put on the stove?

Now Bill and Irene were not coffee-drinkers at all. Not even a cup when they woke up. They were, however, drinkers of spirits.

Chapter 14

Billy's *After Dark* was quite the scene for me. Ever heard of Earth, Wind, and Fire? "Fantasy," "Serpentine Fire?" If not, and you're my age, you started missing out on some wonderful things early in life, brah. This was the shit, brah.

Bill and Irene, as I said, would go out just about every weekend. And they used to go out separately every weekend.

I'm not saying anything about them, I'm not calling him a horndog or her a ho-ho. I don't judge.

I have a real gross story. I've never told Billy about this. I mean, I've only seen my cousin Billy once in over thirty years. That was at my Uncle Reese's funeral. He died at around seventy-two from smoking too much crack and fucking with those young hillbilly crack whores.

True story. After Aunt Wanda died, he started smokin' crack! He was as country as anyone you've ever met, known, or seen in a movie. Farmed tobacco his whole life in Lewis County.

I saw Billy in Vanceburg, at the funeral home.

I have nothing against him, hell, we've been blood brothers from like three on. Remember that, Billy, when we slit our fingers on Oak Point Road and became blood brothers for life while we were getting our skit together for the gong show?

But this involves him, and it is fucking gross!

One night, when staying there, everyone was asleep—everyone. I was in the living room listening to music, and someone pulled in the driveway. It was Irene. I hurried up and acted like I was sleeping, and she came in and called someone on their fancy push-button phone. Whoever she was talking to on the phone at that hour of the night was a real, real close friend, because while they were talking, Irene went, "Oh shit! I gotta run out and get that blanket out of the car before Bill finds it! It has come all over it!"

She came back in and put that come-filled sticky nasty blanket over her son, my blood brother cousin Billy. When she got off the phone, she left again.

I mentioned being taught some things by my cousins Mike and Tony and Rick, the pedophile, who lived at, or near, Pinecrest Apartments on Middle Ridge Road.

I gotta say this. This fucker was a teenager. He had long blond hair. For the fucking life of me, I can't remember his last name. I do remember he couldn't play baseball or basketball worth a fuck. He was as nonathlete as my sissy gutless turd uncle Charlie Hammond. The only sport he played was called How Much Can I Eat at Once?

One day, after this piece of shit started his faggot pedophile games with me, I got sick to my stomach. Really. I did. Not like this was my first cock rodeo.

I've never been stupid, just innocent. Even if it was a brief faint wisp, I was, at one time, innocent.

This scum fuck, one day, while he was trying to play basketball with me, started touching me on my ass. Ya know, the old that a boy! Shit ball players do when they hit a home run or score a big basket? Did it quite a few times. Made me uncomfortable as fuck, and I even told him so.

What did he do? Laughed it off and said some shit like, "Sorry, accident." Whatever it was.

Now I remember him playing catch or basketball with me just about every day. Or I'd be ice-skating on the pond, and he'd come out and stand on the edge of the pond. This went on for a while.

One day, we were walking back into the parking lot of Pinecrest, and there was a little building there for the kids who actually went to school, to stand in out of the elements while they waited for the bus. Was basically a shed.

Rick got me in there and went, "If you do this, it will be doing us a lot of good." And just like that he asked me "Suck my dick and be real, real gentle, please."

I took the head of that motherfucker's dick in my mouth and bit down as fucking hard as I possibly could.

He was screaming and wailing like my dad was on the couch with the shotgun up to his chin that night in Wellington! I looked at him and said, "Is that okay?"

Rick never asked me to suck his dick ever again. He never played catch with me or watched me ice-skate after that either. Sick fuck.

Chapter 15

Now this cocksucker bullshit is going on right around, right before, the Billy's *After Dark* scenario plays out in my life.

I'm not sure if you're aware of this, but my dad's dad, Valloyd Deed Becker, was the nastiest piece of shit I have ever or will ever meet. No matter how long I float in life's sewer, I will never meet anyone as nasty as that pile of fuckin' goat shit. And I've met Don King.

Once, I was in eighth grade, had Mr. Satorious for history, we were given an assignment. There was a choice: you could do a family tree, a history on your roots, or you could write like a two, three-page paper on any president of your choice.

I went home and told my dad I needed to know all I can about our family because of my project. He went, "Just do the paper on a president. Nothin' you need to know about your family. It's fucked up. That's all you need to know." Somethin' like that.

What's fucked up about my family, Dad? Peter August Becker was Valloyd Deed's dad. Pete was a big man, I'm told, six feet something, three-hundred something, big man. Used to take his lunch to work in a peck basket. When he died, they had to bury him in a piano box because they couldn't find a casket big enough.

I never knew Pete, he was dead before I was born, doesn't matter. From what I've gathered, he was a real piece of shit as well.

It's my understanding Peter was a deacon of the church. Four Square Church, right there on Cooper Foster Park Road and Terra

Lane in Amherst, Ohio. One of the finest most God-fearing human beings ever to grace earth. So myth would have it.

I've been told Pete wasn't a drinker, but he was an eater! I was also told some other things about Peter August Becker.

Peter took his job as deacon of the church so seriously, he was always on call for the people at the church. Especially the women. During the day, while the men were at work, Peter would have his son, Valloyd Deed, drive him around to the parishioners' houses—because he didn't drive—and Peter would fuck all the women. That is all I know about my sweet dead great-grandfather.

That's the stock I come from.

Chapter 16

What were you doing when you were nine? I was going to Billy's *After Dark*.

I remember getting real sick one night. Ruth Ann, Billy's aunt, was babysitting. She was married to a guy named Ted.

Well, this one night Ruth Ann was watching us, she had a guy named Terry over, not her husband, Ted. Terry was doing his best to get his dick in Ruth Ann in the family room. I was downstairs playing pool, and I came up the stairs and opened the basement door, and there was Terry's hairy ass, up and down, up and down on the couch.

They didn't really act scared or surprised or anything. Terry just went, "Somethin' wrong?"

I said, "Not really. I was just bored."

So he went, "Look, there's a whole bunch of little green bottles of beer in the kitchen refrigerator, help yourself to a couple and go back down and shoot pool, and I'll be down in a bit."

The little green bottles of beer were Little Kings. I ended up drinking seven of them, and while Terry and Ruth Ann were in the heat of a fuck in the family room, I went up those stairs, opened the door, and puked my fuckin' guts out all over the goddamn place! Right in front of them! *In the Long Run.*

Sure did! She told me I had to clean it up. I didn't. It was carpet too. Light-blue carpet.

I did get in trouble for that. My mom was told but not the Bud Man.

45

This is just the kind of shit that went on at his house. I mean, when his cousin Brenda would babysit, she'd always have this hot girl with her named Ada.

These girls were in junior high or high school, and they taught me all kinds of stuff I've been trying to practice daily since!

Looking back, I wonder if this was sexually abusing a kid? I mean, I was already fucked with by three pedophile faggot sick fucks; I was nine, ten at the time. I already knew I liked pussy. Getting to taste the fur pie was a lot, I mean, *a lot* more fun, pleasurable—you name it!—than my cousins and Rick and their dicks being displayed!

Looking back, staying at Billy's and all this perverted shit going on probably saved me from a lifelong struggle about my sexuality. Thank God, whoever that non listening motherfucker is!

I mean, I in no way intend to write a smut letter here, but I have some questions! Hopefully I pray to God (whoever that nonlistening motherfucker is), even if I know you and hate your guts, I pray to God (whoever that nonlistening fucker is), you were never sexually abused as a kid or adult. I don't hate anybody, really. It burns energy to hate.

But I gotta say this, a couple of the fondest memories I have as a youngster are Brenda's big tits smothering my face and Ada What's-Her-Last-Name telling me to "do it here," harder while she sucked the pee-pee!

Chapter 17

Fifth grade. Ten years old. The start of a friendship that would end in death at nineteen, and the start of a long, long walk down a dead-end road. I started boxing amateur.

One was to be my sidekick in some of the dumbest most retarded, ignorant, stupid shit I ever did as a kid. The other was a long strange ride. I'm still trying to put a finger on the latter. All these years later, it still gnaws at my innermost being.

Kenneth Paul Carney Jr. "Call Me Ken, Not Kenny," you fuckin' dirt ball!

Mrs. Timm's class. Central school, 1980. No need to worry, I'm still in some of those brain-buster classes!

The intricate details of our initial meeting are as follows: First day of school in fifth grade, there was a science project set up in Mrs. Timm's class. Had these little rockets, these rocks, you know, science shit, and Kenny got caught stealing some rocks, and at recess, he accused me of ratting him out.

Now he had no clue who I was, and I had no clue who he was. Went like this, he accuses me of ratting him out, and I tell him to fuck off, I wasn't a rat. He pushed me, and I hit that fucker with a left hook to the body, and he crumpled and moaned and cried and couldn't breathe, and I thought I killed him.

He was tall and skinny, and I knew a body shot would crush him. It did.

That very same day, at that very same moment, on the playground, we became friends. Real pals.

Now I don't know what you were doing in fifth grade, but we were doin' shit most kids in fifth grade weren't! Kenny lived on Naragansett, over by Kmart. As a matter of fact, he lived right by Williamsburg Height Apartments! Hey, I lived there!

There was a Clark gas station on Cooper Foster Park Road that Kenny used to hang out at all the time and smoke cigarettes when we met. The guys that worked there, I remember a Greg, would take power shits that competed with Aunt Flushie's! And he and a bunch of other guys would give Kenny and me smokes and beers and weed. I remember a guy who worked there was complaining his jaw hurt; he'd been in a fight the night before. Kenny and I were eating Burger King and asked him if he wanted any. He told us to fuck off. Turns out, his jaw was broken.

By the middle of fifth grade I was trying to get a feel for if I was gonna be able to get some pussy off Billy's babysitter or should I stay at Ken's?

Again Ken's parents went out every weekend. His dad was a drummer in a band, and they gigged every weekend. I suggest, if you're a parent, maybe, just maybe, you should quit whoring around and stay home with your kids and raise those little fuckers right! Just a thought.

Kenny's dad, Ken Sr., was an architect and his workroom was in the bottom of the house off of the family room.

The entry to the garage was off the family room as well.

We spent all of our time in that family room if Kenny's parents weren't home, and in his room if they were.

Kenny's dad always had political aspirations; he wanted to be the county engineer. He eventually became Lorain County's engineer, and I believe he still is some thirty years later.

Kenny's dad was always throwing some type of party somewhere. I mean, always. He had case after case after case after case of every kind of liquor you can think of in his workroom.

As soon as his parents would go out, the party was on!

Did I mention Kenny's babysitters? Wow! They were as cool as Brenda and Ada! I mean, there was Tina, Gena, they'd have friends come over. Good times.

In the garage at Kenny's was the pool table and the Corvette. We played pool on the table and used to get the weed and Coke out of the glove box in the Corvette.

Neither one of Kenny's babysitters would let us do the coke, but they'd let us smoke the weed and drink. God (whoever that non-listening motherfucker is) bless them!

Chapter 18

There was a time, when I was a young kid, my dad's sister Susie and her boyfriend/husband, Charlie, would take me a lot.

They did all kinds of stuff with me. Took me to Cedar Point, used to take me to a lot of places. Used to let me stay at their apartment whenever I wanted. I mean, it was as if I had a place to go when the shit got really weird!

They knew a lot of what was going on. They knew Valloyd Deed raped my mom, they knew my home life was fucked.

Trust me, these fuckin' people are not normal. I mean, they went from treating me like I was their kid to treating me like a hardened criminal—at five, no shit. The instant they had their daughter, Erin, I was discarded and told something like, "We have a family now, Bruce. But we'll call you!" Kinda like a nice Lonnie Dillon speech.

No big deal, right? I mean, get over it, you fuckin' baby!

It shouldn't have been that devastating to me, but it was. I mean, looking back, I was five years old, and I needed help, and the people helping me turned their backs on me, a five-year-old kid, because they had a kid. Oh well.

Please understand, as I've gotten older, I realize they wanted me nowhere near their precious child because I was Bud's and Carol's kid. I am grateful they abandoned me because through the years, Charlie's sissiness was sure to rub off on me! And I no doubt would have acquired their shitty ability to lie.

You have never met a sissy like Charles Gene Hammond, I promise. This fucker was as big as an offensive lineman, fucking huge. He wasn't in-shape huge, he was a big fat blob of shit, the eat-and-eat-and-eat-and-eat fucking huge. Strong as a fuckin' ox and scared of a girl in pink panties, really.

Every motherfucker with the Becker gene is eaten alive with some kind of *ism*. My dad's sister is eaten alive with the obsession of eating more than anyone ever has before! And lying. At these times, when I'd stay with Susie and sissy Charlie, if they ordered a pizza, they each ordered a large. Susie would get eaten up with guilt, just like an alcoholic. "I bought a dozen Dunkin' Donuts and hid them till everyone went to bed, then ate every one of them!"

Charlie owned a Texaco gas station for a spell in Oberlin. That's about twenty miles south of Amherst. I would go there with him and help him work; it was never fun. Me, being as young and inquisitive as I was, did not understand Uncle Sissy.

I mean, he hated Greek people. He hated the entire Greek race because Susie had gone out with a Greek guy one time before they started dating. Didn't fuck him, so she says, just went out with him. He wanted to drink beer, not eat. So, Greek race, sorry, you all suck 'cause Susie Becker went out with one of you once before Charles Gene Sissy Pants Hammond got to ride that heifer!

He used to call Susie from work and have her hold on while he went out and pumped gas. Then he'd come back in, and they'd continue on with their conversation.

The calls were long distance, and they couldn't figure out why he was losing money at the gas station! And they call me stupid. Go figure.

There is no way in hell there would ever be a fair, honest, open discussion about anything that ever happened when all this shit was going on. I've tried. Honest. Multiple times.

So I figure I'd get my message across this way. See, I really don't know these people. Haven't known them in over forty years. I never knew Erin. Looking back, Aunt and Uncle Fat Ass were afraid I'd be a bad influence on their daughter because I was Bud's and Carol's kid.

I'm okay with that. Have been for years and years now. I'm grateful for that as well.

Susie has always been a soap opera slut and a talk show slut. *Oprah, Dr. Phil., Donahue, Jenny Jones*, shit like that. I would love to get that stinky cunt on Dr. Phil!

My first question would be, "Why, when Bud was beating the shit out of me, did you not help me? Why, around that same time, instead of helping my mom with us kids, after she had knee surgery, did you call Children's Services on her, saying we had no food, no clothes, no nothin'? The only thing that accomplished, after they came in and saw we did have everything, was get my mom a lady from there to come help with us kids. You tried to fuck my mom, and it backfired on you, you stinky lying cunt."

Susie would never admit to any of this shit because she is a liar. She is also a devout Christian. It's the Aunt Flushie connection. Right here and now, I offer the opportunity for her to meet me any-where and have a discussion about anything that takes place in this fragmented rag known as my life.

Sue, you are a nasty stinky cunt, really. A fake plastic monkey cunt. An ovulating monkey cunt, and you are nastier than one of Charlie's shits. I almost forgot, you are a liar too.

Now I don't know much about their son, Ryan Barrett (I was named after a TV character) Hammond, at all.

But let's delve into this stud's life. What I know of it anyhow. His dad got him a job at Ford. Sissy Pants Jr. had to start in Michigan. Eventually he'd gotten back to Ohio, the Avon plant. He couldn't move to Michigan because it was too far from Mommy and Daddy's house. So he commuted the two and a half, three hours every day from Mommy and Daddy's house in Amherst. Needless to say, he didn't keep the job long.

Been a few years ago, I was in Amherst. I was walkin' in a bar, and I saw coz Ryan standing outside, smoking a cigarette. He made sure to let everyone see him smokin' that butt. Then as I was walking in the bar, he went, "Please don't tell my mom and dad you saw me smoking. I'll get in trouble."

Twenty-seven years old and afraid to get caught smoking fuck-ing cigarettes by his parents! I was smoking in front of my parents at fifteen. I was in rehab, someone had to bring them!

Cuz Ryan sure has let me know through social media what a badass he is. He told me, on some kind of social media site, that he was sorry my boxing career didn't work out. Being a wiseass. Of course it didn't work out. I didn't win the title, make millions, and afford the amounts of cocaine Michael Dokes used to buy! I was a club fighter.

I had 131 amateur fights, and I had 27 pro fights. I was 116–15 as an amateur and 15–12 as a pro. I was stopped six times as a pro and twice as an amateur.

Not very impressive by any stretch of the imagination. I do, however, have a question for my gutless sack of shit cousin, who was named after a TV show character—how many fights did you have and win, or lose? How many times have you been on national TV?

The height of this piece of shit's athletic career was playing Little League baseball in Amherst, Ohio, where he rode pine, got to play his three outs in right field, and got to strike out once a game. Maybe he scored a couple walks in his career.

This fuckin' sack of shit, who was too goddamn spineless to work a job three hours from Mommy and Daddy's, has the balls to say my dad was a water boy for the real soldiers in Vietnam.

My dad was a first lieutenant in the army. He was with MACV Team 45. Fucker did his year over there in *the shit*. Far from a sissy, Ryan, was my dad. You have him confused with yours.

I will give this little spineless nut sack some credit, though. He didn't turn out to be a big fat blob of shit like his parents and sister. Fucker is a bean pole, looks anorexic. The reason for this is he has always been embarrassed because his parents and sister look like Divine, remember her, the actress? The egg lady?

His sister is an outright fucking genius, so I've been told. Makes cake, tons of it. Successful yuppie, Erin is. She's also in her forties and still plays with Barbie dolls and has tea parties the way she did when she was young.

The only reason I know all this is because her mom tells people this shit!

Speaking of Vietnam. There's this family from somewhere in Indiana, their dad's name is Bob, Mr. Bob Jernigan. I remember going to see you guys when I was real young. Every time Mr. Jernigan talked to my dad, he addressed him as sir.

Every time Mr. Jernigan did that, I would laugh and go, "That's my dad, not sir!"

And every time I said that, the one time I really remember him saying it, stressing it home to me, he was sitting in his easy boy in the living room, and it was dark out. It was early 'cause it seems like his kids were getting ready for school, and Mr. Jernigan called my dad sir, and I laughed, and he had a heart-to-heart with me.

I do not recall it verbatim, but I do know he told me that he and my dad were closer than my dad and I, and he was alive because of my dad, and my dad was always sir. Did I understand? As Mr. Jernigan was saying this to me, my dad was just sitting there, watching me listen to Mr. Jernigan.

Kinda like the watch-up-the-ass scene of my life.

Not long after we got back to Ohio, my dad got a letter in the mail saying Mr. Jernigan had died. My dad never talked about Vietnam, about as often as he spent time with the family. That wasn't very often, if you haven't figured that out by now. He did, however, let me know, if it wasn't for Mr. Bob Jernigan, he said he'd have been dead in less than two weeks over there. He also told me Mr. Jernigan did two tours, and while he didn't die *in* Vietnam, he said Vietnam killed Mr. Jernigan.

I hope and pray Mr. Bob Jernigan's kids and family have had nothing but happy, prosperous, joyful lives. And continue to do so.

Chapter 19

Now there was an incident in my life that let me know exactly where I stood with all these people. When I was in first grade, and we lived at Pinecrest, my dad came home drunk one night and beat the living fuck out of me. I couldn't go to school for, like, three weeks because the swelling was so bad. Got a new pair of boxing gloves out of the deal, though.

My mom had just had knee surgery, and she couldn't walk. We lived on the second floor. Bud came home drunk one night, and I either woke up to piss or was already up. Either way, he beat the living fuck out of me. My mom somehow got down the stairs and went to Valloyd Deed and Dot Head's house, less than a mile up the road. Valloyd Deed didn't want to get involved. Next stop, Fat Fuck's apartment, another mile away. Charlie didn't want to get involved. Next stop, my mom went to her sister's and husband's, Aunt Sharon and Uncle Jim's house, on Oak Point Road, same one Bill and Irene lived on, about five miles out. Uncle Jim Hollingsworth came to the rescue!

One night, when I was sixteen, and my parents were getting a divorce, I was lying in my bedroom trying to drink myself to oblivion, and it wasn't working. I took a walk over to the Fat's and got them up in the middle of the night. Told 'em I had to talk. I asked them why they refused to help me when Bud was wailin' the shit out of me, and they both looked at each other like, *Wow! Where did that come from?* And they both said my mom never stopped at their house that night.

Then Charlie no-nuts leaned to Sue and went, "He's drunk. He'll never remember this anyhow." And they said my mom never stopped there—she, my mom, was lying to me.

I remember, you fat fuck. Hey, Sue, remember me telling you and Debbie that the reason we were born is to do what we can while we're here, while you two were discussing life in the car? How old was I, one, two? We were on fucking Broadway in Lorain, by a clothes store.

Chapter 20

Life at Central was a fucking blast! I mean, having to get in three fights a day because everyone wanted to beat the boxer up. No one ever did. It was a blast. Even the losers.

These were my junior and senior years, looking back. I mean, the Dirt Ball Gang was formed. Deana was letting me get sticky fingers behind the stage in the gym. I remember Mary Beth playing that game too, with me. Darlene comes to mind. These girls were, I guess, slutty, but they couldn't compare to Billy's babysitters or Kenny's babysitters. I mean, c'mon. I haven't even gotten to my babysitters yet.

The three original Dirt Ball Gang charter members were Ken Carney, John Maroney, and me. We used to ride our BMX bikes to school every morning and go uptown behind Third Base Inn in the alley and smoke our cigarettes and weed.

Then we'd go to the school and play animal ball on the basketball court till bell. Animal ball didn't last too long before the principal made an announcement it had to stop because it was too dangerous.

It was basketball with no rules, and you killed the guy with the ball. People were getting concussions, broken arms and legs—shit got pretty nuts! Of course, not everyone wanted to play. I mean, Rob Zeim, Brad Riggs, the Dirt Balls, Nick Horvath, Bryce Rogers, David Gray? Yeah, they played. Let's just say, it was a rather violent game, and not all chose to participate, and it didn't last too long.

One time, I got a detention for fighting, and my dad asked the circumstances of the situation. After explaining to him what happened, he wrote on the back of the detention I was not going to serve it. My mom called the school and told the principal, Mr. Currier, I would serve it, ignore the note.

Well, after school, I went in the library and gave my slip to the detention hall monitor; it was Mr. Simpson, the special-ed teacher, that day. He asked me who wrote the note on the back, and I told him my dad did. He asked me what my dad did for a living, and I told him he sold cars. Mr. Simpson went, "I wouldn't buy a car from someone like your dad."

Now I kept everything from Bud, everything. Except shit like this! I told the Bud Man that night what Mr. Simpson had said in front of the entire detention hall class.

The next morning, Bud went to school with me. We were in Mr. Currier's office when Mr. Simpson came through the door.

My dad said something like, "What the fuck is wrong with you, you goddamn motherfucker!"

Mr. Currier immediately said to me, something like, "Bruce, I think us adults can handle this, you can go to class now."

That day, Mr. Simpson came up to me and apologized and asked me if my dad was always that way. I invited him over, but he never came.

Things I remember about these years aren't anything special. I mean, Kenny and I were doing shit high school kids did.

Chapter 21

In 1981, I won my only national boxing championship. "Let's Get Physical." I never won another. From 1981–82, going from twelve to thirteen years old, every bit of confidence I had in my being left me. I mean, to this day, I can't figure it out. It's like, one day I was sitting somewhere, and every single solitary thing I had witnessed and experienced up to that point in my life hit me right between the fuckin' eyes *hard*. "All of My Love."

I got to seventh grade and was completely lost. My nose was all red from zits, and people thought it was from boxing. Oh yeah, another three fights a day because everyone wanted to beat up the boxer. No one ever did.

As far as the scholastic part of this year, till I left school, I never tried to learn, not one new thing. If I couldn't get it on the first try, fuck it. Here's where things get a little more fun than not, though, in-the-moment fun anyhow.

I have mentioned some pretty nasty cunts in my life up to this point. I must say here, the smell continues. There were two secretaries at Nord Junior High. Mrs. The Old Lady I Can't Remember who was a pleasant kind person. And Linda Carnes.

She was a mean hateful cunt. To certain students, she was as pleasant as summer's eve. But to others, like me? What a douchebag cunt is all I can say to the memories I have of Linda Carnes.

I flunked out of seventh grade at Nord. I got suspended a lot for fighting. We were getting high and starting to get drunk before school. Not every day, but it was something we did regularly.

Everyone used to stand at the end of a dead-end street and smoke right by the junior high and high schools, but it was off school property, so they couldn't do anything.

My mom was a sales rep for Philip Morris by now, and I used to sell sample packs of Merits, Benson & Hedges, Marlboro at the guardrail before school for a quarter a pack, six cigarettes a box. I did okay at that.

We moved to Sheffield Lake, about twenty minutes east of Amherst, for my second stint in seventh grade.

I was fighting amateur and doing okay. I mean, I would beat anybody in a fight. If it was a fight show. If it was a tournament, I always, like almost always, made it to the semifinals or the finals. I always knew before each and every one of those fights, I would lose because I didn't deserve to be a champion.

Chapter 22

We moved to Sheffield Lake, Ohio, in 1982, I believe. It was my second have at it in seventh grade. I was as miserable as any human being ever has been on earth without killing himself, I promise.

Carl "Stuff" Griffith lived in Sheffield Lake as well. He fought amateur and went on to have a pretty good pro career. We were always friends, even though he fought for Tom Gray in Lorain, and I fought for Jim Kelly out of Cleveland.

I went out for the football team, and right away the coach was sayin' shit like, "You ever run track?" We had to do a mile a day, and I and this other kid, a skinny hippy long-haired dude, Jimmy, would lap the entire team and be done way ahead of them.

In all honesty, I remember this prick beating me every day by more than a few steps. He'd beat me by like, ten, fifteen seconds every day. The prick! That was the only reason I'd show up at football practice, to run and race him. We never said we were racing each other. It was an unsaid understood thing.

No. My football career at Sheffield Middle School didn't last too long. I fought every day I was at that fuckin' school. I'd come off a suspension for fighting and get in one that day.

I swear, I never went looking for fights. I never started fights.

Some fights that stand out at Sheffield Middle School bother me. I mean, there was this kid, David, and I beat him up in the locker room during gym class because he had bumped me hard, and I thought he did it on purpose.

If I could, I would apologize to him today and do anything in my power to show him I am sorry for that, to this day. I mean, I realized by that night it was an accident, and I was a thug, asshole. I just couldn't let anyone know I had feelings.

This cat Scott and I got into it in the hallway. That always bothered me because I knew he hurt like me inside. I could just sense it. He came by my house one night, and we were gonna fight in the street, and we ended up shaking hands.

Jerry Palmer I remember because one, that was the big one! The one that got me expelled from school! Jerry was in eighth grade and had a full beard. The day we fought, I was running home. I used to take the road to the railroad tracks to my neighborhood, and this big old Cadillac slammed on the breaks, burned rubber, and this big burly monster went, "I'm gonna kill you! Jerry's fucked now!"

To this day, I have never run so fast! I hope Jerry didn't get fucked too bad, and I hope his life is whipped cream and titties today!

Chapter 23

I didn't know I was being expelled. But my dad was home one day and went, "The school called me today at work saying you need help, and you aren't ever welcome in that school again, ever! What the fuck happened?"

I told him I got in a fight, that was that. We were in the process of moving back to Amherst, so I didn't miss any school, thank God! Now when we got back to Amherst, it was like I never missed a beat. It was springtime, and school was almost over, so everybody'd hang out after school and do whatever kids did that age.

My friends and I tended to smoke weed, you know, drink beers and booze, stupid shit thirteen-year-old kids do!

One day, not long after being back at the confines of Walter G. Nord Junior High School at all, I mean, the fuckin' door hadn't shut when the gossip was abuzz! "Hey, Becker, Adam New is gonna kick your ass! He wants you bad, Becker!"

Have I mentioned the Becker new saga thrilla trilogy embarrassing beatdowns?

To this day, Adam New is at the top of the list when it comes to retarded people I've known. The high school wrestling coach named the practice dummy Adam. For three years in Little League, he was my catcher on the Beavers, and he was always nonconfrontational, and we got along. Those same three years always turned into Adam wanting to beat Brucey up during the school year.

I honestly don't remember the first tiff we had. I do know I cracked him and drew a little blood.

The second go-round is a little more memorable. It happened my first stint in seventh grade, in Mr. Reed's physical science class. Adam hit me in the back of the head, and I turned around and cracked that fucker right in the goddamn mouth, and he started bleeding!

Mr. Reed came over and grabbed me by the arm, and I hit him in the face. Not hard. I mean, I caught myself, but I hit him, and he had a look on his face of complete fear. I was scared because he was scared!

Mr. Reed did not like me. He looked exactly like the cartoon character Wally Walrus. He had this big white beard, he'd pick his nose, and put the boogers in his beard, and he'd dig them out with his lips. It was fuckin' gross!

Now after moving back to Amherst, and all the buzz about Brucey gonna get a beatdown from Mr. New, it happened.

It was springtime, and after school, Shane Rapose and I went to the cemetery across the street from Hastee Tastee and O' Armour's Hot Dog Heaven and got stoned on some refers.

We all know what comes after that. We walked over to Hastee Tastee, and I got myself the biggest twist cone they had. I probably got two. As Shane and I were enjoying our delicious Hastee treats, who came along but Mr. Adam New with a couple of girls.

I said to Mr. New, "Adam, please quit fucking with me, please. I have no desire to beat your ass again, really."

He retorted, "You be at Bobby Benson's party tonight, and I'm gonna kick your ass."

Never had anything against Bobby Benson. Hell, he was on my Rainbow League team! I had spent the night at his house during that time and pissed the bed. Didn't do it on purpose, just did it in my sleep. Sure. I was embarrassed as fuck! Never stayed at Bobby Benson's ever again.

As we grew a little older, we drifted into different social groups. There was the preppy clan, and us burnouts were called freaks. Then there was the frock. He was the dude who played sports and got high and drank. He was a freak and a jock.

I was a freak, and Adam was a preppy. Me going to that party would be like a gay priest going to a swinger's club in his priest garb. Just wasn't going to happen.

As we're having this discussion, Mr. New pushed me up against Hastee Tastee, and I mean, he pushed me hard. I came off the wall and hit him with one right hand, and I knocked out four teeth. Blood was gushin' out of his mouth like a river. He had braces, and his mouth was a mess. I asked him if he cared to scrum anymore, and he said no. I got my swirls from Shane, and we walked to my house. We lived on Harris Street this time. That was that.

That night, my dad was bringing me home from the gym, and we passed Rapose's house. There was a cop car there, and my dad went, "Wonder what Shane did now?"

I knew Shane hadn't done shit other than hold my ice cream cone! Soon as we walk in the door, my mom went, "The cops were here looking for you, Bruce."

"What the fuck is going on now!" the old man bellowed so goddamn loud they heard it in South Amherst. I proceeded to tell the old man what happened, and he went, "We better get a lawyer."

I was fourteen years old and charged with my first crime, I think—felonious assault. The end result wasn't bad. I never went to any kind of court for anything. My parents ended up having to pay $100 restitution. Aside from the jillion I'm sure the lawyer cost, that was it.

From that day to this, Adam New has yet to fuck with me again.

Chapter 24

I never went looking for fights. I mean, there were a few times in my life at this age, I hurt some people I felt really bad for, because after thinking about it, my reason for getting physical with someone was when they put their hands on me in a threatening way, and when I'd reflect, I'd see where Darryl Hoover, or the kid from Sheffield Lake, David, were probably just scared like I was, and meant nothing by the physical contact they made with me. To this day, I feel bad for that.

On the other hand, there are some people I have had to scrum with and felt pretty goddamn good during and after the humiliating ass whippings I gave.

Dan Carnes. Remember that stinky cunt I mentioned earlier, Linda? Danny Boy is her beloved son! One day after school, I was cutting through the locker room to go out the back of the school toward the guardrail and home. Remember, I sold sample packs of cigarettes, had to get my money.

As I was going through, Dan Carnes was in the locker room with a grade school kid, and they were the only two in there (pretty weird now that I think about it). This little kid, I mean, he looked like about a third, fourth grader, went, "Come here, I wanna tell you a secret."

So I leaned down, and the fucker started pulling my hair like it was some kind of see-how-hard-you-can-pull-it toy!

Dan Carnes went, "My mom told me to fight you and pull your hair and kick you and beat your ass, not boxing either!"

All I can think was, *Where the fuck did this come from?* I mean, I had never had any issues, run-ins, nothing, we never even said hi, Dan the dickhead Carnes and me. Now he's telling me his cunt mom told him to pull my hair and kick me? What the fuck?

Sometime after this, Stuff was spending the night with me, and we got drunk on a bottle of Wild Turkey and went uptown of Amherst to Danny Boy's Pizza parlor to hang out, like kids our age did. As we were literally walking out the door, who was walking through the door but Dan Carnes himself!

I confronted him, and he was telling me he didn't want to fight, he was sorry he had that little fucker pull my hair, blah, blah, fucking blah, fucking blah! I had a good alcohol buzz going, and I was in the zone.

Let me paint a picture for you. At fourteen, I fought at 125 pounds. Dan Carnes was as big as a tight end or linebacker. Him next to me was like me next to that asshole kid he had pull my hair. Big size difference.

As poor Dan gave me his countless reasons for not wanting to fight me, I kept reminding him what he told me his cunt mom said, and I was here, and now for you to kick me and pull my hair and kick my ass to kingdom come, and not boxing either!

This went on for some time, and we ended up in the Amherst Hospital parking lot with a crowd gathered around. I egged this dickhead on for a long time, and he refused to touch me.

Finally I told him, I went, "Look, if you apologize to me and address me as Mr. Becker, it's over. We can let this go." Danny Boy said he couldn't do that, and I cracked that fucker right in the mouth, hard.

I let him know he was not going to get away with having a third-grade kid pull my hair, and he was going to suffer some consequences. I thought I was being fair. I mean, call me mister, and it's over, and you can't do that after what you did to me?

He said, "I apologize, Becker." Probably three times, and every time he did, I cracked that fucker, hard. After about the third shot, Dan went, "I'm sorry, Mr. Becker."

Being a little pissed it took so long for him to see the light, I told him he had to get on his hands and knees and say it. He said he couldn't, so I cracked again. Didn't take long at all, and I had Dan Carnes on his hands and knees, saying, "I'm sorry, Mr. Becker. I'll never do that again."

When he stood up, I hit him again and told him he was a sissy for being a bitch and not finishing the problem he started. And to this point in life, he hasn't. Not to me anyhow. I've only seen him once as adults, and it was when we were in our early twenties, and when he saw me walk in the bar, every bit of life in him left. You could see it. He didn't say he wanted to fight, pull my hair, kick me, nothin'. He walked out before I had a drink in my hand.

Chapter 25

I never went looking for shit like this. It just seemed to always follow me. I was much more interested in having a good time. By the time we were in seventh grade, when Kenny and I drank together, we always each had our own bottle.

I am so well aware of how ludicrous, insane, so much full of bullshit, and downright what a goddamn lie that sounds like. I promise. All I can say is, ya should'a been there and poked around, please.

School in eighth grade was a stellar year. I mean, something I might have forgotten to mention before now is John Maroney's sister was in high school when we were in junior high. Laura. She drove to school. John had a key made to her car and he, Kenny, and I used to ride around every morning before school and smoke weed and drink beers. High school homeroom was 7:45 a.m., junior high was 8:45 a.m. We had an hour a morning to learn how to drink and drive.

This fucker John would pass school buses when it had its flashers on, lay on the horn, flip the bus off as we passed, and throw fuckin' beer cans out the window and then fly up the road in a residential neighborhood.

How we never got caught, I'll never know. We'd get to school, and people would be talking about us everywhere.

Parties. All kids go to parties, no? There was a time when I was in eighth grade, my parents were split up. My dad went to work on a Monday, and about two months later, he called wondering if he could come home. He was in the state of Delaware, with some skank named Phyllis, and the party got old, I guess. He wanted to come home, and my mom asked us kids what we thought, and we said not to let him come back. She did.

During the time the Bud Man was in Delaware, my mom had to go to Richmond, Virginia, for a week for a conference for work. She's a sales rep for Philip Morris at this time. I took a note to school saying I was staying at Ruth "Rufus" and Leroy "Reroy's" in Wellington, and there was no way that the old rapist or his douchebag wife could get me to Amherst every day for school. So I'd be missing that week. I told my mom I was staying at Chuckie Boesel's house that week. He lived uptown, across the street from Wyvill's Texaco station.

I stayed at home for that week and did absolutely nothing but drink and smoke weed with every burnout from junior high and high school.

Darious Phillips' mom worked at the Lawson's store uptown. Mrs. Phillips worked there for probably fifty years, literally. She may still work there. Darious would come over every morning with a dozen eggs, a pack of bacon, and a case of Genesee Cream Ale and Boone's Farm wine that he'd stolen out of Lawson's. He'd leave for school, and through the day, it would start, people knockin' on the door. Tony Roberts, Brian Meyers, Kenny Phillips, Darious's brother, Chuckie Boesel, Kenny, and all his Dirt Ball friends, people I had never met before.

I never had more than two or three people in at a time, and we were never loud or did anything to bring attention to the house.

I remember a Sunday during this weeklong party that was just a total blowout. I mean, there were three of us, Kenny, Chuckie, and me. We had bottles of booze and cases of beer. We drank our balls off all day on this Sunday.

Here's how my mind remembers things. It was the Sunday that NBC *Sportsworld* showed the replay of the Salvador Sanchez-Wilfredo Gomez fight.

Kenny was upstairs in the bathroom, dry-heaving into the toilet while sitting on my mom's makeup bench, swearing up and down he was okay. He had his bottle of Mr. Boston vodka sitting next to him, and he was swigging between heaves.

Chuckie and I decided to go for a walk after the fight ended. Soon as we got up Harris Street and turned right on Cleveland Avenue, I hit an uneven part of the sidewalk and fell flat on my face. I mean, flat on that fucker, no cushioning the fall at all. I didn't feel a thing. We both laughed. We made it to Wyvill's Texaco station about two blocks over, and we were talking to the guy working, Brian somebody.

Chuckie hung out at Wyvill's when we were kids. He lived right across the street above Charlie's Bar. I gave Chuckie a bloody nose there; we were probably four or five years old. Bud Man worked there, and he had taken me up, and he encouraged us to fight, so we did. Busted Chuckie in the nose, and it was over.

We're in the gas station talkin' to Brian, who was also an ambulance driver, and he's tellin' us stories, and this guy came in, Hank Sharp, who knew my dad, and we talked for a minute with Hank, and we got the hell out of there.

Brian later told me Hank Sharp told him he couldn't believe how punch-drunk I was at that young age! I was so wasted drunk I couldn't walk, and this prick thought I was that punch-drunk fifty, sixty amateur fights into my career! Funny.

I had nine green garbage bags full of nothing but liquor bottles, beer bottles, egg cartons, bacon packs, and emptied ashtrays in a week. I cleaned the living shit out of that house, and when my mom got back, she never noticed a thing out of place.

Chapter 26

There was a point, somewhere along the line, during this part of my life, I decided I was going to move to Philly and be a garbageman. I couldn't even accomplish that.

Somewhere around this time, we were thirteen, fourteen, we started driving regularly. Kenny's mom and dad split up, and he ended up staying with his dad.

The story Kenny told me one day in school is as follows. He said he couldn't stand his mom's boyfriend, Jerry, and after an argument, he told her it was him or Jerry. He said he got home from school the next day, and his shit was packed.

Personally Kenny's mom, Dee, was a nice lady, and I doubt very seriously she picked Jerry over Kenny. She told Kenny to cut the shit and quit drinking and doing drugs and get his fourteen-year-old ass together was what happened.

And Kenny said, "Fuck you! I'll live at my dad's, where I'm basically on my own!"

The babysitters were long gone, and it was a free for all. I mean, you have to understand, Ken Sr. was a playboy's playboy. The architect with aspirations, you understand. He had quit hiding the coke and weed in the Corvette eons ago. As we got older, we got more and more greedy with Kenny's dad's drugs, and he didn't like that!

His old man put dead bolt locks on his bedroom, workroom, master bathroom, and all the closets in all these rooms.

It did not do him one bit of good at all! I mean, this fucker had six, eight locks on all this shit before it was over, and he never kept Kenny out of anything ever, not one fucking time! Up till high school, we had a grand old time on Ken Carney Sr.!

Kenny would go, "Fuck it! Watch this, peckerhead!" And he'd just bust the goddamn door down completely!

His dad was never around. Kenny's grandparents had like, a 1974, maybe, Plymouth Duster, I believe, and they ended up putting it at Kenny's house for room in their driveway. Kenny finagled a key from his Uncle Jim, Ken Sr.'s brother, who lived with his parents, and we were set.

We drove everywhere. On weekends, we'd go to Cleveland and cruise around downtown. I trained on Thirty-Fourth and Superior, and there were a bunch of little stores and bars; The Wicked Witch was one of those bars. We'd go in there and drink. We'd also use food stamps to buy beer in the stores. This was back when food stamps were paper money. Six-pack of Pabst cost you $10 in paper food stamps back then.

My family wasn't on food stamps, and Kenny's sure as hell wasn't. They were easy to come by back then.

We would get all fucked up and head the thirty miles back to Amherst before his dad got home.

Something that always confused me and totally fucked me up about Kenny is, he played the drums, but his favorite musician was Ted Nugent. His favorite drummer was Bonzo.

Aside from the Cleveland trips, Kenny'd pick me up during the week late at night, and we'd cruise around and drink. There were times when we were at Nord, he would drive that Plymouth to school and park it in the high school parking lot. Of course, we'd end up skipping and riding around all day.

Chapter 27

Kenny's house wasn't the only rodeo in town. There was "Trigger's", as well. His mom and dad went out every Friday and Saturday night, and they never came home before daybreak. His dad claimed stake in a redneck bar called Still Country, or some country shit like that. Right there on Route 113, just west of 58.

This was like my eighth-grade year. Me being a failure, I got to get acquainted with the younger kids. Trig's parents were the most amazing people ever! I mean, did you know any parents when you were fourteen, fifteen who not only bought beer for the kids but bought kegs of beer for the kids? Barry and Mary did.

Every weekend, for like two straight years, was a blowout, bash, barn burner, brew ha, ha, fucking drink fest with a bunch of junior high and high school kids.

I mean, his parents should have been put in prison for destroying young lives! I'm just kidding. His parents did have a sour taste in their mouths because of me, so I was told. After I got out of rehab the first time, I was over at one of Trig's bashes, and someone told me his parents didn't like me there because I was a bad influence because I was an alcoholic.

Trig never told me that. His parents never told me that. I remember being over there and watching Bramble beat Mancini. I had just gotten out of rehab and wasn't drinking beer, I was drinking near beer that lasted probably a weekend.

There was some crazy shit that went on at Trigger's house! I mean, sexually, holy fuckin' Christ! Gena, Kenny's old babysitter, would have a line of guys out the door and around the block waiting on their turn for a blow job! She wouldn't let you fuck her. She had a boyfriend in Florida, and she said sucking dick reminded her of him.

"Mighty Slidy" earned her nickname one night, when she fucked every guy in the house, some of us more than once, and was lying in Barry's and Mary's waterbed begging for more!

Of course, I was the one blamed for the cum stains on their bed. I mean, Bar might have had a chat with all eight or so of us. But if he did, he did it individually. In my case anyhow.

Of all the things that went on at Trigger's house, two things stand out. The first is calling Kenny early in the morning. It was summertime, and the sun was just coming up, and everyone in the house, even Mary and Barry, were sleeping. There were probably five to ten kids there, sleeping, Super Slidy being one.

There was at least a half-keg of beer left, and I was up drinking and called the Dirt Ball. He answered, and he told me I had to get to his place, right now! Immediately! I tried telling him I was sitting on half a keg of beer on ice, but he'd hear none of it! He insisted I get over to Naragansett, pronto!

I took Slidy's car because the keys were out, and so was she, like a light! We're talkin' like a mile here. I had no license. I wasn't allowed to get one. I got over there, and he took me to his room, and Kenny lifted the mattress of his bed, and under it was nothing but money!

He proceeded to tell me how he was hangin' out at Clark the day before, and he saw the key to the safe sitting on the shelf, and he took it. He went back that night and used a glass cutter to cut a piece of window out, got in, opened the safe—*bam*! He scored like $6,500 cash! We took the change—box weighed a ton—and drove Slidy's car to Oak Point Road and ditched it in the weeds as we drove. Then went back to Trig's and called Eddie Cantu.

Eddie was eighteen and still in school. He had a '73 Mustang that was blue with the big white stripe from front to back. It looked bad as hell! Fucker was a four-banger, and he told everyone it had a

283 Cleveland in it! Bucket seats. Passenger's was broken. Held up from back with a board.

Eddie, Kenny, and I went out to the Cleveland airport and got a hotel room and partied our balls off! We were ordering beer room service; one of the bellhops told us he could smell the weed as soon as he got off the elevator.

That was about the only joy I got out of that stolen money that summer. Kenny had fun. One of the things he did was take about $4–$5 large of that money and bought a '67 Le Mans, and totally redid it. I mean, motor was brand-new, transmission, he had a Pioneer stereo in it, shitload of speakers, top of the line, you could reverse sides of the cassette at the push of a button, new rims, everything inside and out. The only thing it needed was a paint job.

Ken and I were on probation at this time, and part of our probation stipulations was to have no contact with each other outside of school grounds, during school hours! That meant we couldn't call each other, nothin'! Yeah. That worked. Sure. I wasn't allowed to get a driver's license either.

Terry Yepko was our probation officer, and I ran into him one night in a bar when I was in my early twenties, and he remembered me, and we had drinks and talked. He said he wasn't a PO anymore, but he said in the time he was, he dealt with thousands of kids, and he could count on one hand the number of full-blown alcoholics he worked with, and Kenny was one.

Funny how all this ties in. The LeMans, Trigger's, probation, karma gods showing us what stealing gets you, even if you yourself didn't steal it but were partaking in the festivities of stolen goods. Just a wonderful fucking lesson every sixteen-year-old kid should learn.

I gotta tell you the LeMans story before I tell you what placed us on probation. I mean, this is funny! I spent the night at Trig's one night and called Kenny, and he came over in the LeMans. He had Gary Luman with him.

Kenny wasn't crazy about hangin' with the crowd at Trigger's, so we left. I got in front (bucket seats), Gary in back, and Kenny drove. We went all over Lorain County, literally. For hours we rode around and got fucked up. From Gore Orphanage to the Amish Country, where Sam and Aug stayed with Dan and Shirley.

Gary Luman had a way of pushing my buttons, and after hours of this shit and drinking and listening to Iron Maiden through the stereo, loud, I slapped him across the face, and Ken got pissed, and we were all gonna fight, and I was dead, and fuck you too.

We were on our way to Cleveland when this argument started, and I told Ken to just take me back to Robbie's. It was only like one, two in the morning, and all the lights were off, door was locked, strange.

I got back in the car with Ken and Gary. Gary had gotten up front and was going to let me have it back, but I said I would ride in back. We turned left out of Hidden Valley subdivision, onto Oberlin Road heading west, and there was a sharp snake curve right there. Kenny nailed it, and we were flying. It was drizzling steady out. Had been for a while. Then we were up on the bridge over Route 2, then he was pumping the brakes, and we hydroplaned right into an oak tree where Oberlin Road dead-ended into North Ridge Road, right by Penton's Market, almost across the street from where I lived as a kid and saw John!

When I came to, Robert Plant was wanting his lemon squeezed, and Kenny was sitting in the middle of the road laughing, and Gary was lying on the passenger side of the car, in the road, with blood all over him, and he was unresponsive. I thought he was dead.

Kenny was making no sense. I told him I had to go, that I was going back to Robbie's to call an ambulance. I told him we weren't supposed to be together; we'd get in trouble. He said okay, then once I started running toward Trigger's, he was screaming to come back. I didn't.

There was a car coming, and I hid behind some trees until it passed. I was a Bronco. It stopped. How ironic; turns out the guy who stopped and helped was also named Carney! He was a shop teacher at Marion L. Steele, our high school. No relation to the Dirt Ball.

I got back to Trigger's and started bangin' on the door, and Barry was like, "We're all in bed! Come back tomorrow!"

I'm screaming, "Bar, I gotta call a goddamn ambulance! Seriously, c'mon!"

He opened the door and asked me what the hell was going on, so I told him, and he said, "Someone has stopped by now. Don't call an ambulance, lie on the couch."

I hit the liquor in the living room closet as soon as he went back to bed.

The next day, when my mom picked me up, and we were heading home, we were at that very intersection, and my mom went, "Look, someone hit that tree!"

The entire side of my body was screaming, *No shit, Mom!*

Needless to say, the car was trashed. Gary, turned out, was okay. Seems like I remember they thought he might have had head trauma but didn't. I know I partied with him again after the wreck, and he was the same old Gary Luman to me! Kenny was okay, as well.

Chapter 28

This had to be '85 because the Christmas of '84 wasn't normal. Not even by my family's standards.

I spent the night at Ken's one night, and we started drinking, and I told him, in passing, that we should go to New York City for New Year's Eve this year and watch the ball fall. This was about a week before Christmas.

Well, I got fucked up that night and passed out in Kenny's bed. I don't remember passing out, all I remember was that prick waking me up, refusing to let me sleep!

"C'mon, you peckerhead, let's go to New York!"

"Kenny, fuck you! I'm tired!"

"C'mon, you fuckin' dirt ball, peckerhead, fucker! We're going to New York! My old man is passed out cold! Let's go!"

So I got up, and we planned our trip to the big city! Basically we took a boom box (the Plymouth didn't have a tape player), a shitload of tapes, some food, a couple of cases of different types of booze, the sack of weed from Kenny's dad, a film jar full of hash, and a freezer bag with the white powder in it.

We also had a knot of cash from his dad, some credit cards, and checkbooks we had come across, and the all-important thermos full of coffee.

The first stop when we left was my girlfriend's house, Bindy Chesterwood. I was mad at her, so we turfed her yard. Kenny was driving and lost control and ended up going across the street and getting stuck in the neighbor's yard. I got us pushed out, and we were on our way!

As we're driving a couple of hours, the sun was coming up, and I started to feel nervous about the situation we created, and I told Kenny we should go home. He went, "Fuck it! We're already in trouble, just stay drunk, and you won't care!" So I did.

Now what you have are fifteen, sixteen-year-old kids driving a stolen car, higher and drunker than any two people have ever been on cocaine and booze, neither with a driver's license, and not a fucking clue as to what they were doing!

It took us three days to get to New Jersey. It's a nine-hour ride! The first day we were on a highway, and we kept seeing the same signs over and over and over and over. We finally got off and went to a gas station and asked this big burly hippy kinda guy in bib overalls, how to get to New York.

He went, "You guys are jerkin' off in the wind! It's a billion miles that way!"

We had spent the better part of an entire day going around in a goddamn circle! We were on some kind of bypass in western Pennsylvania/New York region of the world, I think.

We stopped and got a hotel room, and I washed my clothes out. They were covered in mud from when I pushed us out of Bindy's neighbor's yard, started in on a fresh bottle of vodka, and passed right the fuck out!

The people at this hotel were looking at us funny when we checked in. I mean, we probably looked nine or ten years old! Kenny had all these credit cards, he had his dad's driver's license, and knot full of cash.

At this time, we had been on the road for two days.

That was the best sleep I got on that trip. We woke up some time in the night and contemplated our next move. Ultimately deciding, after some mind-enhancing help, it was best we be on our way.

To this day, I remember him and me sitting at that little table, in that shitty room, seeing who could do more rails and take bigger swigs out of the bottle before we left. By the time we left, we were feeling anything but pain.

Soon as Kenny backed out of the parking spot, he started laying rubber and trying to do donuts like a fuckin' retard!

To this day, I'm not sure where we were. Sussex, Bergen, Warren County? No clue. We came upon a huge bridge, in the mountains, that connected Pennsylvania and New Jersey. There was no toll collector, just a basket to throw the fare in. So Kenny threw the change, in and we started crossing this bridge.

As we're crossing this bridge, we both smelled something horrible! It was toxic-smelling, take-your-breath stinky, shit! For a second, we thought it was New Jersey, till we realized we were in the mountains!

It smelled like the car was overheating. So as soon as we crossed the bridge into Jersey, we got off at the first exit. We were waiting on a van to pass so Ken could turn left into a gas station. When he started to turn, the car jerked, stopped, made a loud bang, and flames started coming out of the hood.

Not huge monster-engulfing flames but flames flickering through the cracks of the hood. The smoke was what was bad. Thick black stinky smoke.

Two teenage kids, high as a motherfucker on cocaine, well above the limit of comatose in the blood alcohol department, and now what? We both got out of the car. Kenny was just standing there. Awkward moment, really.

I walked into a diner, sat down at the counter, ordered a cup of coffee, and started looking at a menu. Everyone in the diner was oohing and aahing about the car on fire in the road outside; I pretended it didn't interest me.

Needless to say, I probably didn't have my cup of coffee yet, and the cops were in there, asking me if I'd mind going outside for a minute.

These cops were questioning us, and we're telling them we were headed to the city to see some family for the holidays, been a long trip—you know, the shit they wanted to hear. "No, sorry, no ID, we both lost our wallets!"

These guys played this game with us for a minute or two, then they put us in different cars. Soon as they did, I knew we were fucked!

"Boys of Summer" was playing in that cop car when I was helped in the back seat, and I remember thinking, *DeadHead sticker on a Cadillac? I'm just fuckin' dead!*

Before the cop said a word, I went, "Do you want me to tell the truth?"

He went, "You better not lie!"

So I went, "We ran away from Cleveland, Ohio."

He got on the radio with the other guy and started all that 1420, 1329, code 5150 bullshit, and off to jail we went!

They didn't put us in a cage. It was a real small town. Turns out, we were fifty miles from New York City. The jail had a glass case with all kinds of drugs and needles, and it had a gas mask used for smoking weed, all kinds of drug shit. Yes. We tried to figure out a way to steal it. No. We didn't.

These cops were trying to figure out what to do with us, and they're getting pissed because they're having a hard time of it. Finally the phone rang, and the cop went, "We're taking them to a JINS home in Whatever County."

That's when the cop who had to transport us got super pissed because it was like a two-hour ride, and no neighboring counties would help him with the transport.

We had no idea what a JINS home was. We thought we were headed to a maximum security facility. After a forever ride, this cop turned off the road and started going up the side of a mountain, and Kenny and I thought we were headed straight to mini-Attica. I was scared as fuck! We just looked at each other like, *Oh! Fuck no! I don't wanna die here!*

Once at the top of the mountain, it was nothing more than a house. A fucking house! So we went in this house, and there's a little old lady in a housecoat who greeted us, and the cop left, and we're in this JINS home.

This lady took in troubled youth for the state of New Jersey; it was called Juveniles in Need of Supervision. JINS. Turns out, they had a nationwide APB out on us.

She showed us to our room and gave us each a Tupperware cup and showed us where the soda was in the refrigerator. During the course of small chitchat, she asked us if we drank alcohol. We told her no. She replied, "Good. I like to entertain, and I keep my booze in the open."

Her room was across the hall from ours, and as soon as we heard her snoring, we were on the prowl for that liquor cabinet. Wasn't hard to find. Right in the living room. We drank a bottle of Black Velvet and hid the bottle in our room.

After getting drunk, I called my house, collect, in the middle of the night. My dad asked me what I wanted to do. I said, "Leave me here and let them do what they want with me, please." And I meant it. He always told me if I fucked up, pray they keep me 'cause it'd be a cakewalk compared to dealing with him. My parents were there about twelve hours later.

Kenny went back with us because his dad wouldn't go get him. We got home on Christmas Eve.

We did all this shit, and now came time to pay the piper. Pretty melodramatic, really. Ken's dad wouldn't press charges for us taking any of his shit, his grandparents dropped the stolen vehicle charge, nothing was ever said about the dope or booze, or any of the stolen shit we had in that car. I haven't a clue why. You tell me.

The only charges pressed were criminal mischief for turfing Bindy's yard before we left. And even as much as her mom and dad hated me, they wouldn't even press charges; the Amherst Police Department did. Ole Chief Lonnie showing me what a bad kid I was and what a hero he was.

We did get placed on probation. Scary stuff. No contact with each other outside school. No drugs. No booze. Call Terry Yepko every week. I did call every week. I wasn't stupid.

Chapter 29

Round about this time, Sam Aguyo got his own apartment in uptown Amherst. Right on Cleveland Avenue. Back apartment, Tim Dipalma used to live there, across from the bank.

Sam was eighteen. His brother, Teddy, is my age. Sam was still in high school and worked at Slutzker's Market, right uptown. Used to tab an eight-pack of Genny Pounders every night. Same Slutzker's Dot Head Becker was a cashier at for years.

I basically lived at Sam's. Hell, you wanna talk about some professional partiers, Brian Meyers comes to mind immediately! Brian was a short dumpy squat redheaded dude who was, to this day, one of the best goddamn backstops I have ever seen live, in person. And I've been to a jillion baseball games. Fucker stopped anything you threw to the plate and had a decent arm.

He was also an advanced partier by high school. Dabbled in black magic. Actually he's the one who turned me on to reading Alister Crowley's *Findings of a Drug Fiend* and was basically a real dude. Not many people like real dudes. I love Brian Meyers to this day and always will. Pal forever.

One day, Brian brought a five-gallon water bottle full of homemade wine over to Sam's apartment. He called it grape moonshine. Free for the drinking. One day, not long after this bottle of wine showed up, I skipped school and went over to Sam's and started drinking this delicious homemade wine.

As the day wore on, I proceeded to get pretty fucked up. I mean, people were coming by all day. Brad Riggs, Tony Scarpetti, Brian, Bryce, the whole fuckin' gang always came by Sam's!

Before you know it, it's dark outside, and I hadn't been home. And I was drunk. In the midst of the hedonistic atmosphere of Sam's smoke-filled can-bottle-laden apartment, there was a knock, pound, wallop, swarp, fucking earthquake going on outside that window!

I opened the door and went, "Who th—"

The Bud Man went in a voice as loud as the biggest loudest jet ever made, "What the fuck do you think you're doing? You little fuck!" And he grabbed me by the shirt and took me straight to the police station.

I was drunk as fuck. Look, if you've ever been superfucked up on booze and smokin' reefers for hours and hours, that's where I was. Plain ole fucked up. And this isn't long after Kenny and I went on our trip. Maybe a month. So Bud was furiously angry with me and wanted to kill me!

I got to the Amherst Police Station, and this cop was asking me all these questions, and I was trying to answer them as best I could. He brought up the charges and the shit we just did I hadn't even been to court for yet.

Finally he went, "Look, you can either go to juvie, or you can go to rehab for your alcohol and drug problem."

My mom was sitting there, sobbing and crying and pleading and pleasing me, to heaven and back, to go to rehab! Mom, you think I was stupid? The cop asked me where I got the booze. I told him a guy in a Cleveland Browns hat had bought it for me at the party shop.

Of course I said rehab, and they made the call. They called Lakeland. My mom came back in and went, "You have to go to St. Joseph's, 4D, for a week because when they asked me if you have ever tried to commit suicide, I told them yes." That's the psych ward of the hospital.

My parents drove me from the Amherst Police Department to St. Joseph's on Broadway, in Lorain. About a ten, fifteen-minute ride.

There we were, drunk as fuck, headed to *One Flew Over the Cuckoo's Nest*! We got there and got to the fourth floor, and immediately things were different from the rest of the hospital. When the elevator shut, it automatically locked! And well, there was a day-room, the short hall, and the thorazine shuffle, long hall, with the rail to hold on to. Cages over everything—windows, doors, everything.

They put me in a bed, and that was that. As I was laying there, some lady kept screaming from another room.

"I talked to Jerry, and he knows the secret, and he told me, and I'm not tellin'!"

I swear, she said that over and over till I passed out. I remember thinking, *She's a Jerry fan too, eh? Cool.*

The very first thing I saw when I came to on the fourth floor, in the wacko ward, was Kenneth Paul Carney Jr. sitting on my bed, going, "Hey, peckerhead, get up! Get up! You fuckin' dirt ball, get up."

He was drunk as fuck, and his dad put him back in there again. He had spent like four or six months straight in there not long before this. Not sure how long, but it was a long fucking time in that place!

The week in the nut ward wasn't so bad. I mean, I had cigarettes. No lighter or matches. There was a little square box on the wall you put your cigarette in and puffed on, and it lit.

Lotta TV watching. There were some characters in there. The aforementioned thorazine shuffle hall was fun to watch. Kenny and I would bet cigarettes on who would win. Funny shit back then.

Before I left, a girl went in there, who was our age, and she wasn't bad-looking. After some snooping, we discovered through Shamoo—this nurse was bigger and fatter than anyone you've ever seen and could not keep her mouth shut—that she was molested by her stepfather. Not sure how long, couldn't have been long at all, Kenny and she got caught in the shower doing the nasty.

Kenny was out at the nurse's station sayin' shit like, "I'm trying to help her! I told her I love her! She's getting better!" Shit like that. I swear, it was fucking hilarious! If you were there, you'd be laughing too! Every lunatic, nut, was laughing their ass off in their own way!

Chapter 30

My first year of seventh grade, I tried out for basketball. Mr. James, the seventh-grade coach, was a midget! He wore the same two pairs of Toughskin corduroy pants the two and a half years I was at that two-year institution.

Mr. James was a great guy. He was a math teacher. I had him when we moved back from Sheffield Lake. He told me he once trained fighters in Toledo, Ohio.

I wanna talk about trying out for the basketball team. During tryouts, I missed a layup. A simple fundamental basic layup, and I was pissed. Next day, Mr. James pulled me out of class and went, "You had the highest scores of anyone that tried out. Welcome to the team, Bruce!"

Gets better. Mr. Lesner, the eighth-grade coach, was funny-looking. Kinda tall, slicked back horrible Pat Riley imitation hairdo, had a mustache that looked like asshole hair around a lip. I'm not being mean. I liked Mr. Lesner. Just callin 'em how I saw 'em.

Mr. Lesner—sorry, Coach Lesner and Coach James took me in their office one day, not long after practice had started, and had this to say to me. "Bruce, your basketball abilities are such that we feel you could help the eighth-grade team out right now. What do you think?"

What do I think? Sure. I'll play on your big boys' squad. All these years later, I know that was a Friday because eighth-grade basketball practice was at 8:00 a.m. the next morning at Nord Junior High gym.

I spent the night with Brad Riggs, who lived in a duplex we would end up living in the other side of before it was over, on Axtel Street, right by the schools. We got ripped. No recollections of anything special happening. I just know we got fucked up. You always did at Brad's.

When I got up for basketball practice, I was still drunk. I stunk like booze, the whole ensemble. As soon as I walked through the gym door, Coach Lesner went, "Bruce, I have to talk to you."

How the fuck did he realize I was drunk already? was what I thought.

We get in his office, and he went, "Mr. Marley (William "Julio Harry Knuckles" Marley), the principal, said he feels seventh-grade basketball is for seventh graders and eighth grade for eighth graders. Sorry. He's afraid you'll get hurt playing with older bigger boys. You are welcome to practice with us today, though."

I felt a lot of things when he said this to me. Relief that he didn't know I was drunk. I really didn't care about playing basketball, I couldn't train and play ball, and you had to have decent grades to play ball. I was passing nothin'. I did practice that day.

Another thing that crossed my mind was, *Hurt by the bigger kids?* I found that most hilarious. I mean, if you're worried about me getting hurt, why aren't you at these fight shows in a three-state, four-state region that I'm fighting these nineteen, twenty, twenty-three-year-old men at? Why aren't you protesting at the gym every fuckin' day when I'm sparrin' with grown men, pros?

I remember a fight show one time, I was about twelve, thirteen, and after everyone weighed in, the guy making the matches went, "All I got in this weight is this guy, Jim, and he's got a coupl'a pounds on ya, and he's twenty-three years old."

Jim Kelly, my trainer, went, "We'll take it."

This was like 1981, '82. This guy had a tattoo, and when we were weighing in, he was talking to some guy about the day he had had at work. I was in middle school.

By this age, I was sparring with pros every day. Grown men. So what, fighting one? 'Bout goddamn time! I remember that fight well. I won it by decision.

Chapter 31

My first stint in rehab was nothing to write home about. I mean, twenty-eight days of classes, lectures, and on Sunday, family day. There was a set of twins, Bon and Harry Graley. One or the other was in with me, and the other one was coming in when he got out. They wouldn't let family members in rehab together.

What this broke down to was, the twin that came for family day every Sunday brought the other a sack of buds, so we'd go to our room, turn the shower on, and get stoned as fuck!

While all this shit was going on in my life, I can remember having the thought, *Someday I'll win the title, and all this will go away.* Behind that thought was this one, *You're a loser, how you gonna win the title?*

Of course, I never talked with any of the counselors in Lakeland about any of my real problems. I never talked to anyone about my problems, for what?

Chapter 32

Well, by this age, I knew what was going on with my parents. I mean, my dad was a drunk and a whore, and my mom was left with us kids. I knew by middle school, my dad made good money, but we never saw any of it.

I'm not saying my mom was an angel. She had boyfriends at times, did shit not conducive to a healthy family life. Not defending that. However, she was never too busy whoring to help us kids, and she never said, "I can't buy you that, I went whoring last night and spent all my money." She always had money for what we needed. Unless my dad got ahold of it first.

Funny, I knew by the time I was probably five, I was never getting married, I was never having any kids, and I was certainly going to be a drunk.

I mentioned my cousin Lenny. When I was little, I'd be riding with my mom in that Impala, and we'd pass him hitchhiking, and she'd go, "Look, Bruce, here's your cousin Lenny, hitchhiking!"

I'd go, "You gonna pick him up?"

"Are you crazy? He's mentally retarded and gets high on model glue! No! I'm not picking him up! And you better never get high on glue or drugs either!" was her response.

I always told her, "I won't, Mom. I'm gonna be a drunk like Dad!"

Definitely by this age, I questioned why I was even born. I still do.

Chapter 33

When you look back on life, you see there were people there who could have helped you. All they had to do was make an effort. Instead, these people went against you and kicked you when you were down and said shit like, "Told you so!" when something bad happened in your life because you fucked up. All because of who your parents are.

I never had any help from my family, other than my mom and dad. I mean, Ma when I was young. But I have no clue whatsoever what it's like to get excited because Mammy and fuckin' Pappy are comin' over. I mean, fuck Mammy and Pappy! Really, all two sets, fuck 'em!

Chapter 34

What's the drunkest you ever got before school and went? Looking back, it seems the only days I decided to go to school were the ones I should have stayed home because of drunkenness.

In eighth grade, Todd Krase kept telling me, "Becker, I can get a bottle. A full bottle!"

He told me this shit for some time, and one day finally, I went, "Look, Todd, bring it over my house in the morning before school." And he said okay.

Todd Krase was a distance runner and a very good one. We used to run miles and miles together in the summertime when we were kids. No way in hell did I think he'd show up at my house with a bottle of booze before school the next morning. He did.

I had told Shane Rapose about Todd and the supposed bottle being brought over, and he was welcome to come. He did.

It was springtime and nippy in the mornings and nice and warm by the time you got out of school. We lived on Harris Street; our backyard and Brad's, on Axtel Street, were connected. About a five-minute walk to Nord.

We're in my room, and Todd whips out a bottle of Black Velvet, unopened seal. We started walking toward Nord and drinking on this bottle of Black Velvet, and all three of us were seeing who could take the biggest chug, daring the next guy he couldn't do one bigger. By the time we got to the guardrail to smoke and hide what was left of the bottle under the pine tree in the front yard of the house located there, that bottle was damn near empty.

I just knew someone was going to get caught, just knew it!

Soon as we got in the school, Todd started his shit. "I'm drunk! I'm fucked up!" I got the hell away from him and stayed away from him all day!

I passed out in third period study hall. When I woke up, Kathy Bigho was sitting next to me. She was my girlfriend at the time. I said, "Hi, Kathy." And I put my head back down.

Then it occurred to me she wasn't in study hall with me. I looked back up, and I'm lookin' around, and Mrs. Ghetty, the study hall monitor, went, "Bruce, are you okay?"

I said I was and asked her what period it was. She said it was fourth, so I flew down to science class. As soon as I opened the door, Mr. Warhola went, "Where have you been, Bruce?"

I told him I passed out in study hall, and I'd go get a pass if he'd like. He said no and to sit down. There was like five minutes of class left.

The entire class was laughing. The whole school knew we were drunk; how the teachers didn't I'll never know. The next period was lunch. I ate and felt brand-new. Just like a champ!

Todd wasn't so fortunate. I was told a teacher knew he was drunk and called on him to read to the class, and when he started reading, he puked all over the place.

I made it through the day and got home, and all was well. My mom had gotten her hair done that day at Marilyn Griffith's house. This lady had a kid, Jeff, my age, and he told his mom what happened to Todd at school that day.

My mom came home and told me the story Jeff told, and I was all, "Wow! Dumb kid! Hope he's okay. Why'd he do that?" Ya know, playin' the concerned worried friend.

My mom went, "Bruce, Todd was over here this morning before school, so was Shane." Oh yeah, they were, weren't they?

I proceed to tell my mom how I was bullied into drinking, I only took a sip, it was their idea—definitely made it look good on me. Please don't think she believed it. Then I asked her if she was

gonna tell the Bud Man. She said no. She went, "It isn't my responsibility to tell him. I don't care if you tell him or not, but keep this in
mind, your dad bowls with Todd's every Tuesday at Park Lanes. Do
you think he's gonna lie to his dad about who he was with when he's
getting his ass beat? Would you rather your dad hear it from you or
Todd's dad, Tuesday?"

That night, I told the old man I took a sip of whiskey, and he
said I better not do that anymore. That was it. He was lyin' on the
couch, watchin' Thursday night football when I told him.

Chapter 35

I did go to school enough in the eighth grade to pass and move on to high school. Not really anymore three fights a day to beat the boxer up. That was a good thing.

I managed to complete my first year of high school. I missed eighty-nine days and did not complete enough days to get the grades I earned. An *A* in English and a *B* in history. That was it. No other grades in any other classes. Bunch of *I*'s. That stands for incomplete.

I found this out when I applied for culinary school, where I spent a couple months before I started cooking my way around the country. You didn't think I graduated, did you?

Funny story about high school. I've bragged and run my mouth about what a badass athlete I used to be, and I couldn't even pass gym class in ninth grade!

Mr. Bunovich, the gym teacher, hated me from day one. School had gone from first semester to second while I was in rehab, and there was a rule at Steele, if you missed more than five days without a doctor's excuse, you failed the nine-week grading period, period. Done deal. Flunky, flunky, regardless of grades. I had gym second semester.

I showed up for gym the first day back from rehab, and Bunovich was like, "Who the hell are you?" I told him my name and that I was in rehab, and he went, "You've missed more than five days. You fail."

That was how I met Mr. Bunovich, the gym teacher. He was short and wide. He ran the bleachers of the football stadium in the morning. He had a buzz cut jarhead haircut. Always wore shirts with

95

the sleeve cut off. Black glasses with the strap around his neck. Fucker was hard of hearing too. And he made good and goddamn sure to let me know he could kick a boxer's ass. He'd take the class outside to run, and I'd stay in the gym and smoke cigarettes. One day, they came back, and the gym smelled like smoke, and he went, "Becker, if I catch you smoking in here, I'll have your ass in a sling!" He never caught me. I used to stand at the doors and blow the smoke outside.

So many things I learned in school. At Nord, we used to take chocolate milk cartons and rinse them out and fill them with vodka and orange juice. Drink three or four of those, the rest of the day went by better. Of course, this continued at Steele.

Missing that much school, one might wonder what a kid does with all his time. Well, one thing my house was known for during this time we lived on Harris Street and Axtel Street was the Barnaby parties I used to have.

There was a local TV station that had a show called *Barnaby*, hosted by a guy named Lynn Sheldon. He always wore loud vibrant sports coats and different hats. He talked to imaginary friends, had pets you couldn't see. He also showed cartoons of Mighty Mouse, Speedy Gonzales, shit like that. It was a kid's show.

I'd walk down to the school every morning and find people who wanted to party, and we'd get the beers together and be at my place by nine because that's when *Barnaby* started!

The first time I ever did LSD, I was in ninth grade. I did it alone, which is not suggested.

We lived on Harris Street, and I bought a dose off of Brad. His older brother, Jerry, who was out of high school, had gotten a sheet. It was a Sunday night, Bradley insisted I not do that hit of acid alone. He's like, "Save it till this weekend, and we'll all do some."

Sure, Bradley. I ate that hit of acid as I was walking through the backyards to my house.

Nothing happened. Nothing at all! I remember sitting in a chair watching TV, while the Bud Man lay on the couch, and thinking, *This shit ain't shit! Wasted three fuckin' bucks!*

Sometime after that, I remember that same TV start slowly dripping down into the table and forming itself back up. The Marlboro clock on the wall had a cowboy on a horse, and he was actually riding all over the wall. I had to get the fuck out of there! I went up to my room and lay on my floor and listened to albums all night long. Purple Haze sounded like pots and pans banging together in a kitchen with someone singing along!

All night long, this went on. I saw things vividly in my mind, I had infinite thoughts about infinite things. Something spoke to me, it said everything was going to be okay, and I just listened to music and watched the movies in my mind all night long.

There's an Eric Clapton song, "To Make Someone Happy," I'll bet I listened to that song five hundred times in a row that night. Talk about touching the core of the soul.

Then it was time to go to school! One of the only days I ever remember completing, from homeroom to last period without leaving the premises, during my high school career.

In first-period science, Tony Deleonus thought I was high on weed because if I showed up to class, I usually was. We were watching a filmstrip with a ship on it, and it kept going all over the wall in weird positions, and I was laughing my ass off!

Nothing unusual happened that day. After school, as I was heading home, I stopped at the bus barns and smoked a joint with someone. As we were smoking, Mr. Boyton, the vice principal, was standing outside the senior lounge doors at the school looking at us. I went home and slept till the next day. That's all.

Chapter 36

Now my first year of high school, I had history fourth/fifth period, lunch sixth period, and English tenth period, last period of the day. Made for a broken day. I mean, you know how hard it was, day in, day out, getting out of that school every morning and sneaking back in for the vital classes of the day?

There was a stretch during this year. I was dating a girl, Stacy Paul, and she had early dismissal because she was a senior and had study hall tenth period.

She lived by Kenny's, and every day for the month or so we fooled around, I skipped English class every single day and went to Stacy's to study while her mom was at work.

I was amazed because I was never turned in for skipping this class, never. Finally one day, I went back to English, and when I went through the door, Mr. Strohm, the teacher, went, "Bruce, hope everything is okay. Heard you were in the hospital."

Oh, okay! All my other teachers were turning me in for skipping, and you had me in the hospital, Mr. Strohm. Okay! Thanks!

Not proud of that. Really, I'm not. Never felt like I was getting over on anyone, none of that. I was just wanting the pussy. Remember, I am a Becker.

That miss-five-days-and-you're-fucked rule really fucked some people up. Kevin "Schmev" Anderson is living proof of that. Schmev was a senior; he was one of the Hidden Valley gang, where Trig lived. And of course, he was a partier.

Schmev found his way to rehab, Lakeland, when he was a senior. When he came back to school, he was under the impression he had failed and wasn't going to graduate because of the miss-five-days rule. So he did what any seventeen-year-old kid would do in that circumstance; he took a gun—a .357—put it up to his chin, and pulled the fuckin' trigger.

Kevin Anderson took his life because he thought he was gonna fail out of school. I remember being at his funeral and looking at him, wishing I was him. I remember thinking, *Wow! He's where I want to be!* It was an open casket.

Nobody ever talked about Schmev after he died. It was like he never existed. I know people mourned, missed him. I mean, Schmev was a great dude. Always smiling, funny in a nerdy way. I never forgot about him. During the time he killed himself, he had let me borrow his REO Speedwagon album *Hi Infidelity*. I still had it when he died. Most people hear "In Your Letter" or "Take It on the Run," and they reminisce about a high school girlfriend or a crush they had on a girl in school. I remember Kevin "Schmev" Anderson.

To this day, no matter where I am—grocery store, elevator, office building—if Muzak starts playing REO, memories of Kevin and me smoking weed in the abandoned barn by Shaun Gray's house instantly flood my mind.

Chapter 37

One day, as usual, I was drunk before school and left the building. I was sitting in Jimmy Moore's truck, smoking a cigarette in the student parking lot, when Coach Zavara came out the senior lounge doors and looked right at me. Jimmy knew I was in his truck, but it scared me, and I bolted.

I went home and at lunchtime went to school. On this particular day, I was drunker than usual. Before eating lunch, I went in the bathroom to smoke a cigarette. I was about three puffs in, and who walked in but Coach Richardson, the head football coach. I mean, he had me red-handed in the middle of puffing my lungs away!

Coach Richardson went, "Bruce, I chew, and I can wait till after school, c'mon now!" And he took me to the office to get my Saturday school suspension. I never served those. If you missed, you were suspended three days out of school.

I went to Mr. Boyton's office and got my Saturday school and went back to lunch. As soon as I sat down with my tray, Mr. Wing, the science teacher I had with the LSD films, was the lunch monitor and came up to me and went, "Bruce, they want you back in the office." I immediately knew I was fucked!

I ate my lunch and tried to cover my breath real good. Probably only one of five times I drank milk in my life! I also ate a couple of cigarettes. Soon as I walked in and sat down, Mr. Boyton went, "Bruce, you've been drinking, haven't you?"

"No! I haven't been drinking."

He then proceeded to ask me what I was doing in Jimmy's truck, told me he knew I haven't been to class all day, asked me again if I'd been drinking, and brought in the bigwig, Mr. Angoloni, the head principal.

Those fuckers interrogated me for a long, long time. Smelled my breath, and they're like, "It's covered up, but you smell like booze."

I just kept denying it. They also kept asking me who I was with. Finally after what seemed like hours of this shit, I went, "Look, I wasn't drinking. I was riding around with a guy who skipped and is older, and he was drinking, and he spilled beer on me. I'm not giving any names, but that's what happened."

Looking back, they couldn't have been retarded enough to believe that, but they told me to go back to class. Fuck back to class. I went home!

Chapter 38

Freddie Spaghetti. This fucker is as retarded as Dan Carnes, maybe more so. He and his badass gangster friend Bologna Sissycow.

You gotta understand something, by this time, I had been in the fight racket probably four, five years. I promise you, if you have never been in the fight racket, you have absolutely no fucking clue what it is about, I promise. I cannot stress that enough. Whatever you are, and whatever you do, whatever kind of brains you have or don't have, high-tech computer whiz or broom-sweeping janitor, anything in between, if you've never been in the racket, you know more about brain surgery and rocket science than you do boxing. Again I promise from the bottom of my heart.

On the other hand, if you're a degenerate street thug with a penchant for percentages, and you're good with numbers and the ability to do a multitude of things, such as threaten to stab someone in the guts if they don't give you the cash, stab them if they don't, refuse to pay people monies you actually owe them, rob, lie, steal, cheat, and buy off whatever you can't win fair, you and I should talk.

One of the very first things you learn when you walk in a gym is the intimidation factor. You're walking into a controlled-violence situation where everyone is a badass. No different than the streets, other than the controlled violence part.

Ever notice that? Everyone everywhere is a badass. They've done this, they've done that, waiting to do the next badass thing. But in the meantime, no, I couldn't spar for six months. Doctor said it could kill me. Fight you? I almost killed a guy fightin' last year. That's why I'm on probation, or I'd kick your ass!

Then there's the badass who talks and talks and talks and talks, and he's friends with a bunch of them there gangster boys from Lorain. You know, thugs?

Freddie was from Lorain. The first six digits of Kenny's and his phone numbers were the same, 282-771——. How fuckin' weird is that? They didn't know each other or live by each other.

Freddie Spaghetti used to come to Amherst and hang out at the baseball fields and let everyone know he was from badass Lorain, and he'd get his gangster friends to kill us if we fucked with him.

One day, I was down at the baseball fields watching Bindy play, and Freddie is flappin' his gums at me, tellin' me I ain't shit, he'd get his brothers to fuck me up, shit like that. I can't recall verbatim what I told him, but I can assure you, it was along the lines of, your mom is a stinky cunt, fuck her in the ass, so six weeks later, she can squeeze out another inbred bung hole baby like yourself, then you'll have company. Whatever it was, I can assure you, it let him know where I stood.

Freddie said he was leaving, and he'd be back. I assured him I wouldn't be hiding. Well, as the games rolled on and then ended, I was walking Bindy home. Yep. Same yard Kenny and me turfed. This was the preturf summer.

She lived right by the schools and the baseball fields. We lived right on the opposite side of the schools. As she and I were walking toward her house on Sunrise Drive, we heard a car squealing tires, burning out, doing *Starsky & Hutch* shit right there in the serene neighborhood of a bunch of well-off comfortable white folks!

Then a bunch of brothers started running toward me, with Freddie Cockroach leading the way, screaming all kinds of mean nasty things! I just made it to Bindy's garage, I mean, just, and Freddie Spaghetti put his foot through the glass window of the door as I shut it, and blood was gushing and flowing, and well, it didn't look good! All his brothers jumped in the car and left poor Freddie there.

Cops came. Freddie was hauled away in an ambulance. I think his buddies may have taken him, and I was free to leave. Soon as I walked through the door, the Bud Man said, "What the fuck happened to you?"

I went, "Nothin', why?"

He went, "Then why the fuck do you have blood all over you?"

"Oh! That. Well…" And I proceeded to tell him what happened.

His solution was to get the baseball bats, hammers, screwdrivers, and ice picks, go pick up Chuckie Boesel, a friend of my dad's, and go looking for these guys. We found the car in the parking garage of St. Joseph's Hospital, and we just parked there. We were there quite a while, and the cops came up to us and suggested we leave. We did. I never had any trouble out of Freddie Spaghetti after that.

Sure, we talked. He told me he couldn't walk for the entire summer. Cut an artery, the whole ensemble.

Chapter 39

It's around this time I had a fight in Dayton, Ohio. Fought a kid from Kronk, and Emmanuel Steward was there. I lost that fight by decision to a kid named Toureque Fikes. As I was sitting there, crying like a bitch because I lost, Emmanuel Steward came up to me and went, "Son, quit crying. If that was a ten-round fight, you stop my guy in six. You're a pro, not an amateur. Here's my number, call me." He gave me $100 and told me to get some ice cream.

Just like that. So I headed up to Detroit to embark on taking over the junior welterweight world under the tutelage of Emmanuel Steward.

It's around this time my parents were getting divorced, and life was as fucked up as ever.

My mom's company car was burglarized. Thousands in cigarettes missing, a cashbox—everything gone. She swore up and down the Bud Man did it.

Looking back, on one hand, this was a great opportunity for me. On the other, it was a fucked-up situation.

During this time, I was having some serious problems with my legs. I would take thirty steps or walk up ten stairs, and I'd feel like I ran a hundred miles. My legs would go numb. They took me to the Cleveland Clinic, Emmanuel had some doctors look at me, all kinds of shit.

The end result was potassium deficiency, and I forget what else. I remember a doctor at the Cleveland Clinic saying it sounded stress-related to him.

My Kronk experience was good and bad. Mostly bad. The house I lived in had ten people living in it. Johnny De La Rosa, from the Dominican Republic, was there. He grew weed in the neighbor's backyard. He fought for the junior lightweight title. Michael Moorer was there. Keith Vining, JL Ivey, Anthony Lopez, Stevie McCrory didn't live there, but that fucker was always over, drinking beer with us, he had just lost a title fight to Jeff Fenech when I was up there.

All these people there, and every single one of them were great guys! All of them except one. To this day, the biggest most racist scumbag piece of shit I have ever met, Bob White.

From the word go, this piece of shit let me know he didn't like whitey. While at Kronk, we were heading to Indianapolis to fight in the Black Expo. About ten, thirteen people in the van, and I was the only grain of salt. We weren't twenty minutes into the trip, and Bob put on one of those street preachers talkin' 'bout, "Get whitey! Fuck whitey!" All that shit. Not sure who said something, but one of the fighters did, and dickhead shut it off. As he did, he looked right at me, as if to say, *Fuck you, white boy!*

Once, when I first got there, Bob had come downstairs and told me to turn the fights on the TV. I was having trouble, and he started with his white-boys-can't-do-shit-right-you're-an-ignorant-honky shit, and Keith Vining went right the fuck off on Bob! Sayin', "Why you gotta fuck with him, Bob, he ain't done shit to you?"

Basically Keith told Bob to fuck off and leave me alone.

I haven't seen Keith Vining in at least thirty years. I have always, and will continue to always, let people know who Keith Vining is and what a great human being he is. Keith had a really good amateur career. Didn't have a great pro career, but he is a champ of life. He used to help with disabled kids, did all kinds of charity work, great human being. Last I heard, he was running a gym in his hometown.

Bob White? Bob fuckin' died years ago! Racism put that piece of shit in the ground real early. How I found out was, I was in San Antonio, Texas, training with Tony Ayala Sr. I had just gotten in town, and we were eating dinner at Tony's and talking. He and

Emmanuel were partners. We're talkin' about shit, and he went, "Yeah. Bob White died."

I couldn't contain my excitement! I was like, "No shit, there is a God!" Even Tony Ayala Sr. was surprised at my response.

Chapter 40

My mom moved to Kentucky when she and my dad got divorced, and that's when shit got really bad. I mean, Stuff told me when they moved from Cleveland to Sheffield Lake, the counselors took him in the office and said, "Now this isn't Cleveland. Things aren't as fucked up here as in Cleveland. Things are more laid back."

That was twenty minutes down the road. My mom moving from Amherst, Ohio, to Garrison, Kentucky, was four hours and fifty years behind the times. Literally.

All that shit you see in movies about the backwoods, inbred, retarded, holler-livin', incest-fuckin', sheep-pussy-gettin', uneducated, no-nothing hillbillies? It's true.

The cable had thirteen channels; that included the local channels and religious channels you got. I have never liked MTV, but it was never an option on cable there. Religious was free and about three or four of the channels. You got like Lifetime and HGTV.

This was '86. My dad had custody of us because my mom just vanished one day. Talk about turn of events! Turns out, she was getting her ducks in a row to make the big move! New husband lined up, house to live in, the whole ensemble!

As my parents were going through this, my mom showed back up, and we're telling her we weren't moving to Kentucky, and if she did, she's on her own. She assured us she wasn't moving anywhere, and so we went to the lawyers, and he also assured all three of us she wasn't moving. So us kids said we wanted to live with our mom.

I fought in the '86 National Golden Gloves. Didn't fight in the Gloves in '85 because I was in rehab. My mind, at this time, was mush. I mean, it's at this point in my life, it seemed, killing myself really became an option. My self-worth was less than that of a pile of shit. I got beaten in the quarter finals. Didn't care. Pete Cauvillo and I lay fuckin' drunk from the time we got there till the time we left! The day Johnny Avon Jr. dropped me off after getting back from the nationals, there was a U-Haul truck in the yard of the duplex on Axtel Street. My mom was loading it.

I have a National Golden Gloves story for you from '86. Nationals were in Cedar Rapids, Iowa, I think. Every year, they're in a great place, except the year I fight in them! Every year, when you fight in the nationals, you fly there. Except this year! Long ass bus ride, and you couldn't smoke cigarettes or weed!

Upon arriving at the hotel, I got paired with Avon to share a room. He was a referee. Well, one night, we walked to this store and bought a bunch of beers and wine, and we went back to the hotel and started drinking. Before you know it, we're wrestling on the bed like the WWF guys. He reffed that fake shit and was actin' like Hulk Hogan or one of them lunatics, and my sweatpants started coming down.

I started freaking out because my pants were coming down. I went, "Avon, stop! My pants are coming down!"

He was on top of me and had me in a neck hold. He went, "I know! That's where the fun begins!"

As soon as he said that, I grabbed his forearm with my mouth and started biting as fucking hard as I could and wouldn't let go! He went, "Stop! That hurts!"

And I'm like, "I know! That's where the fun begins, you sick fuck!" I more than drew blood, I promise. Took a big ole chunk out of that faggot's arm.

As soon as he let me go, I hit that fucker with a Rocky Marciano Suzie Q, then went Artie Diamond on his faggot ass a little more before I was satisfied he knew I wasn't fucking around. Then he told me to tell everyone we were wrestling, and he hit the corner of the table! I held a team meeting and told everyone what happened. His fuckin' eye was swollen shut and was the size of a tennis ball.

This shit going on, and I gotta go out and fight the next day. And the dickhead still drove me home when we got back! After this episode in his life, Johnny Avon Jr., the faggot, pedophile, amateur boxing referee, from Cleveland, Ohio, joined the navy!

Chapter 41

I'm not certain what order, or how, these events played out in my life, but they did. Jesus Christ! It's as confusing as ever!

When we lived on Axtel Street, in the duplex next to Brad and his family, the neighbors next to us were the Smiths'. Jerry, Joe, and Jessica. They were very religious people when we moved next to them and had quit going to church completely by the time we moved! One of their kids, Joe, had to go to Lakeland because of his chronic pot addiction, acquired since befriending me. He tried to drink with Kenny and me once too.

That's funny because before moving from Harris to Axtel Street, the Reicherts sold their house and moved. Told the Meyers we were a bad family, and they didn't want their kids influenced by us.

There was this family that lived two houses to the north of us on Harris—can't think of their last names—and they had this fat red-headed kid named Tommy. Tommy wore glasses. One day, Tommy poked my sister, Sam, in the eye with a stick. My brother, Augie, hit Tommy with a left hook and laid the little fucker out. I mean, he fucked this kid up. Aug had a natural left hook. Threw it just like Joe Frazier. Fucker was born with that.

Next thing you know, Tommy's dad was baby-stepping his way up to our door. He had some kind of walking ailment, like he had a stick in his ass. I opened the door, and he started telling me Tommy has a disease, he could'a died, Aug was in trouble, he wanted to see my dad. Right then, my mom pulled in the driveway, and this butt plug started going off on my mom! He wasn't three words in, and she started with, "You motherfucker, if you don't get off my property, I'm gonna fuck you up, you asshole! You're lucky Aug didn't kill him!" Tommy's dad left and never came back.

Maybe they had a talk with the Reicherts! One time, while living on Harris Street, the sheriff came looking for my dad, and the Amherst cops came looking for me. As my dad was leaving with the deputy, he went, "Tell your mom I'm in the county."

As the city was taking me, I told Sam and Aug, "Tell Mom Dad's in county, I might be in juvie." I did get home before my mom did; no juvie for me.

Questions. I remember it being questions. I might still remember the questions, and I might still remember the answers. Then again, probably not. That was a long time ago, eh?

Harris Street had the setup. There was a couch on the front porch I used to hide beers under for when everyone went to bed. I could also roll the car out of the driveway.

We lived on Harris Street when the Adam-no-teeth incident happened. It was a Friday the thirteenth, no shit. That night, rumor mill had it uptown at Danny Boy's Adam's older brother, Randy, was gonna kick little Brucey Becker's ass!

Now Randy New was older than me, bigger than me, and he wrestled on the high school wrestling team. Was I scared? Fuck you! I was scared to death! He was also friends with Ken Bauer. Ken Bauer was six-feet-something big in high school. And athletic.

Upon hearing the news I was going to be vanquished by these monsters, I set out to get drunk one more time before my life ended.

I sat on that front porch at 167 Harris Street, on that love seat, until the wee hours of the morning and got drunker than a motherfucker. When I drink, my mind spins at a billion miles per second, non-fucking-stop. Always has. Always will.

Among all the thoughts I had—*I'm fucked! I'm dead! What am I gonna do!*—I concocted a great revenge scheme!

Ken Bauer lived right on Cleveland Avenue. Busy street. If you turn right to go to St. Joseph's Church, that house sits right there on the left. Only house there on the left side before you're in the church parking lot. The front of the house faces Cleveland Avenue.

After getting good and tuned, I went over to Ken's house with a bunch of eggs and a bar of soap. His dad had a big green Ford pickup truck with a white cab on it. I wrote up and down the sides of that truck with the soap, in big block letters, "AN ASSHOLE DRIVES THIS PIECE OF SHIT." Then I smeared eggs all over that fuckin' truck's windows, then threw the rest of the eggs at the front of the house and hightailed it the fuck back to Harris Street!

I probably got to sleep as the sun was coming up. I got woken up at about eight o'clock in the morning by my mom and a police officer, Officer Riko Rivera. I was sleeping on the floor of my room, and I heard a cop radio crackling, and I thought I was dreaming till I sat up.

We went down to the kitchen and got coffee, and Officer Riko started asking me what I did last night, who I was with, shit like that. I told him I pretty much sat on my front porch all night long, my neighbor Donny Alison could verify that. Donny and I were listening to the new Yes cassette in his Jeep stereo. Oh, Skeeter was there too, his brother!

Now look, I was drunk. Fifteen years old, sitting at my kitchen table, drunker than fuck, talking to a cop, trying to explain my actions of the night before, half-asleep, and feeling not good at fucking all! My mom was there, to boot!

Officer Riko was yessing and okaying everything I said, and he went just like fuckin' Columbo. "One more question, Bruce. Do you happen to know anything about this?" And he whipped out some Polaroids of Ken Bauer's dad's truck!

"Me, know something about that? Fuck, no!"

Officer Riko went, "I didn't think so, Bruce, I just had to ask. If you did, and you tell me, I promise I'll do my best to work in your corner and get Mr. Bauer not to press charges. If I find out down the road you did, I will see to it charges are pressed to the fullest extent."

He's sayin' this shit, and I was wiping the shit out of my eyes, and I noticed on my hands, there was nothing but dried fucking egg! Ray Charles could'a seen this dried-up peely come-looking shit! So I went, "Yeah, I did that, Officer Rivera."

I might have mentioned, my dad tried his best to get out of as many as he could working days selling cars. He did go to work one of those days, and he had Mr. Bauer's truck cleaned. Not only cleaned, detailed. No charges were ever brought.

I mentioned Joltin' Joe Smokin' Joe Smith. One night, it was summertime. I was headed to Sislow's house to drink a twelve-pack of beer I had stashed behind their garage. This fucker was on his porch and went, "Where you goin'?"

Told 'em I was goin' for a walk, and he asked if he could go. Sure, why not? Tell anyone about me drinkin' beer, I'll fuck you up! Matter of fact, I'm going to waste one by making you drink it. That way, you drank too. Only one. You get one.

That was my introduction to Joe Smith. Joe wasn't a bad kid. He was the really nervous type who repeated the same three stories every ten minutes because he wanted you to know he saw Stephanie Stanziano's pussy one time, and his dad got a monkey drunk in the army, and I forgot the other one.

Did I mention Joe tried to drink with Kenny and me once? Kenny's dad put him up in the house he owned on E Street, across from his parents' house on the eastside of Lorain, and I took Joe over there one night with me. Was around Thanksgiving or Christmastime. Cold as fuck out.

We each had a bottle of Wild Turkey. By the time we left Kenny's, I could not walk. I could, however, drive. I was in a dealership car, a Cadillac Broham. About a ten, fifteen-minute ride back to Joe's, this fucker was puking his guts out in my car like hell wouldn't have it! We got back to his house, and he sat in the basement with a pot from the kitchen, puking his guts out! Remember that, Joe? I tried to tell ya, ya fuckin' idiot!

I remember having the air conditioner on and the windows down on the ride home. One of those nights.

That took place around the time my parents got divorced. Joe worked at an IGA grocery store in Amherst, and he stole a bottle of Southern Comfort. We hid it in a dugout at the baseball fields and went back that night and drank it. Again he got sick. I never asked him to steal that booze. Never even hinted at it. But I'm certain that had to be my fault, him stealing that cough syrup bottle of booze.

Chapter 42

After trying to stay with my dad off and on for a while and giving the backwoods a try or two, I ended up at Stuff's house for probably about a year. There is not one bad thing I have to say about his parents, Carl and Carol Griffith! Great, great, great, real, real people. Act like a retarded fuckin' dickhead around him, or especially her, and you were gonna be called a retarded fuckin' dickhead! I promise.

I can't say a whole lot about this time in my life. I mean, I was a mental wreck 24-7. Chris Kirk, a kid our age who lived on Stuff's street, had gotten killed on I-90 coming home from the races one night, and I remember thinking how lucky he was. He was an Aerosmith fan, and his dad had a coat made that said "Sweet E. Motion" on the back. I haven't liked Aerosmith since about 1982, '83, but every time I hear that one overplayed cheesy bubblegum rock song, I can't help but listen because I feel something.

Stuff fought for Tom Gray. There was friction between Tom and me. He's the guy I very first started with, and my dad yanked me and took me to Kelly. When I started living with Stuff, I trained at Tom's, and he just never could get over what happened. It showed in all his actions toward me. My confidence in anything I did in my life by now was thirteen tons of stinky raw sewage shit. I had none in anything I did.

Funny, Tom Gray worked my corner for my very first amateur fight, and he worked it for my very last. I remember the night of my last amateur fight because Stuff and I had it out. It was a testosterone thing. He was calling me out, wanting to fight. I was living with his parents and feeling very, very, very uncomfortable. He was pissed because I got into it with one of his retarded friends, Chuck Hasledge, when we were out partying.

So I dropped Stuff off and went to Kenny's on E Street. That was when I quit staying with the Griffiths.

Stuff thinks I'm retarded. After I moved to Texas, he was going to the bars in Amherst saying all kinds of shit about me. He had turned pro and thought he was the shit. He might have been, but the one time we fought, I stopped him in the third round. Hey, Stuppy, you find someone dumb enough to come up with the right amount of money, we can do it again today! Be an older version of Tex Cobb fighting Leon Spinks! You get to be Leon Spinks! I still have all my teeth, you don't. And well, you and Leon are twins in the IQ department.

See, at this age, I can see now where my mind was completely fucked, really. I mean, during this time, I was trying to fit in with a family that was just trying to help me, but it was extremely uncomfortable for me. I asked my dad's sperm donor if I could stay with them, and he said they were too sick. Yet up to the day he died, he paid a lady—I use the term loosely—who took care of Alzheimer's Dot Head, to give him oral pleasure. Apparently you can be on your deathbed for thirty years. Those two used condoms were. At one time, I had a bunch of fuckin' guys hounding me, who were looking for my dad. I had no fucking clue where he was. He had me help him move a bunch of cars one day and told me to never say a fuckin' word about it, and he was going away for a while, and to not drive any of those cars anywhere, stay with the Griffiths, and keep my fucking mouth shut! Life with Bud was not easy.

At this time, my mom was lost in her soap opera of moving back to where her family was from. I say bad things about this place and places like them. There are good people everywhere. There are retards everywhere. I call shit how I see it. So if you're from Lewis County, Kentucky, or the surrounding area, or a place like it, if you have half a brain, you will be able to see where I am coming from. If not, I don't care.

You move from where you are in the hills to a major city overnight and see how you like it.

Chapter 43

I wound up in San Antonio, Texas, with Tony Ayala Sr. I was seventeen. Looking back, this was a great opportunity for me on one hand. On the other, more perverted twisted shit.

Tony put me up with his partner, Joe Sousa. Joe lived, I believe, at 6803 Wheatstone in San Antonio. There was him, his wife (can't remember her name), his daughter, Marie, and his son, Arthur.

Now Arthur and Marie were adopted. Arthur was a big kid. Uncle-Sissy-Pants-Hammond big. He was about fifteen, sixteen years old. Marie was hot! She was about seventeen, eighteen.

One thing about Joe's wife, she was always saying how she was blind and couldn't see shit. And one day, when I was walking through the door, didn't even have it open yet, and she was in the kitchen, she went, "Oh, I see Tony gave you one of his new T-shirts."

It was small print and pretty discreet. I mean, the name of the pit bull was in the left chest of the shirt in, like, two-inch letters. That was the only thing on the shirt, the name of a dog, King. Looked a little bigger than that. No picture, nothin', a name. But she was blind!

Now Arthur, he had stacks of porno magazines surrounding all four walls of his bedroom, and they came up to about my waist. I'm talkin' hard-core freaky porn. The only thing this fucker talked about besides his job at McDonald's was fucking and sucking, that is all! Yes! He was a virgin.

Their house was nice, in a nice area, but it was small. I slept on the couch in the living room. Same couch Robbie Epps slept on, I was told. From night fucking one, Joe and Marie would sit on the floor in the living room and watch The Playboy Channel together. I could not help but watch as well. I say that not in a sexual way. I mean, I was three fuckin' feet away on a couch.

Joe would end up giving her a massage, and it always ended with him playing with her tits, and I wouldn't even be able to jerk off after they went to bed, much less fuck her. Because I was weirded out.

I was telling Tony about this. I told Jesse Benavides about it, Ray Medal, the whole fucking gym! All they did was tell me Joe stories back.

First time that fucker tried to give me a massage at the gym, he tried pulling my fuckin' pants down. I told Tony, and he took me to his house, which was, well, different than Joe's. For starters, he had thirteen pit bulls in his yard and a bunch of pit bull training equipment.

I was in San Antonio a little less than a year, but I just had to go. From a boxing standpoint, I helped Mike Ayala get ready for his fight against Juan Meza. I worked with Mike a lot. Jesse Benavides, Ray Medal, Paulie Ayala. Jesse James Leigha was an amateur at the time. Ask him if I could fight. His dad didn't let us work together often. I'm certain he'd deny all this today, but the truth is the truth. I never had anything against Jesse or his dad. Stand-up people back then.

Jesse Benavides is a class act, and I think the world should know that. He was when I knew him anyhow. Jesse made the mistake of drinking with me once.

All during this time, the one thing I did not have was self-assurance, confidence in myself. Why? I mean, I always heard my dad's sperm donor in my head, my cousins, Rick, the bad shit I had started doing. The one thing I thought I always had was alcohol.

I remember one day, I was sparring with Jesse Benavides, and between rounds, he came up to me and went, "Stay away from Tony as much as possible. I smell that beer you were drinking."

Proud of this today? Do I really need to dignify that with an answer?

Chapter 44

Ya know, gettin' back to that athlete thing for a moment. When I played Little League, was my second or third year, and I pitched as perfect a game of baseball that could be pitched for seventeen straight batters; five and two-third innings of perfect, perfect baseball. All I needed in the field was Adam still-had-teeth New. There were seventeen batters up and not only retired, struck-out retired. Seventeen of those motherfuckers in a goddamn row! Eighteenth batter was up, ninth batter in the order, Ryan Barret (I got my name from a TV character) Hammond's spot in the lineup, two strikes on the prick, and I hit him!

Sure fuckin' did! Hit 'em good too! Next batter up, number 1 guy in the order, struck him out. You gotta confirm this with Tommy Capaso. He's an Amherstonian, and that fucker knows everything about sports from the beginning of fuckin' time! Especially local shit. Used to be that way anyhow. His brother, Mark, died when I was living in California with J Dub. These guys lived by J Dub. Tommy got a job at the *Journal* while still in high school and retired from there.

They were water boys for the high school football team. These two were something! Never played any organized sports, but if there was a neighborhood game going, they were the first to go and the last to leave! They loved baseball, basketball, and football. Tommy saw Queen's News of the World Tour, lucky fucker! I was too young.

These two knew everything. This is before the Internet. Fuck, Internet? Pong wasn't even a vision yet.

I was a water boy for the varsity football team. Was in third and part of fourth grade. Coach Toth. Larry Toth. Had a ball! Kevin Criss "Brillo" and Les Dostal were the kicker and punter. They used to go back to the actual football stadium to "practice."

These fuckers would go to the Tuff Shack and get the weed, and guess who smoked with them?

Goddamn! I forgot all about this segment of my life! Coach Toth went to Kent State, and he roomed with either Lambert or Ham, whichever one went there, and all his speeches were about that! Coach Toth was something. Took the team to Massilon to scrimmage the Tigers. They were a state powerhouse. I remember their quarterback's name was Ofenbecker.

Comets got beaten soundly, but I remember Coach Toth reading off stats about the scoring they did and the yards they gained, and the whole team went nuts!

My fourth-grade year, Andy Stainbrook's younger brother started hangin' out, wanting to be a water boy or something. He was in, at least, middle school, and the fucker was bullying me one day at the Tuff Shack, and I hit that fucker in the eye with a Nolan Ryan fastball, in the form of a goddamn rock, sure did. I was scared to death of this fucker. He was ten times my size trying to bully me. He didn't know me. He didn't know where I had already been in life. Andy Stainbrook played on the varsity team. Tight end or wide receiver, I believe. Number 85, I believe. Cliff Azok was 64, Skip Fleming 55, Les Dostal 62, Ken Balko 72; why I remember this, I have no idea. I think Brillo was 6, Phil Parker was 3. After I hit him, I just left and went home. Never water-boyed again. Never did a goddamn thing to that kid, nothin'. "Hot Child in the City."

Chapter 45

Have I talked about the preacher's son and our friendship yet? William Lee Jones, Jr. (Willy) Lee and I hung out quite a bit for a spell. His dad, William, was the preacher at Good God Church in Amherst.

They let me stay with them for a spell before or after I stayed with the Griffiths, I can't remember which. Today I realize these people were horrified with me in their house, and they had no idea how to tell me to leave.

I mean, I was coming and going all hours of the day and night, Willy was keeping the car out all night, I wasn't going to church every Sunday like I said I would, and when I did, I was always drunk, on and on. Steven Bishop.

It isn't like I turned Lee into a bad kid. I mean, long before we started hangin' out, he was drinkin' and smokin' cigarettes and weed and doin' all the things preacher's sons aren't supposed to do. Actually Lee got tons of pussy in high school. Shameful, isn't it?

One time, when I was staying with them, Lee and I scored a vitamin bottle full of Valium. One of those big extra-value bottles full of nothing but pure bliss. Can't recall how we scored them, doesn't matter.

All I know is once I started eating those fucking things, life slowed way the fuck down, and I got really confused about shit.

I have been to one NBA game in my life, and this is why I remember it. It was during this Valium run. One day, I was at Lee's parents' kitchen table, reading the paper, and I went, "We gotta go to a Cavs game! We haven't been to one yet this year."

To that, Lee responded, "We were just at one last week, when they played the Lakers." Then he showed me the stub and the date on the paper I was reading to prove it!

Lee had a younger brother, Borgy. Year or two younger than me. Borgy ended up dating this girl, Billie Hoazillo, and he got her pregnant. Now remember, his dad was the preacher man at the church, and he went and did this.

Couldn't have been a week or two later, I was staying at Tracy Boose's and her husband, Eddie's. I forget his last name. I went to school with Stacey.

They lived above a dentist office on Park Avenue in downtown Amherst. I was at the bars till close and went up to their apartment to crash, and guess who had found their way there? You guessed it, Billie Hoazillo. Wide awake. Layin' on the couch. Wonderin' what I was up to at three o'clock in the morning and was it okay if she stayed on the couch. Do I have to say what happened?

Not long after that, probably the next day, Borgy got word to me; he wanted to speak to me. Needless to say, I don't think I've been back to the rev's house since. No fear, no worry. Just didn't want to start more shit than Billie's pussy already had.

I saw Lee when we were in our twenties. I mean, I went to his wedding, stuff like that, but really, it was a chapter ended.

I tried to reach the ex-reverend and apologize to him and try to let him know I'm a fucked-up human being trying to take responsibility for doing rotten things like I've done, but I've yet to hear from him.

I understand. I would be a total sack of shit retard Valloyd-Deed-like person, if I was able to find fault in their bitterness toward me at all. I hope the entire family is doing well.

Borgy, did you retire from the navy? Mary, are you a banker like your mom? Lee, still pissed at your wife, who put on all that weight, and still smoking cigarettes to show her?

Last time I saw Lee was—wow! What, 1992, '91? Long time ago. I hope the entire Jones family is doing well. And I want them all to know they have the right to really hate my guts, and I can't say I blame them.

Rev Jones came to see me the second time I was in rehab and tried to tell me God loved me. Never forgot that, Mr. William Lee Jones Sr.

Chapter 46

All this shit was goin' on, and I was supposed to be going to school somewhere along the way. Remember those brain busters classes I was tellin' you about? My sophomore year, I was back in those classes they put me in when they thought I couldn't color between the lines.

During my sophomore year, I got in the habit of going up to Johnny K's quite often with some guy named Eric. Can't remember his last name, but I went to school with him, and he drove a pickup truck. I know for a fact we were in Johnny's by 9:00 a.m. because that's when *Donahue* came on, and God forbid we miss *Donahue*! I just realized Eric had a touch of the Susie Hammond lyin' sluts when it came to the talk show thing. He told me he had to drink a beer every morning after he brushed his teeth because he hated the taste of toothpaste!

I was quite the regular at Johnny K's for a while. I mean, I lived close by. I already knew half the crowd, they were my dad's and uncle's friends, my underage friends Kelly King, Stan, Kenny Leman, whole bunch of serious fuckin' drinkers.

It all came crashing to a head one day when the *Lorain Journal* did an article on me about boxing, and the very fucking last sentence in the article said I was a high school dropout. I should be in eleventh grade.

Went into Johnny's that day, and as soon as I opened the door, he went, "Bruce, I know your dad since we were kids. We played softball together. No more." Totally understandable. Wasn't mad. Didn't try to sneak in after that at all. The ban lasted about a month. Maybe two.

Chapter 47

Do you remember the last day of school, ever? I do. Funny. I remember my first day of kindergarten at Shupe. That was where I had Mrs. Poplar.

Anyhow last day of school ever was way more interesting than the first day ever. Bud and Carol were getting divorced, and I lay on my floor and drank on a bottle of Yukon Jack and listened to music all night long.

Homeroom was 7:45 a.m., and I could literally throw a rock and hit the student parking lot. Back then, probably the school building. So I did the right thing. I threw some clothes on and headed down to the school to see if anyone was smokin' weed behind the bus barns and to see who had showed up early with a vehicle.

There was nobody smokin' weed behind the bus barns, or cigarettes. No one was even at the fuckin' bus barns yet! There was one car in the entire student parking lot. One car.

It was a Nova or Chevelle, I forget. About a 1969 to a '72, '73. Bill Hart was driving it. Bill Hart was definitely a Dirt Ball. Rumor had it he had shot whiskey under his fingernails to get a better buzz one night at a party. Personally I drew the line at the aspirin-in-the-cigarette-tobacco thing when it came to drug experiments.

Anyhow we "hey, what's up?" each other, and he told me to get in. He said he had to run up to Lawson's to get a pack of cigarettes, did I care to go with him? As I get in that grumblin' machine, I mention in passing, I had a few chugs of Yukon at the house, did he care for any?

Bill Hart, may God bless his soul, said something along the lines of, "That sure will go good with this!" And he pulled out a joint. Not a big fat sack but a big fat joint. I ran back to the house and got the bottle, ran back to the student parking lot, and jumped in the car with Bill. We went straight to Lawson's and got a pack of smokes, and the cruise began.

Not an all-day cruise. We rode around and smoked the joint and hit on the bottle and went back to the school as the student parking lot was filling up.

I walked through the senior lounge doors and down the longest hall in the school. At the intersection of Longest Hall and shop classes corridor, the corridor Mr. Carney, the car-wreck-stopping-to-help teacher, taught in, there was a bathroom. I went in that bathroom and looked in the mirror and said, "No, sir! Not today!"

You guessed it, Stevie Wonder could'a seen I was fucked up! Eyes were slits, cheeks all red. Yep. Fucked up. Walked out of the bathroom, back up Longest Hall, and right out the doors to the sanctuary of the floor in my room, with the music.

No. I'm not proud of that. Never have been. That was, however, the very last day I have ever stepped foot in Marion L. Steele High School as a student. My grades that year were, again, an *A* and *B* in history and English.

The English class I had as a freshman only had one freshman in it—me. It was some kind of required class, and it was mostly juniors, a few seniors in it. My sophomore year's English class had all sophomores and kids who, well, couldn't color between the lines.

While in Detroit, I came home, and I went to a school dance, and Mr. Boyton approached me and said school dances were for students. I told him I had enrolled in Detroit, and he asked me why they never asked for records. He didn't make me leave the dance. That's the very last time I ever graced the halls of that fine learning institution.

I did get my Good Enough Diploma. One day, while at my mom's and Duke's, my new stepdad, my mom was in tears, literally. Begging me to go to school there! I told her she had to be fuckin' nuts!

So she went, "Will you get your GED?"

I agreed and went to the Lewis County High School night class to take the test, and the teacher said I had to study with the class before I could take the test.

I am making fun of no one and have never and will never belittle someone for their mental capacity, unless you are someone like a politician or someone who deserves to be told, in no uncertain terms, what a retard you are. But this class was literally the can't-color-between-the-lines kinda thing, and I told the teacher I wasn't staying. So he asked me to take a pretest, and he'd place me where he felt I belonged, but I had to promise to stay in the classes, even if it was that one; I promised. After he graded this test I took, that took about two hours to complete, he went, "You're ready to take the actual test. I'll call and set it up."

Chapter 48

In 1988, I turned pro. April of '88, I believe. Fought on the undercard of the Roberto Duran—Paul Thorne card. Signed a contract for a six-rounder, got bumped to a four, got paid $1,200 for that fight, and walked away with $550.

Not only do you learn about the unexpected expenses in the fight racket, you get to experience them and many other things you were never taught from a book firsthand!

I signed a two-year contract with Carmen Graziano and Greg Cook. I got $10,000 cash, shared a condo on the island, had a 1986 Mercedes SEL—I think it was a 400—got $125 a week to put in my pocket, and fucked it all up well within six months. The ten large was gone well within two weeks.

Greg Cook was a nice guy. His mom and Graz dated. She was into real estate, Pat, Ms. Cook. At one point, I was staying with them, and when Greg would be gone, or in bed, she'd go outside and smoke and come back in and go, "Please don't tell Greg I was smoking, Bruce! He thinks I quit!"

Greg had one kidney because his sister, who was a nun, needed a kidney, and the doctor said his was the best match. After giving one to her, and her body rejecting it, his one left went bad!

Greg was young, in his thirties, had money, and was quite angry at the world. Especially certain doctors!

He'd take me with him, and he'd go drinking around the island. He wasn't supposed to drink. He'd talk about suing this doctor and that, tell me not to drink. He'd tell me he wished his mom would quit going outside and smoking. We'd go to the Circle Bar in Brigantine—he knew the owner—and he'd drink and talk. And what that did was get me a free pass to the Circle whenever I wanted. They had a Grateful Dead cover band; first set started at, like, two o'clock in the morning. I don't think I ever missed a show. Thursday nights.

He had this dog, terrier type, named Killer. He'd bring Killer on the mornings he picked me up to do wind sprints at a big field in Brigantine.

From 1988 till 1994 is hard for me to talk about. I mean, I'm pretty sure it was '92, I went up to Vegas and stayed with a guy, Randy Smith, who was one of Terry Norris' sparring partners. Joe Sayatovich had gotten word to me through Rudy Elias, the trainer, I was officially done at First Fighter Squadron.

I called Randy, and he said, "Come on up, Joe Frazier, you AIDS candidate you." He called everybody Joe Frazier and an AIDS candidate. Randy Smith was quite the character.

I spent about six months with him at an apartment off Twain, by the fashion mall.

I tried, with all my might, to drink myself to death in Vegas.

I got a job, third shift, at a 7-Eleven not far from the apartment. The guy who owned it—can't remember his name—was a PGA golfer and a real asshole-dickhead combination.

My manager on that shift was a gay guy who was funny as hell! I went out with this fucker a few times. He looked like a Hispanic version of Kimbo Slice in size, and when he dressed up like a woman, it was hilarious!

The entire time I was in Vegas, I was completely under the influence of alcohol and, at times, other mood-altering substances. Hell, every night I worked and took all the trash out, I was sure to have at least twelve cold ones, if not twenty-four, for later that morning at the apartment!

Nothing good ever happened to me in Vegas, and nothing bad ever happened to me in Vegas. I was sparring with guys at the, I believe, Ringside Gym for a few extra bucks. I got in two fistfights within three minutes of each other, one night. One in a bar and one in the parking lot of said 7-Eleven when leaving said bar. Lots of drinking and drug use. Lots more drinking than drug use.

Chapter 49

Boxing is not a sport nor is it a game. It is people fucking people at any and all costs, period. At any and all levels, up to, and including, death. I can't blame boxing for destroying my life. Not at all. On the contrary, boxing gave me a stellar education and taught me how to survive in life.

After years of total devastation and feeling like a total failure, that is how I rationalized wasting seventeen years of my life.

I got used and burned so many times while in the fight racket I can't count that high! I also used and burned—tried to—as many people who did me.

Looking back, I had some talent. I mean, the second time I went to rehab was at Greg's and Graz's request. They both sat me down and had a talk with me in the kitchen, right there on Lighthouse Drive.

Graz was sayin' stuff like, "Look, all you have to do is dedicate five years of your life, that's all. Five years! If you wanna drink yourself to death and put that shit up your nose in five years, you will be able to do it till you die. Just lay off that shit for five years! What is wrong with you?"

Greg was saying things like, "Bruce, you know Carmen doesn't usually put up with stuff like this from fighters. You saw him kick Lenny out in the streets, and he was a number 1 contender. Carmen believes in you, really believes in you, so how 'bout going to rehab and straightening this thing out? I got a lot invested in you too."

They flew me home, and I went through Lakeland a second time, and when I landed at the Philadelphia airport, I was so drunk

I couldn't walk straight. This was during the holiday season of '88, I believe.

I had a friend, Hugh Scully, who drove for a limo company on the island, and he was there to pick me up in a stretch limo. He was pissed because I was drunk. Hugh concocted a great story for me and told it to Greg and Graz, and he pleaded with them to give me one more chance.

They did. I was shipped off to a rehab in Seaside Heights. I didn't get drunk the day I got out of there, but I didn't feel any different inside. I still felt useless and worthless. No blow jobs at the Seaside Heights rehab either.

One day, not long after this, I was having some kind of mental spell. I mean, you know, a conversation in my head about what a piece of shit I am, and I'm no good, stuff like that. And I'm sparring with a guy while I'm having this conversation in my head, and I am not able to do what I'm trying to do.

The guy I was sparring with was Georgie Navvaro. I dropped my hands and sat on the ropes and let Georgie pummel me. When he refused to hit me because I wasn't defending myself, I started saying real personal stuff to him, and he then proceeded the onslaught.

Graz called time, and I apologized to Georgie, and I thanked him. To this day, I can't explain it, but sometimes, getting cracked in the head with a stiff right hand and a Joe Frazier left hook just feels good. Make sense? Every now and then, to this day, I like it better when the pain comes. Remember that Pete Hamill book? "They ain't got what we got."

Chapter 50

Seems like people have always been enthralled with the world of fisticuffs. I mean, everyone on earth enjoys watching a good ass-beating, giving a good ass-beating, and talking about a good ass-beating. Their favorite thing is talking about all the ass-whippings they themselves have given! However, on the other hand, no one wants to get a good ass-beating or ever talk about the time they got their ass kicked!

I had a guidance counselor in junior high school, Mr. Dean Wegahaupt, who used to tell us, "The more you play with fire, the better chance you have of getting burned." The more you play in violence, the better your chance of getting your ass whipped. I've had mine whipped a lot.

When I was in the fight racket, I saw at least two million guys through the years who had more ability than Henry Armstrong and Joe Louis put together. I mean, world-beaters.

There was a guy, when I was a kid, probably twelve, thirteen, who used to fight for Kelly. Can't remember his name, but his nickname was Kid Chocolate. It was on all his gear and workout clothes.

This fucker had the speed of Hector Camacho and the power of Mugabi. To watch him hit the speed, heavy, and double-end bags was a treat. I mean, to see this guy work out, you'd think he was Walker Smith Jr. reincarnated!

He wasn't old, but he was older than me. He was probably seventeen, eighteen. He was an open fighter; I was a Junior Olympic fighter. First time Kelly told me I was sparring with the Kid, the fear must've shown all over my face 'cause Kelly went, "Crack this prick quick and hard, and he'll quit after one round." Kelly was right. Most people, a very, very large percentage of people, can't accept being beat on. It's called heart. You have it, or you don't.

If I could do one thing over in life, it would be to have never left Jim Kelly. If I would have stayed with him, there is no doubt in my mind, my pro career would have been completely different.

Jim Kelly took care of all his fighters—pros, amateurs, people who trained at the gym, and the people who didn't train and needed serious mental help; James Richard Kelly took care of all these people.

He got Mark Rivera a fight with Evander Holyfield, Tommy Hanks with Camacho, Tony Rodriguez a fight with Camacho. He took Pete McIntyre to the light heavyweight NABF title. He worked with Ralph Moncrief. Jim Kelly was a smart boxing guy and a kind caring human being. I still think of him almost daily. Fucker would steal anything not nailed down. Toilet paper, paper towels, soap, bleach, nuts, bolts, anything he saw lying around at a fight show, or anywhere, he'd have to have it! And every other word out of his mouth was a cuss word; *fuck, goddamn, piss, fuck* again, *cocksucker*, that was Jim Kelly verbiage. Kelly was a good Catholic. May God rest his soul.

Getting back to the violence thing for a minute. Do you like to be hit hard and hurt, possibly knocked unconscious, possibly suffer some broken bones? No? No kidding, me neither!

It is not normal to take physical abuse and go right back where it came from, looking for more, is it? Everybody is a world-class ass-beater and invincible, till they get a whiff of something coming back at them.

Let me say this, the trick to being successful in the fight racket, being a successful fighter, the one key ingredient is this: when someone cracks you with a Larry Holmes jab, right in the nose, and the blood is flowing, and you can't breathe, and it's broken, and your lungs burn, your legs are so heavy they feel glued to the spot, your arms are tied to your sides with silver chains, and the weight of gold ship anchors your belly and ribs and hips, and thighs are sore from being pounded and beat on, you can't see straight, and you have three and a half rounds to go, and getting beaten on is easier than trying to dance or move around, and you've had your ass beaten all five previous rounds, and the only hope is none, and you get back to your corner, and they ask you how you feel, what is your response? By the way, you're making $350 for this eight-round exhibition of pugilism. Minus a C-note for the cornerman and cut man.

Only you can answer that question. I already have.

One thing boxing taught me is as long as I have breath in these weak-ass lungs of mine, you're going to have to kill me to take anything away from me or try to hurt me, because as I said, violence of any kind is not a sport or joke. Ask Benny Peret. You can't, he's dead. Ask Adam no-teeth New.

It is not my job to educate the public on the fight racket. I only have my experience to go by. I've met the nastiest, stinkiest, used condom, used toilet paper, scumbag, douche in the fight racket, and I've met the kindest, nicest, most caring human beings in the fight racket. I must say, I have never met anyone in the fight racket who lies as bad as Susie and dead Charlie Hammond. And that's really saying something, I promise.

Chapter 51

There is not a day goes by that my mind does not let me know I am a failure, and I fucked up. It is not a conscious thought, it's something that just pops in my head at least once, twice, sometimes a lot, every day. It's like that same voice that let me know I was a loser before I ever competed. It just has to let me know I fucked up and failed.

From 1978–19994, there is not one thing you can stump me on concerning the fight racket. Not one. Cut men, the faggots, the fakes, the snakes, I can tell you about fighters you've heard of from this span; I got high and drunk with quite a few of them. And a billion you never have. I was at the sparring session in Atlantic City where they say Tyson got dropped by Greg Page (he was pushed down); it's all useless, worthless memories.

I was in camps and trained at gyms with everyone, from Tyson to Sauol Mamby to just about anyone you can think of from this span. And if you want to match wits on the history of boxing, bring your money. I challenge Mike Tyson to a game of boxing *Jeopardy*. No shit. Sorry, Mike. It would be another KO by on your end.

If you are that interested in boxing, I suggest you start frequenting your local gym regularly for a long, long time, if you really want to see how the circus operates.

If you are interested in boxing, and there is no local gym, just stuff a bag with sand and have your mom or dad or drunkard badass uncle train you. That is no different than your local gym.

Get ahold of a Johnny Bos or a Pete Susens, and you'll be well on your way.

If you have a lot of money and are interested in the fight game, you should contact me immediately. I mean, pronto!

Chapter 52

I have some fond memories of these days. I think it was '93, I had left Vegas and Randy Smith's AIDS candidate Joe Frazier ass. I wound up in Brockton, Massachusetts. I sparred for about six months with Sid and Fitz Vanderpool and Johnny and Angelo Bizzarro.

All I am going to say is this: Fitz was my weight, and he ended up getting a title shot. I owned him. I mean, one day, he went, "You been runnin' or what? You aren't supposed to go all out on me! You're supposed to get tired after three rounds!"

Of course not! But you were me, correct? And you in the fourteen-ounce gloves! I was in eighteens. When I look back at things like this, it makes me sick to know I deprived myself from being successful.

Goody Pettronelli trained all these guys. He and his brother, Pat, had split as partners over a money thing when Hagler retired, and they refused to see or speak to each other. So Pat had the gym till, like, five or six, then Goody got it.

Goody Pettronelli is dead. Anyone who knew him, and is honest, cannot say this isn't true—he was the cheapest cocksucker to ever exist! I mean, this prick made generic toilet paper look like Charmin!

One day, he picked me up where he had me staying, the YMCA 315 North Main Street, and took me to eat breakfast. He was thumbing through a book of houses, talking about how his wife wasn't sure which one she wanted, then left the waitress a tip of about 65¢, literally. I was awestruck! Of course, I had to buy my own breakfast. Had to leave two tips 'cause I was with a cheap fucker!

Here's the deal. It was agreed upon between Mr. Pettronelli and myself that I was to get $250, American dollars, cash, every Friday, after workout as long as I showed up and gave work (I never missed a day). He also paid my rent at the Y during my tenure; that was the deal. I supplied my own food.

Now how many times do you think I heard, "Oh, sorry! I forgot all about paying you, Bruce. I'll have it tomorrow, okay?" Every Friday!

Johnny and Angelo Bizzarro were handled by Don Elbaum. They weren't put up at the Y. They stayed with a Brockton cop, Mike Olyczak.

When I met Mike, it was on. I have to say this. Mike was thirty-five years old at this time, and he professed to be a Vietnam vet, and that's all he talked about. He was seventeen when the Vietnam War ended. That makes him as bad a liar as Susie and Charlie Sissy Pants Hammond.

I knew Mike was full of shit, and it struck a nerve in me because of my dad being in Nam, but still, hanging out at Mike's with Johnny and Angelo was better than the YMCA.

Johnny and Angelo Bizzaro did not drink or do drugs or smoke cigarettes. They thought it was all bad for you. Mike Olyczak was a drunk and a cokehead. Once I found that out, I had a new best friend.

Apparently Mike thought I was stupid. We were drinking wine one night at his house, and he kept running up to his room and coming back down with the sniffles. After about the third time, I went up to his room and caught him red-handed with a mirror full of powder on it.

I'm like, "What the fuck, dude, I don't get any?"

He went, "Oh, this is just something extra I had lying around, here ya go."

So after that, Mike the criminal cop Olyczak and I became pretty good buddies.

I have nothing but fond memories of my stint in Brockton.

First of all, being a sparring partner can be a decent living. Terry Norris used to pay his $750 a week. Tyson was paying crazy money to his. Tyson was paying his like $1,200, $1,500 early in his career. I once saw Jose Ribalta, who was sparring with Tyson in Atlantic City for the Spinks fight, betting five large a whack at the blackjack table. That was sparring partner money.

Anyhow at the Brockton YMCA, there was a restaurant on the bottom floor. There was a juvenile detention center on the fifth floor. I lived on, like, the ninth or tenth floor.

My first day there, I went down to the restaurant and explained my situation, being a sparring partner for Goody, and could I run a tab till Friday, small tab.

I explained my plight to a gentleman who, I quickly learned, owned the establishment, and he told me to sit down, what did I want. I had two drops on wheat, coffee, and a tonic, no ice. Matty proceeded to tell me to watch my back, Goody was no good, good luck getting paid, I wasn't the first he'd met in town with the Petronellis, kinda gave me the Boz Scaggs lowdown.

Matty's family were the only workers in his establishment.

Chapter 53

My stint in Brockton was kinda movie-like, dreamlike. As I think about it, it was like my stay in Macon, Georgia, but in a different way.

What's it like being a drunkard, cokehead, sparring partner living at a YMCA, in a broken town, where you know no one or how anything works there?

As Bill Medley and Jennifer Warnes sing, "I had the time of my life!"

Here was my training regimen: I ran every night. I'll tell ya here and now, the best way to get in shape and stay in shape is run. Put five miles in a day and shadowbox twenty, thirty minutes a day, you're good. Counteracts the Marlboros and booze and weed and coke and stuff.

Goddamn! I haven't given this memory any thought in a long time. I mean, first of all, the janitor Paulie took right to me. Within a week of living there, I had a master key to the entire place. All doors that required a key, I had it.

The Sergios, the people who owned the restaurant, liked me. When I went in to pay my tab, Mattie took it out of the box it was in and ripped it up and went, "Your money's no good here." I never paid for anything at Sergio's Place.

His son, Junior, was a good dude. He was a big hockey fan, as am I, so we used to go to B's games often at the old Garden.

Junior belonged to the Brockton Country Club. That's where I learned coke was $40 a gram in that neck of the woods.

There was a guy living there, Jim, who worked at the Bradley's Department Store warehouse. He was friends with Richie Cormeier. I got to know Jim pretty quick. He did not drink or do drugs. He had worked at Bradley's for, like, twenty-some years. It was a good job. His addiction was scratch-off tickets.

Scratch-off tickets were Jim's addiction. Fucker got paid Thursdays and was borrowing $20 every Friday morning before work. It got to where every Thursday night, in the middle of the night, I'd be high and drunk and going through the list of a zillion things racing through my mind, and giving Jim $20 would be on that list, and I'd go slip it under his door so he wouldn't wake me up when I was just getting to sleep and him going to a sucker's job.

Richie was a good dude. He was like a twenty-eight-year-old career college student who lived at his mom's. He went to the University of New Haven in Connecticut. He took me there with him one time for a weekend, and we told all the girls I played for the Paw Sox. Baseball player is more appealing than boxer.

Chapter 54

The neighbor across the hall smoked Garcia Vega cigars with his door open all day and the TV full blast. The neighbor next to me was a black guy named Pops, and he ran a crack house/whore house out of his room.

Traffic would start about nine, ten o'clock at night and go all night long. Every night, about two, three o'clock, after I got my buzz on, I'd sweep the racket ball and hand ball courts for Paulie. After that, I'd do my roadwork on the indoor track, then I'd retire to the Jacuzzi in the women's locker room with my beverage and bag of goodies. I'd generally go to bed at sunup, and by eleven o'clock, noon, I'd start my day.

There was this restaurant/bar Mike used to hang out at. A Chinese guy owned it. We'd go there and eat lunch. Okay, drink lunch, and that's where he'd meet his coke dealer.

We were out at a nightclub one night, and when it was closing, as we were leaving, I said something to a girl as we walked down this hallway. Wasn't rude, wasn't crass, just something like, "Have a good night."

We got out in the parking lot. Next thing you know, Mike and I have four guys around us asking us what we said to that girl. Even the girl was saying it was nothing rude, but these pricks insisted on being tough guys.

Now we're in a parking lot, four guys around us, we're high as hell on coke, been drinking who knows how long, it's January in

Massachusetts, which means it's freezing out. I had no coat on, and Mike went, "I'll be right back!"

Thank you, cocksucker! I was standing there, trying my best to prolong time so I don't get gang beat, and before you know it, there were like five cop cars there, lights going, sirens screaming, and guys with guns everywhere!

Mike was asking me, "Is this the one?"

I'm like, "Yep! That one, and that one too."

There were four guys, and of the four, one of them had kept his mouth shut and wasn't playing badass over me talking to that girl. When Mike asked me if he was one, I said no.

So three of the four went to jail, and guess who the girl left with when they weren't even trying to pick her up? True story. Ask Mike Olyczak. He's either a retired cop, dead, or in prison. No. Nothing happened with the girl. I mean, we went to Mike's and did coke and drank, but we didn't choo choo train her or anything. Mike even got her a ride home from a cop on duty.

Mike had this pink—I think it might have been a Cadillac. Was a '60s car. Was a badass ride. He was too fucked up to drive. I know. He tried.

Chapter 55

There was a guy who lived at the Y, Eddie. He'd get drunk and sit in the lobby of the Y and watch TV in the middle of the night. He was always in his underwear, and he had already pissed himself the time I'd see him. Every night!

Norm. Norm had crazy Einstein gray wiry hair. He was a little guy. He walked the halls all day long and constantly wound and checked his watch to see if it was ticking, then he'd look at the clock on the wall. He went to AA meetings. Once I found this out, I asked him how long he'd been sober.

For at least two months, he'd go, "Three years, eight months. Right, right." The last time I ever asked him, he went, "Three years, eight months, right, been longer, okay?" I never asked him again after that.

Norm told me one day, he went, "I see you walkin' around here fucked up all the time. I'm not sure how much you like to drink, but Sterno is a good buzz!"

Did I tell you about the asprin-in-cigarette-tobacco experiment my cousins turned me on to and how I gave up on drug experiments after that?

I mentioned this place had a juvenile detention center located in it. I was actually put on the payroll for a couple months as a guard. A third-shift guard. If you haven't been able to tell by now, my third shifts were pretty busy already. I mean, would you rather babysit a bunch of delinquents or do a quick five miles and party till dawn?

That was a nice check to get every week, aside from the $250 from Goodie.

I got that check for about three months. How? Simple. See, I spent a lot of time in that diner. My dad's brother, Russ, owned a sports bar/restaurant for a few years when I was a kid, till he lost it to the mob over a gambling debt.

I used to work the kitchen when I'd be in town. Guess who I helped? You guessed it—Aunt Faye "Flushie the Comody!" Stinky bitch used to do the daily special, and Russ had her running the kitchen. Didn't realize it at the time, but that's where I learned to line cook.

Anyhow I'd help them out at the restaurant if they needed it, and Mattie said I should get paid. So I got paid as a guard at the delinquent home for helping out in the restaurant. Make sense?

Richie had a Mustang GT with a headlight out. I rode in that car from Brockton to Boston, Connecticut to New York to Philadelphia, high and drunk the entire time. We never got stopped.

I remember a funny story involving Richie. One night, we went out. We partied our balls off. Stayed out all night. I had paid for the night out 'cause he was broke. I had let him stay in my room at the Y so he wouldn't be confronted by his mom.

When he left the next day, my money was gone! I looked everywhere! It was gone! I was furious! I called Richie and told him he fucked up, I knew where he lived, I was gonna kill him, all that jazz! For stealing my money! He's telling me I'm nuts, why would he steal from me, fuck me! I went back in my room, pissed!

I mean, you ever lived in a room at the Y? Slightly bigger than a jail cell! Where could that money have gone besides Richie Comiere's pocket? That night, at the gym, I was putting my boxing shoes on, guess what I found? My money! I called Richie when I got home, and we celebrated that night for still being pals. Spent the rest of that knot.

Chapter 56

Now as if my life wasn't fucked up enough, I was about to spend the last few months of this long walk down a dead-end road in Indianapolis, Indiana, with Pete Susens. This had to be '93.

Seems like the last fight I ever had was in Illinois, somewhere in late '93, early 1994. I had about ten, fifteen fights for Pete.

I've mentioned Carmen Graziano, Joe Sayatovich; these guys were big players in the racket. For different reasons. Joe, because he had money and was a middleweight boxer, boxing fan, who wanted a white hope. Graz, because, well, Graz was a boxing guy because he was a businessman who did business in boxing circles.

If Graz and Joe were the crème de la crème, Pete Susens was the sour milk. Fighting for Graz and Joe, everything was up front, taken care of, and you were making top dollar for your appearance. Basically you were fighting one of Pete's fighter's or Jimmy Montoya's guys, making a third what you were and had none of the privilege you did as far as gym equipment, sparring, food, nutrition, judges in the pocket, and so on.

I have to say, the highlight of my professional boxing experience was the time spent with Pete Susens and his family of misfits. For a spell, couple few weeks, Randall "Tex" Cobb was fighting for Pete.

Randall "Tex" Cobb could drink beer and liquor and smoke weed like a real man. This fucker would drink a twelve of Bud while he chain-smoked joints, getting ready to go out drinking at the bars.

Drinking is an endurance game. I mean, fuck all you guys who get up the day after a night out and tell everyone how you had nineteen drinks, didn't get sick, drove home, didn't get stopped, on and on.

The question is, why did you go to sleep? Randall "Tex" Cobb was one of those guys who could drink with you till the sun came up and well into the next day. He was, at the time I knew him anyhow.

There was no roadwork fighting for Pete. There was no training when fighting for Pete. Sure. There was a full gym in the building we lived in. Walked right through it to get upstairs to the living quarters. Okay. I'd throw a combination on the heavy bag every time I passed it on the way upstairs. So I did train.

We never missed a night of going to the bar and getting drunk. Pete drank his Canadian Clubs with Coke, tall glass, and smoked his Marlboros. Talked all night long about people in the fight racket, called me an alcoholic and said I should go to meetings, and cussed because someone was gonna have to drive drunk to get home. Not him, though. Was usually Sean Gibbons.

Chapter 57

Boxing gave me opportunities I didn't see at the time, and once realized, those opportunities were gone.

I mean, one day, at Irish Spud Murphy's gym in San Diego, I saw this guy dressed like a bum. Wrinkled shirt, shorts didn't match, sunglasses on, walkin' around, talkin' to everyone, bein' a real big shot.

I never said a word to the guy. I was standin' outside the gym, talkin' to some people, and this guy came out the door and went to a Porsche, one of those expensive ones. He took a third of a cigar out and lit it, started puffing on it like he was really someone.

Finally I went up to him and went, "Who are you?"

He went, "Have you ever seen *The Karate Kid?*"

Right then, it hit me. The cleft in the chin. It was Martin Cove. He was the "bad" sensei in the movie.

During this time, he was a producer, director, writer—something—of those TV shows *Renegade, Silk Stalkings*, seems like another one I can't recall. All those popular shows on USA Network.

Anyhow we saw each other for a couple of weeks, and one day, he went, "You're a good-lookin' kid, and you have some personality. Here's my agent's number. He wants to meet you."

My response was, "I can't. I have a six-rounder coming up."

Chapter 58

I can now look back and see where all this was set up for failure. I can remember being in San Antonio, and one night, Joe came out of his room naked and started walking toward me on the couch, and I was like, "What the fuck are you doing?"

He said he thought he heard me moaning for help in my sleep.

If Robbie Epps is still alive and not talking like he has marbles in his mouth, I sure would like to meet him!

Shit like this would happen, and I'd lay there and cry and think thoughts like, *Why can't I just go back home to Amherst and fight for Kelly?*

Chapter 59

People are always interested in what it is like to box. Back in those days, I was asked this question at least a billion times, "Does it hurt when you get hit? I mean, you have big gloves on and a headgear on?"

My response to that has always been, "You put a headgear on, and I'll put a big glove on and hit you. You tell me if it hurts."

Some of the things I learned in boxing, I have carried with me through life. Actually if I was ever to sit and really think about it, I'd have to say I am who I am because of boxing.

The longest I have ever gone without a nibble, morsel, taste of food is nine days. Going three or four days with no food is a joke.

I once lost thirteen pounds in one day. I've lost twenty-eight pounds in twelve days. Look, I spent my entire life, at one point, with the scale always in the forefront of my mind.

I don't think that ever kept me from drinking all the beer I could and eating all the tacos and Breyers ice cream I could at once. I promise, it was a lot. It still is.

Weighing 172, and we just got a call for a fight in two weeks. Weight for the contract was 42, give or take a pound? No problem.

You know that magnesium shit, comes in a green bottle, take a capful, you shit your intestines out? I used to have to drink a six-pack of that shit for it to start to work. I still have the innate ability to throw up without sticking my fingers down my throat.

Sure. You get to drink all the water you can, then some. Water is a meal.

Check this out. It's nineteen degrees outside, we have a wind coming off the ocean at 22 mph, it's 4:50 a.m., and you have to get up and go run on the beach.

Or it's twelve degrees outside, shit pile of snow everywhere, wind is only 14 mph 'cause it's coming off of Lake Erie, it's 4:50 a.m., and you gotta get up and run before going to sixth grade?

Rain, snow, sleet, hail, windstorm, subzero temperature, too nasty to run outside? You're right, it is—for sissy bitches who don't have the balls to do whatever it takes it get the job done.

I have a funny story. I was training for the National PAL tournament in 1983. Everything was good. My weight, I was in good shape, wasn't boozing and smoking.

One morning, I got up to run and didn't feel like running. So I put a box of cereal, the milk, bowl, and spoon on the back porch.

I'm not saying my dad made me run or train or box or anything. He didn't. However, once I said that was what I wanted to do, I agreed to do whatever was necessary, end of conversation.

Anyhow I went out to the yard, stretched, did a few minutes of shadowboxing, not sure if the old man was watching, but if he was, it had to look good! Then I started out on my thirty-minute run. I went to the end of Harris Street—a five-second feat—went left on Cleveland Avenue for ten seconds, cut down Axtel Street through Brad's yard to my back porch with the corn flakes. Less than a minute.

As I was sitting on the backsteps, indulging in Kellogg's finest, the backdoor opened, and the Bud Man went, "What the fuck are you doing?"

I went, "Eating corn flakes."

He said, "Why not come in and eat them like a normal person at the dining room table?"

So I did. He didn't yell, scream, didn't say not one word to me. Didn't bring it up again that day at all.

Next morning, he got me up at 3:30 a.m.—just to let you know, the bars in Ohio closed at 2:30 a.m.—and told me to get dressed to run. He drove me to what I always called Pinecrest Hill. Those apartments I bit Rick's dick at is in a valley between two hills. The one going east is steep. I mean, pretty fucking steep.

He parked in the cemetery at the top of the hill and told me to start running up and down the hill; he'd tell me when to stop. I was also told if it took me more than three minutes to get down and up, I was in trouble.

Look, the fastest man on earth on meth, coke, crack, pure ether, and rocket fuel might have a chance. I ran up and down that hill for two hours straight, then he went, "See you at the house in fifteen minutes, son."

And he was gone. It's, from recollection, maybe a mile and a half. I made it.

I lost to Thrac Paulett in the semifinals. That fucker beat me in the semis of the National Junior Olympics, National Silver Gloves, and PAL. Has a southpaw from Casper, Wyoming, I think. He was one tough prick. All these years later, my three fights with him seems like it was yesterday. I remember the trunks I wore in two of the three fights: the purple ones and the blue ones.

Thrac Paulette, you alive, pal? You're one tough prick and a fair fighter, and I hope life has treated you kind. Never heard anything from you after the Junior Olympic years, why'd you quit fighting? You had talent, my friend.

During the finals, Smokin' Joe Walker, a welterweight from Akron, and I got some Wild Irish Rose bottles and Olde English quarts and stopped the elevator between floors at the hotel we were at, The Bond Court, and got fucked up and went back across the street to public hall where the fights were.

The PAL tournament was in Cleveland that year, and Don King was there. And while Honest Don was doing a TV interview, Smokin' Joe kept screaming at the top of his drunk ass lungs, "Hey, Don, Joe Walker, Akron, Ohio, welterweight!" Fucker just kept screaming it over and over!

Honest Don kept looking over at us, him smiling, giving that shut-the-fuck-up look! It was funny.

Bill Murphy owned Irish Spud Murphy's Gym. After living on beer, tequila, and Mexican food for about a year, I decided I'd give the fight racket a whirl in San Diego. The first day I walked into Murph's place and stepped on the scale, I weighed 194 1/2 pounds.

In five months, I was ready to fight. My walk around weight down to a buck fifty, no smoking cigarettes at all, wasn't drinking, then Murph got me a fight in Hawaii.

This was the second time in my life I was supposed to go to Hawaii. The first time, Greg Cook offered to fly me there, but I went to Ohio instead. Fucking brilliant, aren't I?

Anyhow one day, I was training, and another trainer in the gym, Emilio, went, "Did you know that guy you're fighting in Hawaii is a fifty-four-pounder, he's fifteen, and 0–15 KOs, and he's a southpaw?"

Needless to say, I still haven't been to Hawaii. Murph told me I had to be at forty, and nothing else. That is how boxing works.

Murph's gym was named Irish Spud after his kid Irish Spud Murphy, who died after taking a beating in the ring. Murph also had another kid, Rocky, who was a great guy but didn't have much ability. He did have balls. If I recall correctly, Murph put his son Rocky in my place over on the island. Rocky was a featherweight. That's a twenty-six-pounder.

"Hey, I got a six-rounder with a junior middleweight. Pays $2,500. You got a featherweight or junior welterweight for my guy?"

"Sure. My kid. My other kid died because I led him to slaughter. I got one kid left. He's a twenty-six-pounder. You aren't gonna kill my only son left, are you?"

"Nah. My guy'll probably just break a couple ribs. But hey, you'll get to see Hawaii!"

"Okay. We'll take it."

And that's what happened in real life. Rock got his ribs broken over on the big island! But his dad got to see Hawaii!

Murph named his son Rocky because he said he fought Rocky Graziano.

I don't like to talk about boxing. I don't like to think about boxing. I never watch boxing. I never tell people I meet I used to box. So let's not talk about boxing anymore, okay?

I defeated myself in the fight racket. Now I can see today where I defeated myself in the racket of life. It has only been, in about, the last fifteen years I have been able to realize this and try to be that confident person I was at twelve.

Chapter 60

So around '93, '94, I left Pete's fisticuff empire based out of Indianapolis, Indiana, and ended up back on Kinney Road in Garrison, Kentucky.

The pain I felt when my mom picked up and moved to Garrison is indescribable. It hurt as much—probably more in a different way—as being sexually abused.

Imagine wherever you are right now, that is your life. Friends, ways of life, familiarity, dialect, taste of the tap water, what soda pop is called, walking distance to a store twenty-four, fast-food walking distance, civilization is what I'm trying to say, everything. Now if you have kids, say seventeen, thirteen, and ten, move them to a totally different region where they know no one or anything about where they just moved, other than it is backwoods, fucked up! I mean, empty country roads and woods, that's it. Twenty-miles-to-town kinda shit.

See, if you don't have problems with those kids, even if you do, do this experiment and see if you don't have problems with those kids you never dreamed possible. Those problems are going to manifest throughout their entire life.

For years, I hated my mom for doing what she did. I did every goddamn thing I could to fuck with her and cause her problems. Wrecked her cars, would get money from her and not pay her back, would go to the house drunk and raise all kinds of hell. I did my utmost best to show her I hated her guts and hoped she'd die on the spot. Sure did.

Chapter 61

I was extremely close with my mom. Then she went and did something like this! Through the years, wherever I went, I always wound back up on Rock fucking Hill, on Kinney Road, in Garrison, Kentucky.

It would always wind up to that or be homeless. My stepdad, Duke, has never liked me. I could go as far as say hate. I can't say I blame him. I do respect Duke. I mean, the entire time my mom was married to him, she only moved once. That's as far as the respect goes. And that was her choice. He did shit like not buy groceries, the food he'd buy he'd put in his room. Duke worked at the railroad, Norfolk Southern. From the moment my mom married him till the time he retired from the railroad, they were still married, I think, every day he came home from work, he had a case of something.

Toilet paper, paper towels, oil, hand soap, nuts, bolts, tools, lots of tools, Elmer "Duke" Willis had a real bad case of the Jim Kelly's. Fucker made $50,000 a year salary and $175,000 a year in bonus goodies! As I write this, if I was to go steal all of the tools out of his work shed that he took from the railroad and sell them, I could retire from my street-corner hustle!

Remember that sitcom *Soap*? Ever seen *Pulp Fiction*? What about *Paris, Texas* with Harry Dean Stanton? You a fan of Benny Hill?

Chapter 62

Now during these years, there was so much shit that happened I'm certain I can't recall a schmilligram of it. I'm okay with that. Really.

I recall enough. I went to San Diego, California, in 1989. Carmen had kicked me out, and I went to Louisville, Kentucky, for a few months. After spending about six months with a retarded hillbilly who got me three fights paying a whopping total of about $150, I was "Goin' Out West."

Shit gets blerry, as Ray Ray Gray used to say. Kenny died in '89. January 11, 1989, I believe. Or April of '89. I get his birth date and death date mixed up.

I was in Jersey when Kenny died. How I found out was, after talking to my mom on the phone, I went out for a while. When I got back, Dorian Mallomad went, "Your mom called as soon as you left. She said to call her, it's important."

As soon as she answered the phone, I went, "Who died?" I thought it was my dad. And I knew something bad had happened because we had just talked two hours ago for about forty-five minutes.

She went, "There was an accident, and Ken Carney got killed."

I flew to Ohio and stayed at Russ's bar (no mob takeover yet). I got back to Ohio the night before the funeral.

When I got to the funeral home, I was going up to the casket, and Ken Sr. stopped me and went, "I already have six pallbearers, but Kenny would be proud if you grabbed the head of the casket."

His mom and Jerry told me Kenny always talked about me and said shit like he wished he could be more like me. Which didn't make sense then nor does it now.

John Maroney was there, Gary Luman, all the Dirt Ball Gang. I never cried at all the entire time. Kenny was buried in a pair of jeans, a Zeppelin T-shirt, his black leather, and his turquoise pinky ring.

When I got back to the bar, I called my mom and started crying while we were talking. It got pretty uncontrollable, and my mom said she was coming up to Ohio. When she got to the bar in Birmingham, Ohio, from Garrison, Kentucky, I was still crying. About a four, four-and-a-half-hour ride.

I was supposed to go back to Jersey the day after the funeral; I didn't.

Chapter 63

Are you *Dazed and Confused* yet? Do I have you "Going Down the Road Feelin' Bad"? Is the sun shining in the big "Blue Sky," and the rain pouring in your heart?

Funny. I remember this shit from the early, early '70s like it was last week, yet the closer to now I get, the more difficult, blerry, and hard to recall my own life experiences it becomes.

I mean, I was in San Diego four years. I mentioned that construction job. That didn't last very long, couple of months. I did get other jobs. None of those lasted long either.

Look, this was Southern California where rent on a dumpster with a urinal was $1,000 a month. That was in a neighborhood with activity in it, if ya get my drift.

I have to honestly say that Jack Wayne "J Dub" Niskey carried my ass for a solid two years. I would get jobs and give him money, but well, if we were to sit down and figure out how much I actually contributed to bills, we're talkin' one-fifth cents on the dollar here.

Jack never bitched at me, complained, threatened to put me out, nothin'. Somewhere through the course of me staying with him on Bancroft in Normal Heights, he told me I was helping him get over his split with Beth better than he ever could have imagined.

Something I never would have remembered, or even given a second thought to, had J Dub not made such a production number out of it for so long, told everyone we ran into for months about the salsa sandwiches I made for dinner one night.

This is Southern California where there is a Mexican restaurant every other doorway, but we had that El Paso jar shit from Vons.

The only thing we had in the entire refrigerator was a block of Velveeta, that jar of shit, and a part of a loaf of bread that had been in there long enough to reproduce.

I cut the little bit of mold off the bread, layered it with cheese, salsa, cheese, salsa, and put it in the oven long enough to bring it up to temp, Chef.

The entire time I was preparing this gourmet meal, J Dub kept saying, "You aren't really going to eat that, are you?" Fuck yeah, I ate it! I was hungry!

If only all my memories of the Golden State were so golden. Don't get me wrong, I had some—I have to call them—wonderful experiences in Southern California.

My idea of wonderful and your idea of wonderful may have different meanings. I lived fifteen minutes from the beach. There were, let's see, the Old Sod, Rosie O'Grady's, and two or three others I can't recall the names of within crawling distance of the apartment, got to know Montie, the third-shift guy who worked at 7-Eleven by Jack's apartment, free food! And well, it was on.

Having grown up on Lake Erie and spending quite a bit of time on the East Coast, you'd think I couldn't wait to be a beach bum. Never have been a water person.

I did, however, frequent the beach regularly because that was where the drugstore was.

Mission Beach had a roller coaster, and it was *the* spot to score LSD. People sold toilet paper for 25¢ a square outside the restrooms, you could legally drink alcohol on the actual beach but not on the boardwalk, and as I said, it was a really hot spot to buy acid.

You went to Ocean Beach for one thing and one thing only— Boy. I got to know Boy for a while, got to know him pretty goddamn well. Boy will fuck you up, I promise.

When this opioid epidemic exploded some years back, it flooded my mind with so many memories when I'd hear a story of another person succumbing to heroin on the news or a news show.

The how and why I decided to try heroin remains unclear in my mind to this day. Really. This was Southern California, 1989, 1990, and well, seems to me heroin was as popular there then as it is everywhere now.

I was probably strung out for a good six, eight, ten months The one thing I never did was stick. Not one time. Not heroin. The only drug I had ever shot up was cocaine. And that was once only. Comparing a coke high to a heroin high is like comparing getting hit with an Ernie Shavers right hand to getting by Shirley Temple's right hand.

Jack introduced me to this guy my age he used to work with. He said we'd be a perfect pair. He was my age, and he liked to party. He and I ended up becoming like Kenny and me with booze; only with Jason Travers and me, it was dope. J Dub called us Peat and Repeat.

The first time we ever did heroin, we bought it downtown and went back to Normal Heights and snorted it in the apartment. We were back downtown a couple more times that night.

During this heroin experiment, I would do things like disappear for two or three weeks, if not longer, not let anyone I knew know where I was, and I'd go downtown and panhandle, then go to OB to get my shit because it was better than the shit in the alley by Murph's.

Balboa Park was a great place to hang out if you were homeless, a junkie, gay, a prostitute, or just a fuckin' quack. I had my bench.

I'd sleep at the beach or at the gym, wake up, and start the hustle again. I don't have great exciting wonderful heroin stories to tell. I smoked black tar heroin in cigarettes or weed, stinky, seedy, most-times-still-wet $5-a-bag weed, and I snorted brown powder heroin up my nose for a few months of my life. The China White makes you piss yourself. And it feels good, pissing yourself high on the China White. All at the expense of others.

Here is the scam I used to hustle people out of money, plain and simple. This was SoCal, so you were either extremely wealthy or extremely poor. The middle class were people like Kato Kalin and me; we were middle class because we were moochers who didn't work.

When I look back, I still get pissed because that prick got OJ and I got J Dub! Oh well!

Anyhow here's the scam I'd use. Always downtown San Diego. I'd clean up at the gym and hit the streets.

I'd find a guy in an expensive suit, or someone getting out of a $250,000 car, standing at a crosswalk—anywhere I was able to strike up a conversation with a sucker—and I'd start, "Sure is nice out today, eh? I saw Jerry Lewis at a lightbulb store today!" Whatever the fuck popped in my head.

Not long into the conversation at all, I'd throw this in there. "Yeah, I just got out here two days ago from Corn County, Iowa, and my car got towed when I ran in to a store. I had no idea I wasn't supposed to park there. Fuckers got me in no time! I wasn't in the store two minutes!

"So since I've been here, I have been homeless, I know no one, and my wallet is in my car. They won't even let me get it so I can pay them! If I can pay it by 5:00 p.m. today, it will only be $275, tomorrow it goes up another $75. I have $82 of the $275, so all I need is $193." And I'd show the money I had—if I had any—to add legitimacy to the bullshit story.

People don't give you pocket change for that story I just told you. They give you tens and twenties, and people offer to take you to get your car with a credit card, get you lunch. I stayed high on heroin for a good eight, ten months on that scam alone.

Chapter 64

Now another vivid memory I have and will never forget, I hope, is the one of the day I decided to stop doing heroin. I was at J Dub's apartment cleaning up, washing my ass, brushing my teeth, and I looked in the mirror, in my eyes—totally by accident because I didn't like to look myself in the eyes—and something said, *Just fucking look at you, you fucking bum!*

Something like that anyhow. It was a voice telling me to straighten up. I looked at my body; I was skinny, my eyes were sunk in three feet behind my skull, I was dirty, I was a junkie mess.

Instead of bailing out of Jack's before he got home from work, I waited on him to get home, and we had a talk. I told him I was on heroin and wanted to get off it, would he be pissed if I stayed there full-time again if I got off the junk? The amazing part of all this was, I was sleeping like a homeless person, and I always had a key to J Dub's apartment. How funny is that?

There were a couple times during this run, Jack would come home, and I'd be there, and he'd yell at me and tell me to get my shit together. He cared about me, I was gonna end up dead. Basically the same speech every junkie has heard from a loved one.

He told me I could, but the first time I did brown again, as he called it, I was gone. I haven't touched it again to this day.

Have you ever detoxed off heroin? I don't mean at a facility with medical staff and all that shit people think you need to dry out. I mean, on a couch in an apartment with no help? I puked and shit for about seven, eight days. Ate meals of soup broth, and crackers were possible after a couple days.

I also drank a lot. There was a liquor store right by the apartment, and they had fifths for like four, five bucks. That's funny. Writing that had me thinking about all the garbage bags Kenny, Chuckie, and I filled when we were kids during that blowout. I was drinkin' this shit like it was Gatorade.

Chapter 65

Now again, this was 1989, 1990, hell, maybe '91. I don't know, I can't recall, it doesn't fucking matter, okay? It was in between these years, probably. It was before cell phones were stuck to everyone's head!

El Cajun is a suburb of San Diego. When I was living out there, El Cajun was known as the meth capitol of the world. At least that's what all the tweakers out there said.

I had never even heard of this shit before moving out there. Even after hearing about it, doing it wasn't a priority of mine at all.

One evening, Jason came and picked me up and took me to a steak house on El Cajun Boulevard. That's a few blocks south, I believe, of Adams Avenue and Normal Heights. Can't remember the name of the neighborhood, but it had the ho stroll on it.

Anyhow he took me to this steak house and went, "Get anything you want, on me, anything!"

I was like, "Dude, what the fuck, dude! Why you buyin' me a steak and treating me like I'm somebody?"

Jason just assured me to eat well, and all was fine. So I ate a steak, I'm sure, with the fixings. Steak medium rare, baker with butter, sour, extra butter, extra sour, salad with blue cheese on the side, coffee, and a soda—no ice—to drink.

After eating our meal, we went back to Normal Heights, and he parked in a cul-de-sac not far from Bancroft—actually it overlooked Jack Murphy Stadium—and he pulled this little white bag of powder out.

I'm like, "Dude! You have coke! Please tell me that's just a sample of the kilo you have!"

He went, "It isn't coke. Just do these two lines." He had put two out on his driver's license.

I did them, and nothing happened. No change at all! Jason went, "You're going to be up for three days, I promise."

I'm not believing that at all. That's when he said we did meth, and he explained what I had gotten myself into.

I guess somewhere along the way, I started tweakin' pretty fuckin' good because I remember walkin' to 7-Eleven a hundred times to buy beer and gum, beer and gum.

Sometime in the middle of the night, I was on my hands and knees, scrubbing the living shit out of the walls in the dining room of the apartment with a toothbrush, chewing gum, feelin' pretty goddamn good, thank you!

I was scrubbin' and chewin' and scrubbin' and chewin', and apparently I was scrubbin' and chewin' a little bit too loud because it woke J Dub up. When I turned around, he was standin' in his bedroom doorway, scratchin' his head, and he went, "Dude, you're tweakin', good night."

And Jason didn't lie, I was up for three days. I knew nothing of him or his past problems with meth. This was my first meth high, and it was as fucking strange and weird as anything I have ever experienced, as far as drugs anyhow. It makes your mind work kinda like it's on squiggly, but you don't get the visuals like you do acid.

That night, or the next day, his girlfriend, Jennifer, called Jack and told him Jason was on meth, and he said he was going back to Seattle. She said it was my fault Jason did meth, she hated me, don't ever let me call Jason again, you get it, fuck off!

Well, Jason ended up not going to Seattle, and from that point on, we never saw each other again. He always lied to Jennifer when he'd come see me. He'd say he had to work over, and he picked up a lot of Saturday shifts.

Those Saturday shifts he worked killed me! I'd be out all night drinking, doing whatever else I did, and I'd be ready for bed by 4:00 a.m., 5:00 a.m., Jason would come over at *seven* o'clock in the god-

VALLOYD BECKER

damn morning, and Jack would let him in, and those fuckers would beat on me till I got up. He and I would leave the apartment and start doing meth.

Somewhere along the way, our neighbor Doug bought a house in Claremont and asked J Dub if he wanted to move in. I was a consolation prize.

Jason would go over to Doug's and climb through my window to get me up. If you ever have a hangover, headache, shits, blerry vision, feel like death, if you smoke some meth, you'll feel like a champ instantly! We'd smoke meth and go to the park by the house and play basketball at 6:30 a.m. on Saturday mornings.

168

Chapter 66

Seems like after living at Doug's for a while, I ended up on the streets. I mean, I stayed at the gym, Murph's, every night Emilio would let me, but I'd have to wait till Murph was gone for the night. And I'd have to be gone before Murph got there the next morning.

He'd moved his gym from, like, Ninth and Broadway to Twelfth and C Street. When it was on Broadway, I stayed there in a room with a cholo who ripped me off and Mike. I hadn't fucked Murph out of his free trip to Hawaii yet, so I was still his boy.

Look, this Mike guy, you think you're fucked up, you think you know some fucked-up people? Murph let him live at the gym for the tradeoff of him keeping the gym clean.

Mike kept that gym so goddamn clean you could eat off the floor! The one thing Mike never cleaned was himself. I stayed in the same long unventilated, no-windows, stuffy, sticky room with him for quite a few months.

Not one time did he ever take a shower, ever. This was Aunt Flushie's twin brother! I even asked this fucker why he never took a shower, and he said he didn't like them, and he didn't want to waste water, there was a shortage. No shit. This cholo fucker, who stole my jewelry from me, George, who was Mexican and spoke a little Spanish, gave him the nickname *bostoso*. He said that was *stinky* in Spanish.

Mike was a guinea pig. He would go in to hospitals and take drugs that weren't on the market yet to see the effects, side effects, etc. He'd get decent money for doing these tests, $1,500 or better for a test, as best I can remember.

He tried to get me to do them, but I just couldn't bring myself to. Look, heroin, I know what I'm getting. Coke, meth, booze, weed, Valium, any other shit I did? I knew what I was getting into. This shit no one knows about? I'm good.

I might be a drunk and somewhat a junkie, but maybe I was afraid I'd quit wanting to bathe if I did those hospital experiments with medications!

For the most part, all I have to say about my time in Southern California is I stayed fucked up for four years at other people's expense, I was given another chance in the fight racket, and well, I have a bunch of stories to tell! That's about all.

Chapter 67

Seems like I might have mentioned, somewhere along the way, I have met some of the nastiest, most cockroach-like people in the fight racket. And I have met some of the most kind, generous people on earth in the fight racket.

It was during the time I was sleeping at Murph's, trying not to let him know, living out of a bottle and a baggie, a kind, warm, caring, amazing individual took me in to his home and treated me like I was somebody.

One day at the gym, Murph was going off on me, cussing me out. He had seen all my clothes in a locker and freaked out! "Get the fuck outta my goddamn gym! I train sixty-eight world champions here! I ain't got time to fuck with a bum like you!"

Shit like that. Murp was a fucking quack, really. Christ! He got one of his kids killed, and one almost killed!

Orlin "Shot" Norris Sr. was at the gym when this Murp (as I called him) explosion on the junkie took place. Shot went outside and told me to put my stuff in his car.

He owned two houses in Campo, California. That's about sixty miles east of San Diego, in the Black Forest. Cowboy Joe's First Fighter Squadron was in Campo.

Shot had me stay in the house next to his families. Another fighter, Jeff Leggett, was also in the house. I started running every day, eating right. Shot was working with me on the pads in his yard. No drugs, no booze, no cigarettes.

After about four, five weeks of this, one day, Shot went over to the house I was in and went, "C'mon. We have a meeting."

He took me to Cowboy Joe and Rudy Elias, the trainer, and had me spar four rounds. When I was done, Cowboy Joe said, "Son, I'm lookin' for a white hope. You're it. Nobody who fights for me uses that lip shit I saw you spit out when you came in the barn, son."

Joe left, Shot took me back to his place, and he bought Jeff and me some beers to celebrate.

Orlin "Shot" Norris, Sr. was a very giving, kind, wonderful human being.

Always laughing, always smiling, always in a good mood, cared about people. Orlin "Shot" Norris is one of those real-life heroes you hear about but wonder if they're real. Shot was real.

During this time, his two sons, Orlin "Juice" Norris Jr. and Terrible Terry Norris, were world champions at the same time. Orlin, he, I think, had the WBA cruiserweight title, and Terry had the WBC junior middleweight title.

Orlin had split with Joe as the trainer, Able Sanchez had, and those two were a team. Terry still fought for Joe.

Juice and I hung out quite a bit. As often as he could get away from his wife anyhow. They lived in a San Diego suburb, can't remember which one. When he'd go out to his parents, we'd get fucked up.

Two things Orlin "Juice" Norris and I had in common: we loved Coors beer and ate Copenhagen lip shit. He'd get too drunk to drive back to San Diego, and he'd stay at his parents. Shot told me one time, he found Juice passed out on the bathroom floor.

We went to the Black Forest one time and got fucked up. His parents didn't live far from the Black Forest camping area. There was an alcoholic border patrol guy who used to hang out with us. Fucker'd be drinking beers at seven o'clock in the morning. We were in Orlin's Mustang. When we were leaving the park, he crashed through the fence at the guard shack and just kept on truckin'! Funny shit.

Chapter 68

I can look back now and see, by the time I started fighting for Joe, I was done. I mean, even after all the drugs and drinking, physically I was good. I could still fight. The problem and trouble centered in my mind.

Hell, he was paying Lalo Perez $250 a week to spar with me. He had beaten world-ranked guys.

I tried a couple of times to talk to Joe, let him know some of the issues I had rolling around in my head. He'd just go, "Son, you're a man. Sort it out. We got a fight coming up."

Not to mention the constant struggles with everyone in the camp. Look, I fought 140. These guys would be at camp, people like Rodney Toney, Earl Butler, Engles Pedroza, tons of fucking guys. All of them were bigger than me, could fight, and figured they could treat me like their bitch.

Earl's room was across the hall from mine, and one day, he had his music blaring super, super loud. Might have been his first day there. He was from Baton Rouge, Louisiana. Rodney was from Boston.

Anyhow I asked this prick eighty times to turn his shit down, and he kept laughing at me. I left my room through the window, as I always did, and went to the woodpile and got the ax. The woodpile was by Rodney Toney's trailer, and he came out and asked me what I was doing. I told him what was going on, and I was going back up to the house to kill the new piece of shit.

When I got back to the house, Rodney was already there telling Earl he shouldn't fuck with me. Fucker still wouldn't turn his music down, so I threw a pool ball at him, six ball, hit him in the arm—I was trying for the head, I promise. I threw it Nolan Ryan-like, had bad intentions, and started going after him with the ax. I chased that fucker all over that ranch. Finally he said he was sorry and wouldn't turn the music up so loud anymore.

After that, Earl and I were cool. Hell, one time, we were all at some kind of press conference bullshit, and Earl turned to me and went, "Hey, let's go outside and be black for a minute, Bruce!"

No shit. So I did. Earl was a cool dude. He fought Tommy Hearns.

Rodney and I were tight. Every night after training, we'd sit in his trailer and play hockey on Nintendo and smoke Mexican seedy weedy and drink beers. He was fucking this girl from Sam's Club. We just called her Sam's Club.

"Hey, white boy, crazy fucker, we can only play best of five tonight, Sam's Club is coming over with my weed and money."

Joe Sayatovich knew nothing about the fight game. As in, he didn't know dick about boxing. However, he was a multimillionaire who knew what boxing was all about—money.

All I had to do was beat eight bums Joe put in front of me, and I was on my way. I couldn't even do that. Joe Sayatovich's asshole had to smell like Marty Denkin's cologne because he sure did have his head up Joe's ass far enough! And I blew it, choked, fucking failed an easy test.

Boxing was a business to Joe, and after I lost my second fight for him, he sent me packing.

Chapter 69

I had my last fight in 1994, I think. My only goal on earth, when I realized that dream was a bust before it ever started, was to not see 1995.

For the next twelve years, I did my very best, I promise, to not see the next day.

Drinking is an endurance game. I mean, minus the meth and blow, have you ever gone on a three, four, five-day bender, nothing but booze? I'm not talkin' Kinclaith and pale ale either, Cutty and PBR. No sleep either, bitch.

Chapter 70

As I grew older, there were things that would just not leave my mind. I mean, I was scolded and told what a piece of shit I am so many times, regardless of what I accomplished, those memories would always be in the forefront of my mind.

The only thing I found enjoyable on earth was to be fucked up to the point of vanquished.

If I could have done that without getting into trouble—legal trouble—regularly, I would have been dead some time ago now.

I went to culinary school around this time. As soon as you hit campus, every swinging dick in the place were talking about how they worked there with so and so, and they have the best recipes for raviolis and shrimp, and they're on their way to Master Chef status, and they're twenty-three years old and have been cooking thirty-six years.

There was a pub on campus. Literally seventy-five yards from my dorm room door to the nearest stool at the bar. Insecure? Out of place? Uncomfortable?

Look, to get in this school, I needed two reference letters from places I worked. Mattie wrote me a scholarly letter explaining all my fine qualities as a human being and my master skills in the kitchen.

He actually wrote both letters. He used different letterheads for each one. I was a decent line cook. Line cooking and knowing food is like saying you were a passenger in an airplane, so you can fly one.

I lay drunk for a couple months at culinary school and got in trouble for writing a girl I had talked to at the pub one night, a

Penthouse Forum letter and putting it under her door that night. I was told had I signed it, I wouldn't have been in any trouble.

Didn't get kicked out of school. I just decided to leave about a month after that because I felt really, really inadequate. As with high school, quitting is better than failing.

Chapter 71

Looking back, the smartest thing I did while at culinary school was start talking to the guidance counselor, Jack Rittel, immediately.

Have I mentioned my stellar high school career? Have I told you the one about me watching boxing film in my head, from sixth grade on, as the teacher talked about the lesson at hand, while generally comfortably intoxicated or high, or both?

I had no idea how to study, take notes, nothin'. In a nutshell, let me tell you how fucked up in the head I was when I journeyed to culinary school.

I always had trouble with math. Actually started in third grade; Mrs. Games' advanced class threw me for a loop. So they put me back in the regular class, or slow class, can't recall.

Anyhow second day of school, I went to the guidance counselor, Jack, and he suggested I go to tutoring.

That night, I went to tutoring, and the guy helping me whipped out some huge culinary math problem and went, "Here's a good one to help you understand culinary math. There's a 1/16th of nutmeg per 47 ounces of flour, minus 8/16ths if you use self-rising flour, plus don't forget your all spice, 9/8ths of a gram, shit like that. What do we have?"

That is how fucked up, delusional, backward, foreign, and impossible this math shit appeared to be in my mind. He started to explain how to do the problem, and he went, "Wow! This is a tough one!"

It was pig Latin to me. I looked at it and concluded an answer in no time. He quit working his problem and checked mine, and in a real sarcastic, wiseass, dickhead way, he went, "Are you a fucking joke?"

There I was, puking my guts out at night because I was so fucking stressed, and this asshole wanted to know if I was joking?

He went, "I'M HAVING TROUBLE with this goddamn problem, and you have it done in ten seconds! How'd you do it?"

I gave an honest answer. "I don't know."

The day of the math final, the professor, Joel, told me as he handed me my test, "You need a 75 percent on this to pass my class."

Fuck you! I got a 78 percent! Yes. I was drunk.

Back to Jack. He was a cool dude. Beard, hippy-like, John Lennon glasses, the tweed-coats-with-jeans-and-a-T-shirt kinda guy.

There was a kid in my class, Alfredo, can't remember his last name; he was from Arizona. I called him Alfredo Sauce. I liked Alfredo. He was a cool dude. He and I came from different planets. He was always joking, laughing, saying he was confused, didn't understand a thing the chef said in class, yet the fucker got 100 percent on every goddamn thing he did, everything!

And he didn't study half as much as me! One day, I ask Rittel about this. I mean, yes, I laid drunk, but while doing so, I did study. Studied my balls off! And eked fucking by. Jack also knew I drank. I was honest with this guy.

He told me the reason Alfredo Sauce was able to be airheaded and ditzy and still be a genius in class was because he had a happy, positive, normal childhood. While I, on the other hand, had a rough one. He said that influences learning capabilities quite a bit. So I did learn something at culinary school that stuck!

Chapter 72

Seems like this was about '95. I traded a riding lawn mower I got from my dad for a 1978 Chevy Chevette and basically lived in that car for two years.

During this time, I spent an entire summer following The Allman Brothers Band around, living out of that Chevette. From fucking Tennessee to Toronto in an eighteen-year-old Chevette! All stops in between! Smokin' and trippin' and drinkin' the entire time.

I also started working in every type of restaurant you can think of. I mean, country clubs, private clubs, independent restaurants, chain restaurants, retirement centers, nursing homes, to this day—and not that I'm above it—I have never had to get a job at a fast-fast-food joint, i.e., McShit, Booger Queen, In N Out Your Asshole Soo Fast, Jack Me Off in the Box, places like that.

I also tried every day of my life to figure out how I could die. By this time, I had put a gun to my head more than once and just could not pull the trigger. Too chicken shit for one. And another thought I used to get was, *So many people hate you. They're going to be ecstatic when you do this!*

So behind blowing my brains out, I'd have this thought, *Let them do it so they get four years in jail!* Then I'd get fucked up.

Chapter 73

So about all I can see of these years is I stayed drunk. Get in the occasional trouble drunks do—fights, DUIs, public intoxication, shit like that. Then 1997 rolled around.

I had been on a good long drunk. Don't know how many days. Have no idea how many towns or states I went through. I do remember leaving Indianapolis on a hot sunny day and making it to Louisville, Kentucky, sometime in the night.

I remember drinking into the next day and deciding I should go to my mom's in Garrison. Three hours away.

I was on 64 east, heading toward Lexington, and I could not see. I couldn't focus on anything, I couldn't hold a thought, felt overwhelming fear; I mean, mentally I was in the midst of a meltdown.

I got off on Lexington and parked the car and started walking around downtown, trying to clear my head. As I was walking, I saw this hot girl and went up to her and started talking to her. I would like to say I was flirting with her and being amorously beautiful, but in reality, I was probably being an asshole. Take *probably* out of the equation.

We talked for a couple minutes, and as I was getting a bit vulgar in the language department, I reached out and grabbed her butt. She started freaking out! I started freaking out! I apologized and started walking away, trying to show her I didn't mean to scare her, and I wasn't going to hurt her.

She followed me. I went to my car and left. I was in an '89 Nissan Maxima with a moonroof. As I was driving through traffic, I noticed a guy climbing through the moonroof! I stopped, and he got out of the car and asked me what I did to that woman and took my car keys. I said nothing and took the keys from him and left.

I got to Garrison and slept for about fifteen hours straight.

Chapter 74

When I woke up the next day, all I could think was, *What the fuck is wrong with you?* I had this huge blue gym bag you could fit a dead body in, literally. I packed it with everything I needed to live on the road, and I took Kinney Road to the AA Highway and started walking.

The cops had called my mom and said they had three felony warrants for me. I figured I'd like to see Macon, Georgia, before I spent twenty years in prison.

The next three days and nights, I spent walking and getting rides through the states of Kentucky and Tennessee. I walked the back roads, not the highways or interstates. I made sure to have plenty of Mad Dog, or an equivalent, when I knew my day of walking was coming to an end.

It wasn't that bad, really. I mean, that fuckin' bag weighed a ton, but I got used to it. Carried it like a backpack.

The trick when hitching is to not drink when trying to get a ride, for lots of reasons. Your safety, number 1. And if people see you've been drinking, they won't pick you up. So that's where the bag of weed and corncob pipe come into play!

My third day of hitching, I was worn out, so I got on a Greyhound somewhere in Tennessee. One of those towns where the bus station is at the general store in town, headed for Macon.

I got to Atlanta about midnight. My bus to Macon wasn't till 9:00 a.m. It's seventy miles.

This dude I met and I conspired to go find a liquor store, but the guards insisted we'd be murdered if we left the bus station, so we stayed.

I also met this redheaded hippy chick who was waiting on a friend in a school bus headed to Oregon. After talking for a while, she invited me to go with them! Her friend was supposed to be there at 5:00 a.m. and hadn't shown up by 9:00 a.m., when my bus left for Macon, so I headed south on the Greyhound.

Chapter 75

I had a plan. A solid concrete plan. I was going to stay at a homeless shelter, get a job line cooking, save some money, and be "Going Out West" again. Figured statute of limitations on one count of sexual abuse and two counts of wanton endangerment—the charges they charged me with—couldn't be more than five years. Oh yeah, I got charged because that guy jumped on my car when I was driving. That was one count of wanton endangerment.

So the instant I got off the Greyhound in Macon, there was a homeless guy, wino, whatever you choose to call him, standing there.

There was a Checkers next to the Greyhound station, and the guy who owned it let the homeless sit there and drink as long as it was in a paper cup, and you didn't stir shit. That was cool of the owner. I ended up drinking there a time or two. The owner put up with *no* trouble. That's all.

Anyhow I ask this wino where a shelter was, and he walked me to the street and pointed at a building clear at the other end of town, with a big cross on it, and went, "Right there."

I made my way to this shelter and went in and explained I was from out of town, just got there, was there a bed there, how do I stay there, I'd been on the road three days, and I was exhausted, can they help me?

This guy was real friendly, I'm thinkin' Andy fuckin' Griffith already. And he explained he had a bed, I could have it, I had to work for them at their store in turn for staying there; if I got a job, I had to work it around working at their store.

Now it's about eleven o'clock in the morning, and I told the guy I was exhausted. He said no problem. I could get a shower and take a nap. Maybe get a bite to eat.

So I took a shower upstairs and went back downstairs and asked him which bed was mine. He retorted, "Sorry, they called from the store, and they need your help, bad! They're on their way to get you!"

All I wanna do was eat and go to sleep, and I gotta go work at some fucking store I know nothing about! Well, they picked me up in a box truck and drove about three to five miles outside downtown Macon, and we got to the store.

It's a Goodwill-type deal, and they "needed" me "badly" to help sort out donated clothes!

So I went over and started helping this guy, Eddie, sort clothes out of garbage bags. Kids here, women's there, men's over there, it was a no-fun repetitive game of bullshit.

I was not helping Eddie long at all, and he went, "Man, you look like shit!"

I explained I've been on the road three days, hitchhiking to Macon, just got there, gave 'em the dirty laundry.

Eddie went, "Come with me." And he took me to his room. He lived at the store. His room had two beds—it was cold as a witch's tit—with air-conditioning—this was the end of June in Georgia—it had cable. He went, "Lie in this bed, I'll be back to get you."

Eddie woke me up a couple hours later, and I was in complete psychotic freak-out mode. That was the first real sleep I'd had in a solid five days. My mind was working a little more clearly, and my first thought, when I realized where I really was, was, *How in the living fuck did I wind up here?* And, *I gotta get out of this place!*

I went out to see if there was a phone I could use in the store. There was a sign you could see one hundred yards away, from the back of the store, that read "DO NOT EVEN ASK TO USE THE PHONE."

I went out the door and up to a gas station on the corner with a pay phone. I called my mom collect, and she accepted. I told her where I was and could she send me some money so I could go back?

She responded, "I don't have it. You got yourself there, get yourself back. But I'd go somewhere else."

We said we loved each other and hung up. I went back to the store and got in the box truck with the rest of the herd and headed back to the mission downtown.

As soon as we walked in the door, he came up to me, the Andy fuckin' Griffith guy, and he was furious! It was funny, him yelling at me in his southern drawl and me having no idea what he was talking about!

He went, "Where the hell were you!"

I went, "What do you mean, I'm right here!" It took me years to figure out he meant where did I disappear to for two, three hours at that store!

Anyhow I felt really, really uncomfortable after that, so my mind said, *Let's eat here, get our shit, and quietly disappear with the wind.*

I still remember that meal to this day. It was spareribs, collard greens, mashed potatoes, cornbread, iced tea—no, *sweet* tea—and peach pie, no shit. At a fuckin' homeless shelter! To this day, one of the most enjoyable meals I have ever had.

I ate till I was content, climbed the stairs, got my big blue body bag full of my life's belongings, walked back down the stairs, slipped out the side door, and not a soul saw me.

This was downtown Macon, Georgia, a place I had never been. I had three felony warrants on me, I had about $50 left to my name, and well, that's about it.

There was a Mexican restaurant/bar about a block or two away from the shelter that had a sign out that said "2 for 1 Happy Hour," so I decided to wander in and have a couple cocktails.

There was nary a soul in the place, and I asked the bartender if the sign was correct, so I got a couple of drinks and a couple of beers, and we started chatting.

He said, "Where ya comin' from or goin' to with the big bag?"

I told him I was from Cleveland, and I came to see where the Allman Brothers were born.

I asked him if it was safe to sleep in Rose Hill Cemetery, and he said it was. "But," he said, "if you go across the street, there is a hippy bar, and you'll find somewhere to stay tonight."

I slammed my drinks and headed across the street.

There was a guy opening the door as I crossed the street. I was the only one, besides him, in the place. His name was Tim. He owned the joint. He asked me about the bag, and I again replied I was from Cleveland and came down to see where The Brothers were hatched. As soon as I said that, he went, "You're getting drunk on me!"

Look, it might be seven o'clock in the evening. I was physically worn out, mentally drained, still trying to figure out how I got myself in a fucked-up situation like I was, and well, find a hippy chick or sleep with dead people!

Ah yes, Tim, my pal, a bar owner, offering free flow of the tap simply because I trudged to the birthplace of something so unexplainable, so spiritual, so moving, so comforting; I was in good hands!

As the night wore on, I got extremely drunk. There was a live band, the entire bar was out back smoking weed at one time or another, and I met two dudes, two pals, Beaver and Bo. No shit, they were friends.

I explained my situation to them, and they went, "You can stay with us tonight. We're both moving back home tomorrow, or we'd let you stay with us till you got on your feet."

I asked these guys if they knew where I could get some shrooms, and they said they had just gone shrooming last night. They went, "When the bar closes, you can stay with us and eat some. They're still wet, but you can eat 'em."

I was physically exhausted; mentally I was scared, stressed doesn't even begin to explain it. I'm in a town eight hundred miles from anyone I know, that I have never been to. I had just put in a solid six, eight-hour shift of drinking draft beer and cheap whiskey. The bar closed, and we're off to Beaver's and Bo's.

They lived downtown. So we walked to their apartment, and they broke this newspaper out of a closet full of mushrooms. One of 'em went through and got a pile and said, "At a glance, these are the best ones I saw. But eat all you want. That door is to the backsteps outside, if ya gotta puke."

I started eating these shrooms, and one of 'em got one out of the pile that was real wet and soggy and gross-looking, and he dared me to eat it. I did.

Well, next thing you know, I headed to the backdoor and puked off the landing onto the yard. As soon as I puked, I felt the weight of the world lift off my shoulders. I went back in the apartment and lay down on the floor.

Again this was the end of June in Georgia. Hot? Fuck you! You beg for hot! That isn't as bad as this shit.

I remember lying on the floor, and Tom Snyder was on the TV. I had my eyes closed, and it felt like I was floating through nice cool clouds. Tom Snyder's laugh put me to sleep.

Chapter 76

Beaver and Bo woke me up at seven o'clock in the morning and said they had to go to work. Check this out, these guys rolled me a joint and gave me a ride to Rose Hill Cemetery, right to Duane and Berry's gravesite. They said I was safe there to sleep, and left.

Well, I lay down between Duane and Berry and went right back to sleep. I woke up some time later because I felt like I was trapped in a sauna at 19,999 degrees with no way out! Hot! Hot! Hot! Hot as a motherfucker, Jack!

I sit up from between Duane and Berry, and what do I see? A big long black-and-white bus, with "PRISON" on it, and a bunch of guys in white-and-black jumpsuits, cleaning and weeding the cemetery!

"Time for Me to Fly!" I grabbed my bag, headed downtown again. Not very far, ten to twenty-minute walk.

Look, it's "Can you Loan Me a Dime" time. I was down to my last twenty bucks. It was midmorning, early afternoon.

I went in this restaurant/bar, The Rookery, and I sat at the bar, ordered a draft and a shot, and lit a cigarette. Just as the shot started to take its effect, as I was taking a puff of the Marlboro, some guy went, "Do you smoke?" Really, no shit.

My cigarettes were on the bar, so I pushed them toward him and told him to take one. He went, "No, do you smoke weed?"

I was thinkin', *Wow!* I mean, the accent, the mannerisms, the way he so politely just came out and asked that, *He knows I have these warrants, how?* All kinds of shit ran through my head!

I told him yes. He asked if I had any. I had that one joint from Beaver and Bo, so I told him I had a joint. He asked me if I'd sell it to him! Fuck no! I won't sell it! It's all the weed I had!

He went, "I run a gas station/self-storage unit with my mom, and I never get a day off. I'm off today, and I'd really like to smoke some weed!"

I asked him if there were any empty units, and could I stay in one? He said yes and yes. So my new best friend and I went outside, up the sidewalk, sat on a bench right on Cherry Street, and smoked that joint I had been given by Beaver and Bo at lunchtime, in downtown Macon, Georgia!

This guy told me he wanted to drink some more and go play some pool. I explained I was broke, and he said it's on him. I liked Georgia a lot already!

We walked to the other side of downtown to O'Neilly's, and after he let me rest at the park across the street for a while, we went in, and he started buying pitchers and shots, and we started playing eight ball.

Listen, have you ever been physically and mentally, just completely, drained? I mean in a sphere, a realm you didn't know existed? Physically the road had taken everything I had. I was "Running on Faith" and fumes.

Mentally all I could think was, *I'm fucked! Twenty fuckin' years!* Shit like that.

So this guy and I, my new pal, were in the middle of shooting a rack, and what walked through the door at about four o'clock in the afternoon? I was literally lining a shot up when she came in. A fuckin' chick with a pool stick! A pool stick and a rack of her own! I miscued!

Next thing you know, she and I were talking and shooting a 34C. She could really play pool too! The guy, my pal, decided he was going to go and told me where the gas station/storage unit was located, I was still welcome.

I can't throw a bunch of colorful adjectives in there to describe how drunk I was. Let's just say fucked up, okay?

This girl took me to Engleside Pizza in her 1973 Volkswagen Bug and fed me and bought me another beer I really needed and took me to her place. She had a black Lab, Holiday. We talked a bit, I let Holiday know I was a dog-over-people kinda person, and well, do I have to say what happened?

Okay. Here's a blow-by-blow (no pun intended). Little Martha and I were in her bed, and we were going at it hot and heavy. You know, balls deep into the nasty. As I was on her, doing the "Ride My See-Saw," my mind started doing its thing, thinking.

I mean, what a week I'd had! I was thinking about the night I slept under a bridge somewhere in Kentucky, and all I had were two cans of hot beer (I drank 'em), getting a ride from some guy from West Virginia who played those holler-church tapes, not having a can opener, the girl at the bus station in Atlanta, Tim, Beaver and Bo—all this shit just socked me right in the head at once!

I was thinkin' all this, and I was physically exhausted, and I was fucked up, and I started laughing my ass off at this thought, like I was on an acid peak, *Now you have a full belly, you're drunk,* and *you're getting some!*

Little Martha went from praising God in a deep moan and groan to sitting up on the bed like she had been electrocuted! Holiday even sat up and looked at me (she was on the bed)! Then almost in a giddish way, Little Martha went, "Is everything okay?"

I told her it was my overactive imagination and explained the thought process in my head and lay down and died.

Have you ever woken up in a strange girl's bed, eight hundred miles from anyone you know, with three felony warrants, zero money, a forty-pound bag of shit you have to lug around, no hope, sixty seconds into being conscious, wishing you were dead, wondering how you were gonna get drunk that day, and if any of this shit was even real? I have. It sucks.

Chapter 77

After lying in Little Martha's bed for a while, petting Holiday, I made my way to the living room and met Little Martha for the first time, as sober as I ever got, just woke up. Wishing I'd die, of course, because we were in a complete fucking mess!

I was extremely uncomfortable. I was also not looking forward to leaving the confines of this cozy apartment with the cool dog, the rack of jugs, and security! To live in a cemetery. So after some coffee and get-to-know-you chat, I told Little Martha I was going to be living at Rose Hill Cemetery, I'd be looking for a job cooking, I hoped to see her around, and thanked her for the southern hospitality.

She went, "Why don't you stay here and get a job?" *What?* That would be a great idea!

Couple months after not letting Papa Joe know she had a roommate, she took me to meet him at Engleside Pizza for lunch. We professed our undying love for each other, she told him she hadn't had to take her medicine, and she wasn't purge-eating and throwing up since she met me (learn something new every day!), I had a job, "Endless Love."

Papa Joe just looked at me and went, "Where you gonna be in six months?"

He put $20 on the table and said to Little Martha, "We won't tell Mama Pat about this one, Martha." He kissed her and left.

We went back to the apartment, and I showed her some tricks I had learned with whipped cream.

I was in Macon about seven months and had about probably ten jobs. The one that lasted the longest, the last one I got, was about four, five months.

Anyhow I started living with this girl I just met yesterday, I got a job or nine, and life went on.

Chapter 78

The being wanted was always in my mind, but it subsided a bit once I started my everyday groove in Georgia. It did fuck with me, though. One time, Little Martha and I were tripping on mushrooms, and we went for a ride out in the middle of nowhere, in the middle of the night, and there was a fucking road-block! She was driving, and they didn't ask me for shit. As soon as we went through that roadblock, two deer walked slowly across the road and looked at us, then ran off. Trippy.

So the third day of living with Little Martha, it was the Fourth of July weekend, 1997. The Allman Brothers were playing in Conyers, Georgia, outside Atlanta, where they had the equestrian competition during the 1996 Olympics.

I had no money, no hope, no love, no nothing. Little Martha was in between jobs, and she had sparse change in a jar. She did, however, have a '73 Bug and a FINA gas card Papa Joe was kind enough to give his little girl, in case of an emergency! If having trouble getting to a Brothers show wasn't a dire emergency, dire emergencies do not exist!

We had no money to buy tickets but figured we'd go up and tailgate, maybe score some good drugs, listen to some good stories. We stopped at a FINA in Macon and filled up and bought some beers and headed I-75 north for about an hour and change!

We got to the show way early, about eleven o'clock in the morning. There were a few people already there, playing guitars and drinking beers, so we parked and mingled in. It was an all-day show. Only

195

other band I can remember being there is Blues Traveler, but I'm certain there were a few.

Anyhow as we're sitting there, we saw all these people walking through the gate to where the show was, so we followed them in, and they all headed to the bathroom. So we followed. It was the concession workers; they were changing into their uniforms! We were in, no questions asked!

We met back up outside the restrooms and contemplated our next move. I mean, we didn't have the uniform—a black T-shirt—and the gates weren't open yet. There was a remote radio broadcast set up, so we went and sat outside the tent and acted like we were rockin' out to the music on the radio every time security came by!

Finally one of the DJs came up to us and asked what we were doing, why did we keep getting up and acting all fuckin' goofy and retarded? I gave him the scoop, and he went, "Fuck it! You're in! What do you want from Taco Bell?"

Just like that! Great show. Jack Pearson was playing with The Brothers. Oteil Burbridge had taken over bass; I think Warren and Woody were muling full-time at this time.

Things with Little Martha weren't always so carefree and vibrant and mystical.

Have you ever been lugging forty pounds of shit around, everything you have on earth, in a strange place, with three felony warrants, met a girl at five o'clock on a Wednesday, and moved in with her eleven o'clock Wednesday night? If not, let me warn you, there is going to be a few issues.

One of the issues she had, not far into this adventure at all, was my drinking. Had to be well within the first week. In the getting-to-know-you phase, after moving in together, Little Martha let me know she was a wine collector and did I like wine? Nah, not really. Not a big wine guy.

However, if that's all there is to drink, I'll drink it. She didn't have a big collection going, a good twenty, thirty bottles. Wine was always just so fucking easy to drink! The first argument we had was over me drinking all her wine while she was out looking for a job. And her six-packs of imports after I drank my twelve shit beers.

We'd go to the bars every night to listen to music and drink and smoke and have a gay old time! I was working second shift, so after work and stopping by the bar till close and coming home at 3:00 a.m. became a problem, because Little Martha acquired a day job that required her to be up at 5:00 a.m.

What can I say? After a while, she was freaking out, calling me crazy, needing help, psycho, all that jazz. For a solid three months, I never let her know I had those warrants. I saw no reason to bring it up, did you?

Chapter 79

So "As Time Goes By," I got a job in the kitchen of a retirement center for the duration of my stay in Macon, Georgia. The guy that ran the kitchen, Rusty Brown, was a cool dude. The owner, Ms. Amy, was a sweet lady. He never could figure out why I was a basket case who couldn't grab my ass with both hands. I mean, I'd fuck up heating up frozen biscuits!

He was always positive and upbeat, Rusty was.

Look, going to Macon, Georgia, for me, was like Dorothy going to the Land of Oz. Everybody *loved* music, everyone partied, and everyone did trippers! Shrooms were free, and doses were cheap, and everyone had them!

Little Martha bought a little glass pipe, and I smoked so much weed in it I burned a hole in the bottom of it! She was pissed!

We made the rounds nightly—I did anyhow—to O'Neilly's, Tim's, The Rookery, all the hot spots, Liz Reed's, where the action was.

There were a lot of trippers in Macon. Seems like every other day, I was dosing. Here's an LSD trip that will have you wondering if any of this is real at all. One night, Martha and I had no weed, no money, no alcohol, no nothin'. We're riding around, and she ran into a dude she knew, and we started talking.

He had a sheet of acid he's trying to get rid of. We had no cash, but Little Martha had a checkbook and $16 in the bank. So what does logic say? Write a $15 check for four hits of acid. That's what we—she—did anyhow.

We went back to the apartment and dropped that acid. That was the first and only time in my life I ever had sex while tripping. We hadn't been at it fifteen minutes, and I had to take the acid shit from hell! Kinda ruined the mood! Oh sure! We laughed about it for the next three hours!

It was during the course of this journey when things took a turn for serious, and we were talking about deep shit in our lives. This was when I told her what I did and was wanted.

She confessed some pretty dark deep shit to me too, so I felt comfortable telling her. All she said was she had a lawyer friend we'd talk to when we weren't wiggin' nuts and big tits.

Chapter 80

This retirement center I worked at was something. I mean, it was well-to-do people living there. I remember a Ms. Green who used to ask me to go to her apartment to move something, fix something, basically *I'm lonely, can you spend some time with me?* Then she'd try to give me $5 or $10; I never took it.

Part of my duty was to go over to the clubhouse and serve. The clubhouse was optional, and most—some—of the people who could still get around pretty well would go over there and eat lunch.

There was a lady, Ms. Hendricks, Ms. Jean Hendricks, who lived there in the independent section, her own apartment. There was also a semiassisted and a fully-assisted section of the grounds. It was a pretty big place.

Anyhow I'd go to Ms. Hendricks' apartment after I got off work, and we'd talk. She had been an educator. When she retired, she had been dean of students at Mercer College, right there in Macon. She had a stroke, I believe, and had to retire.

I was going by Valloyd in Macon, not Bruce (remember, on the lamb. Nobody is going to think Valloyd is a peculiar name. Especially in Georgia.), and Ms. Hendricks would go, "Valloyd, you have so much more to offer the world, why do you waste it in a kitchen?"

In my mind, I'd be thinking, *If you only knew. Whatever little hope I now realize I did have is now gone! I'm gonna rot in prison when I get caught!* I'd leave, get drunk, and go to Little Martha's, where, by now, only Holiday was happy to see me. I always had a box of food.

This went on for a few months, and things got, shall we say, hairy? I mean, she's finding out what a prize I am, and I was finding out people were fucked up everywhere, including her—especially her!

We did have some fun times, though. She took me to the Hitchiti Trail, I believe it is, about forty-five minutes from Macon. The Tumbledown Creek empties into the Ocmulgee River. There's a trail that runs along the creek to the river. There are mushrooms of every color growing in this forest! Went there a handful of times and never saw a soul. Great place to trip. There was a peach orchard nearby, I remember.

Chapter 81

This all played out through the course of the summer, and fall set in. Tim wasn't so trusting of my Yankee ways anymore; he needed money by the drink. Reality was starting to put the "Stranglehold" on again. Little Martha was not love personified toward me; she was venomous and witchy, voodoo-like. None of it good, all of it scary! Sweet solace by day. Pleasant dreams by night? Ha!

I'm not sure which catastrophe led to Little Martha putting me out. The yelling, voicing my concerns over the black cloud hanging, not working every day, being drunk, taking her car, making sure we were always real low on weed, what the hell did she have to worry about? We've known each other three, four months! We've lived together three, four months!

To this day, I'm not 100 percent sure where I met Scott. I wanna say at Tim's bar. Anyhow Scott was about 5'4", and he weighed about, at least, a solid 280. It was all gut! First time I ever saw him, my first thought was, *There's two-ton Tony Galento!*

Scott wore a hat, one of those flappy hippy hats. It was multicolored and fit his personality to a tee. One day, I came home, and all my shit was on the enclosed porch with a note saying to fuck off in a nice way, or the cops would be called.

During the course of the summer, Martha and I went by Greyhound to Tennessee and met my mom, who gave me her car to use, a wanted felon. I loaded that car with my shit and went to Scott's apartment, and he invited me with open arms!

Now once at Scott's, guess who was over there as often as me and me living there? You guessed it—Little Martha! Spending the night, the whole ensemble! One day I asked her why we couldn't just go home, and she said because I hadn't suffered enough.

I had not been drinking for a week or two. I was trying to show her I didn't have to, and I was trying to get my mind in the game at hand, was my thinking anyhow!

Chapter 82

This dude, Scott, he was a big, big, big doser! He ate acid the way I drank booze, full throttle plus ten! He told me he did a whole sheet at Woodstock 11 by himself (that's one hundred hits in three days). One evening, when I got home from work, he asked me if I wanted to dose. It was a Friday, and I had that weekend off, so I told him yes.

I took a shower, ate, and got ready for the journey ahead! He asked me how many hits I wanted, and I told him I didn't care; I mean, I always did two or three, even really good acid! He ripped off two ten-strips and went, "Let's start with ten!"

We ate ten hits of acid at one time, and when those started knockin', we ate a couple more. We walked all over downtown Macon. I found a big brown leaf that was really hard in texture. It kept moving on its own, so I picked it up.

We sat and listened to tons and tons of his albums. I remember listening to Floyd's "Alan's Psychedelic Breakfast" over and over and over. We were both tripping on the way the guy was saying, "Lots of marmalade, please!"

I called off work that Monday because I hadn't been to sleep at all. I was still wigging nuts and really tired of it!

Little did I know at the time, but that job and a lot of other things were about to change in ways I never conceived or wanted! I haven't felt the need to dose from that day to this.

Chapter 83

Life was moving along, and I was waiting for the bottom to fall out. I was on this not-drinking kick I talked about for a week or two, and one night, Martha came over and asked Scott if he wanted to go out to dinner. I said I was available and had money but was told I wasn't invited.

Again finding words to describe the feelings I had when I had these warrants is hard. You're constantly looking behind you, you cringe when you see a cop, if a cop makes eye contact with you, you know he knows, you don't rest well, it's a fuckin' mess, I promise.

Feeling the way I did inside, and her saying that planted the seed. As soon as they left, I went to the store and got a twelve-pack of sixteen-ounce beers and a bottle of something cheap, I'm sure. Went back to Scott's apartment and started drinking and blacking in and out immediately.

I remember seeing him at Tim's bar, Scott, and it seemed like we had words, and I beat him up pretty bad. I have a memory of being on the ground and a bunch of people kicking the shit out of me. I have a memory of coming in and out while I was driving. All this stuff is a blur. It's as clear now as it was all those years ago. I have a memory of going by Tim's bar. It was on the right-hand side as I passed on the side street near his bar.

The very next memory I have is this: I came to, driving a car at a high rate of speed, and I saw a guardrail coming up, and I went, "Oh! Fuck!"

The next thing I remember is coming to and feeling something really heavy on my legs and trying to pull away from it and a bunch of voices screaming, "Don't move!"

So I knew I was in a wreck, I wasn't dead, and the cavalry had come to rescue me! My leg was killing me, bad! The car was on it. It was flipped upside down and had me pinned to the ground.

I was in and out of consciousness, and once when I came to, I was on a stretcher, and a cop was asking me questions. He asked me if I had been drinking, I said yes. He asked me if I'd take a breathalyzer test. When he asked that, my mind said, *You were just in a horrible wreck. If you pass back out, he won't fuck with you!* So I threw my head back, sighed—the whole ensemble—and started snoring real loud!

When I did, every swinging dick there started laughing so hard I thought they were gonna need an ambulance! You ever laugh really, really loud at church, school, court—somewhere you shouldn't be loud—and you hold it in, and your stomach is contracting in knots, you're laughing so hard? That was me on that stretcher, and then I went right back out again. Next time I came to, I was naked and freezing my ass off in some kind of *Star Trek* contraption.

I was in the hospital in Macon. I had wrecked the car in Cobb County on I-75 southbound. When I came to, I tried to move my hands before I opened my eyes to see if I was handcuffed to the bed. I wasn't.

So I started plotting my "Alabama Getaway." I went to the desk, and they said they couldn't release me because of the amount of alcohol in my system, it was dangerous. I needed to be observed, a bunch of shit I knew wasn't factual at all. I mean, I listen to Dr. John! And he wasn't dead at that time yet!

I kept going out through the day to try to get released, and they'd say the same thing. I'd take the elevator down to go outside to smoke. My left knee was the size of a basketball, I had to hobble on it. It wouldn't bend at all. I called Rusty somewhere through the day to tell him I was in a car wreck and wouldn't be in today. It had to be hours after my shift started.

As the day went on, I got superscared! I mean, I was fucked! I called Rusty back and asked him if he could go get me from the hospital. He said no, he had to work his other job on base that night, but his wife could go get me.

That evening, I was standing outside the hospital in my hospital pajamas and gown, smoking a cigarette, wishing I was dead, and some lady in a brown blazer suit went outside, lit a cigarette, and went, "You were in a bad car wreck."

I went, "Yep."

She continued, "You're from out of state."

"I am."

"Well, you were just on the six-o'clock news, and you're going straight to jail!" Those words no sooner fell out of her mouth, and Rusty's wife, Sharee, a lady I had never met before, and their two kids pulled up in the van. I jumped straight in and couldn't wait to be gone from that hospital! In my pajamas!

Chapter 84

Sharee took me to their house, and when Rusty came home, we talked, and he told me he didn't understand why I went to Macon. I needed to go back home, and he told me to go in to work with him the next day, Ms. Hendricks wanted to see me. He had told her what happened.

Ms. Hendricks was one of those stereotypical deep Southern women, completely engulfed in the Jesus thing. She never pushed it or said I needed it or any of that. She just made good and sure to let you know the good Lord is why she was who she was!

Ms. Hendricks insisted on buying me an airline ticket home. I kept refusing. My wallet, everything, was at the hospital, and I sure as fuck wasn't going back there! So getting on a plane was a roll of the dice without ID. This was pre-911.

Finally I called to see what a Greyhound ticket was to Lorain, and she gave me the cash for that trip. Another long trip on poor man's airline. When I got to Lorain, I had nowhere to go, so I checked in a rehab.

Now after about a few days in this place, I was shittin' my pants, playin' in it, smellin' it, and asking you if you saw the egg man in the lights too. I was a fucking mess!

This was one of those everybody-welcome-regardless-of-ability-to-pay places. Sort of like jail—it was full of guys in the system on the move, but not quite jail.

After not being able to douse my brain in alcohol for a few days, my mind started really fucking with me. I mean, this warrant thing was eating me alive, cartoons were playing in the windows, I was sick.

There was a counselor there, Chuck, I think was his name. He was also an ambulance driver. He told us how one time, in a car wreck, the guy kept screaming, "DON'T CUT MY COAT OFF!" 'Cause they had to save him. It was a biker coat. Chuck said he had a Harley, like a '70s something. He always said it was *functional*; I never forgot that. He always stressed the word *functional*. Reminded me of an article I read as a kid that pitted style over substance.

After another sleepless night and this black dude testifying and screaming to Jesus all hours of the night, I decided the best thing for me to do was go back to Garrison for Christmas, as it was maybe a week away. Get a lawyer and turn myself in.

The guy who was the head counselor was, at least at one time, Bobby Lesko's sponsor. I can say that because Bobby's dead. Bobby was my first sponsor ever, when I was fifteen. He got sober at twenty-four. He died sober at fifty-two. His sobriety date was Valentine's Day. I went in his office and told him my situation, and his solution to the problem was to tell me I had to get my shit and leave, pronto! What the fuck was I gonna do now? I was furious! I got my clothes and walked to my cousin Michelle's, Uncle Bill's daughter, and her boyfriend, JJ's, house behind the Mr. Hero on the east side.

They lived at the end of a dead-end street. I was calling anyone I could think of to try to get the $65 I needed so I could get a Greyhound to Portsmouth, Ohio, spend Christmas with my mom, get a lawyer, and turn myself in.

I called my dad's sister Sally in Amherst, and she insisted I give her an address where I was so her husband, Charlie, could go give it to me. As soon as I did, I knew I was fucked.

I kept sitting at the dining room table, smoking bowls, getting up, looking out the window. After a while, I was sitting at the table, smoking a bowl of weed, and JJ went, "That's strange. There are two cop cars parked on our street! Just sitting there."

As I said, they lived at the end of a dead-end street. I told him they were there for me, and he asked why. I started smoking as much weed as I could, and in no time, the cops were coming up to the door and knocking. JJ went to get it, and I went, "They're here for me, I'll get it."

I opened the door. They asked me who I was, I told them they're there for me. They cuffed me and put me in a car.

The cop transporting me went, "Aren't you the boxer?" Told me he fought amateur for Primo's AC, and we were at the jail!

I spent about a week at the Lorain City Jail before being moved to the Lorain County Jail. There was a guy, Fred Riley, who I went to school with, who was a guard at the city jail. He'd get me out of the cellblock to look at the law books, and he'd give me cigarettes to smoke and coffee to drink. He did this every day till I got moved. I never forgot that, Fred.

Now one day, sitting in this cellblock, a young Puerto Rican kid got put in, and as soon as the door closed, he went, "Anyone got any papers?"

There was no radio, no TV, no newspapers, no nothin' in this cellblock, and this prick wanted to know if we had any fucking rolling papers?

We all "fuck off" to him, and he went, "That's too bad 'cause I have this!" And he pulled a quarter bag of weed out of his pants! "There was a band playing in my head and I felt like getting high!"

Well, you know that thin paper that institution toilet paper is wrapped up in? It makes for perfect marijuana cigarette rolling material. I had a Bic from Fred, so we were good.

I was in cellblock A. As soon as the door opened from the main hall, you saw inside cellblock A. There were like six or eight cells in this block. The doors on the cellblocks were bars, not doors. We're in the back cell, smoking weed like hell won't have it! Getting stoned, having a ball!

The trustee came by and told us, he went, "I can smell that shit in cellblock C! Be careful!"

Not long after that, about four guards came through the door and opened our cellblock and told us to get against the wall. I had that Bic. The only place to hide anything in jail is your asshole, so I stuck that Bic in my sock and figured I'd bite the bullet!

Of the guards in there who searched me but Fred Riley! He felt that lighter and looked at me and felt it again, and I gave him the nod, and he moved on! They didn't find the weed on the kid either! True story.

Chapter 85

So I spent Christmas 1997 in the Lorain City Jail. We had a bologna sandwich and a dried-out orange for dinner. Ah, but I had cigarettes and coffee for dessert! I spent New Year's Day in the Lorain County Jail. Kelly King's brother (friend of Bud Man's) worked there, but I didn't get any perks in the county. Can't remember what we had for New Year's dinner. Had to be good.

I'm in the Lorain County Jail a week or two. Right after the new year, 1998, they came and woke me up at, like, three o'clock in the morning.

"Get your shit! They're here to get you!" the guard yelled it real loud so every fucking body heard him in the entire pod! Again it's the middle of the night.

I went out to the booking area, I was handcuffed, and picked a phone up and went to make a call. And I'll bet I had sixteen guards on me like that, Jack!

"Put the goddamn phone down!"

"Stop!" Shit like that. All I wanted to do was let my mom know I was being extradited back to Kentucky.

Check this shit out. It's freezing cold outside. Wanna know how cold Cleveland gets? It's the same exact weather Chicago gets.

Anyhow these two Lexington cops asked me if I wanted to smoke a cigarette. Are you kidding me, I wanna eat some too! I hadn't had one in a couple of weeks. I had a pack of Camels, and they put one in my mouth and lit it; I was cuffed.

As I stood there lighting that cigarette, the cold wind felt so, so, so wonderful! It was ripping through me and making me freeze instantly, and it felt amazing! Ever been locked up?

I took the very first hit off that Camel, and I got light-headed, dizzy, my head was spinning from a loud guitar, and I fell right the fuck out! No shit! I came to immediately. I mean, I was never out cold. Just the most intense, most beautiful, most amazing head rush of all time!

I sat up and started to try to pick my cigarette up, and they were like, "Oh, no! You've had enough!" Best fuckin' buzz of my life, it was.

I've made the trip we were on a billion times. I mean, they took an extra two hours to get to Lexington. Not that I cared, and not that I told them anything. They did have Ted Bundy Jr. in the car, so they had to take every precaution. The only conversation I had with them the whole trip was, I asked them where they ate, and they said Red Lobster.

Red Lobster? Why not try something not in your neck of the beans and cornbread woods, say.

Say, Presti's maybe? I mean, they have Red Lobsters everywhere, only one Presti's! I guess being out of the beans-and-cornbread region threw them for a loop!

Once we got through Cincinnati, they stopped at an Arby's and asked me what I wanted to eat. I told them a cup of coffee and a cigarette. One went in and came out with a kid's roast beef and a small soda, no fries.

Chapter 86

They got me to Lexington and got me booked, and I got placed in my cellblock. What I can I say?

I was charged with one count of sexual abuse and two counts of wanton endangerment. All I could think was, *Sexual abuse? For grabbing a woman on the butt? Wanton endangerment? What the fuck?*

I was placed in a cellblock with fifteen individual cells in it. Mentally, at this time, I was a shell of a broken being at best.

In this cellblock, of the fourteen other inmates, about seven or eight of them were facing murder charges, seems like four or five of those were death penalty cases; there was an armed robbery suspect, or two, and it seems, at first, I might have been the only white boy in there. At times, there'd be four or five of us white breads in that block.

There was a guy who came from death row. He was trying to get his sentence commuted to life. He was a white guy. Look, this was jail. It never closes, ever, for any reason. It's open now.

I spent sixty days in here before I got bonded out.

I'll bet I had been to jail a hundred times before this, literally. Five DUIs, five thousand fights, public intoxication, sleeping in my car, all kinds of stupid retarded shit I've been to jail for. But never like this.

There was a TV in the pod. Of course, it was impossible to watch because it was always on something I had no interest in, always loud, and everyone was always standing around it, screaming and being assholes.

This was the summer steroid kings Mark McGuire and Sammy Sosa were trying to hit three hundred home runs each. Didn't matter, wasn't basketball or football or Jerry Springer.

Now if you've never been to jail, I'll do my best to paint you a picture. It's always loud, people screaming, yelling, this is 24-7; there are always lights on, the average IQ of someone in jail is smaller than their shoe size, unless they wear a size 10 or above (dick if they're white), everyone is a thief, liar, backstabber, piece of shit, and well, I used to frequent jail often, what can I say?

My cellblock was right across the hall from solitary/suicide watch. That's where the real quacks were. Locked 24-7, no blanket, no nothin'. Fuckers over there screamed and yelled all night long.

I was in this fucking mental ward about four, five days, and they got me out of the block and took me to a small room. I was thinkin', *What the fuck now?* Some guy came in, took his coat and scarf off, told me to move to the other seat, sat down, put his feet on the desk, and went, "What happened?"

I went, "Who are you, my attorney or a detective?"

He took his feet off the desk, whipped out a business card, flung it at me, and went, "Are you satisfied? What the hell happened?"

My mom (as usual) got the money together to get me a lawyer, five large. Now this guy, Andrew Stephens, never should have accepted my case. The minute I started to tell him what happened, he went, "YEP! YEP! Marcell Smith! Randy's girlfriend! You grabbed her vagina, bruised her, they have pictures! She's tougher than a knot on a pine bark! She's from Scott County!"

I mean, he freaked me out even more, and I didn't think that was possible after my own attorney told me this shit.

I was in this jail sixty days, and my mom bonded me out. Duke put his house up as collateral.

We got stopped on the way home in a small town, Millersburg, on the way to Garrison. Goddamn! Freakin' out the whole time! Thinkin' they decided to not release me, that kind of shit!

Now being out, being able to think a little bit, I thought I had some hope. I gotta say here, my first bond hearing, Stephens said he didn't receive payment, so he excused himself as my attorney, a public defender got me bonded out at the higher court. This was all remote TV shit, I wasn't in the courtroom.

Later that day, I believe, he said he received it, he made a mistake. Why I kept this piece of shit I'll never know. I mean, I had no money to get another attorney. I mean, the first time I went to his office, I was sitting on a chair across from him, and I asked to see these pictures, and he said he'd have them in a day or two.

The pretrial we went to, the first offer was one-year probation. Yes, to sexual abuse, a felony, mend the two wanton endangerments down to misdemeanors. When we got back to his office, I went, "I'm not accepting that. I didn't do any of that shit you said I did. I need to see those pictures, all kinds of stuff!"

He got right in my face and pointed his finger at me, and his exact words, my defense attorney's, were, "If you don't accept this, you will do ten years, I promise!"

He told me I dragged her with my car (she was never closer than five feet, ten feet from my car), ripped her clothes, skinned her, bruised her—this was my own attorney telling me all this. I asked for the pictures and proof, but all I ever got were two police reports: Marcell Smith's and the guy who jumped on my car. Neither one mentioned any of this shit at all.

I also found out, years later, Attorney Marcell Smith from Lexington got caught fucking a guy in public and got arrested. How many Marcell Smith attorneys with slut tendencies are in Lexington, Kentucky? I know I've met a ton of Valloyds throughout the years who boxed and did dope. So I'm guessing there's a slew of slut attorneys in Lexington with the name Marcell Smith who have slutty behaviors. I tried to tell Stephens I was in a conversation with her, I thought she was receptive to being perverted. He refused to listen to me at all.

"THAT'S RANDY'S GIRLFRIEND!" was all I heard a million times. Other than that, "You'll do ten years" a million times.

I sure do wish this would be looked at. I mean, what I did was *way, way* wrong. I have never denied what I did, ever. I felt like a shit bag for doing it.

But a convicted sex offender, really? What I did, while wrong, wasn't done in a threatening way. I have no excuse for what I did. It was wrong. Shouldn't grab strange women on the butt. Look, you an attorney? Tell me I have hope of clearing this up all these years later. Yeah? I didn't think so. Ted Bundy for life.

Chapter 87

They didn't need a prosecutor for this case, I promise. It was during one of these strike-the-fear-of-God-in-me meetings, he also told me probation would be five for five, in all likelihood.

Five years' probation for five years in prison if I fuck up. To this day, I haven't heard that from the court.

During this bond freedom, one of the things I had to do was go to Lexington, to the probation department, to be assessed. As soon as the lady started asking me questions, I interrupted her and went, "Lady, I am not going to get probation. I refuse. I am going to go to prison and do my time."

She said, "Okay. That was easy! Have a nice day!" And I left.

Look, I had been locked up two months. That counted toward my sentence. Seven months, twenty-one days, killed a year in Kentucky at that time with good behavior. I was 40 percent done with my time, only an idiot would be tied down for five years if all he had to do was five months, twenty one days with good time!

Here's another thing that happened during that free-on-bond stint. This is thirteen years after I had dosed for the first time.

I went to Louisville, Kentucky, one weekend, and I was hanging out in a bar, and I left with two girls, roommates. Now look, I was not trying to get laid, nothin', my mind was warped! I was just trying to live while I could. With me, that meant drink.

Bars closed at 4:00 a.m., and we walked to their apartment. I remember one saying she was a nurse. I asked one of them if they had any weed, and they said yes and got a wooden box out and started going through it, looking for the weed, and she went, "Oh! There's a bag of shrooms!"

Now normally, when I hallucinate, things have to be right—all things—in my reality. Things were not more wrong in my reality at this time than ever before, a hundredfold! But almost instinctively, I went, "Can I have some of those shrooms?"

She said, "Why, of course!"

I gave up a guaranteed threesome to eat those shrooms. The girls were even trippin' on that. I mean, I tried, but I was wiggin' fuckin' nuts! My mind was overwhelmed with everything going on, and when I started tripping, all I wanted to do was be alone.

This has always tripped me out. I mean, obviously I didn't tell these girls they invited Ted Bundy into their apartment. I just told them I had a lot going on in life and was stressed. They understood, were kind, and helped me enjoy my shrooms under the guise of a live lesbian porn movie.

Here's the part that trips me out. While these two were tongue-lashing each other's gash, I was looking through their CDs, and what do I find but Eric Clapton's '70's blues something, and what's on it? "To Make Somebody Happy!"

The porn show had long ended, but that song, again, guided me to a safe secure spot.

When I went in front of the judge, he was reading through the paperwork, and he went, "Probation is recommended."

And I had to have Prosecutor Stephens tell the judge I didn't want probation, I wanted to do my time.

Chapter 88

So after a month or two of freedom, I go right back in the same hole I crawled out of. Murderers, robbers, rapists, death row was still there.

Couple of things I remember about this time. During one of my court appearances, I was in a blackout. A full-fledged I'm-fucking-wasted-on-pills-and-booze blackout. I woke up on my sister's couch in a suit and tie at, like, the middle of the night, and I freaked out! No idea how I got there, nothin'! She lived in Maysville. About sixty miles north of Lexington.

And when I told the judge I wanted to go to prison, my mom told me he addressed the court and said if everyone did what I did, they'd have a serious problem. I didn't hear this. I was in the holding tank by then.

Chapter 89

So I get put back in the killer pod and, a week or two later, got shipped off to the "Big House." Not the Big House in Macon The Brothers lived in, the Big House in Kentucky where criminals go.

I cannot put in words my mental state at this time. Low self-esteem would have been a gold medal. My attorney, Andrew Stephens, knew this and played on it.

Look, here's how smart I am. The two lowest rungs of shit in jail are sexual offenders and people who fuck with kids. When I got put in jail in Lexington, and everyone asked me what I was in for, instead of saying something cool, like murder or drugs, I said, "Sexual abuse. Grabbed a woman on the butt."

I only got in one fight in the Lexington jail, with some piece of shit in on a murder charge. He tried to take the phone out of my left hand, so I cracked the fucker with my right. Typical bullshit squabble. I made my call.

There was another piece of inbred shit in there, Harold "P." He was in on a death penalty case involving murder and coke. His dad was a jailer. This piece of shit's cousin was also in our pod for something. It was a family affair.

P's dad used to bring him weed every day. I got invited to smoke but never did. During this sixty days, I'd just sit and wonder how I got where I was. I mean, killing myself whenever I got out was definitely the plan.

I didn't do anything but sit and think those sixty days. All there is to do in jail is sit and think.

The monotony would get broken up occasionally. You were not allowed in your cell. When you came out in the morning, they were locked. They'd open back up at dinner for a few minutes, then close till bedtime.

Sometimes at dinner, I'd just stay in my cell when it closed for the night. If you got caught, they put you in the hole across the hall. I never got caught.

One night, I stayed in my cell, and I woke up to two people being inside it! That is a *no-no* in jail! One was this big huge muscle-bound monster, white guy, and the other was a black guy I'd rap with.

I went, "What the fuck you doing in my cell!" And I looked out of it and saw why.

The death row cases had joined together as a team and destroyed the pod! Ever been to jail? The only thing in there is metal and steel. Okay, then maybe some more metal and steel. They broke the TV to pieces—the only thing to ruin—and were screaming and yelling and having a gay old time!

This muscle-bound guy, he was the size of Chuck Wepner, but he was chiseled, he was crying like a bitch! "I wanna go home! I'm sorry! I didn't mean to do it!"

That was when he told me he was in for molesting his daughter, and he did it, and he was so sorry. I put him out of my cell right then and told him not to talk with me anymore while we were incarcerated together, or I'd tell everyone in the pod. He was telling everyone he was in on attempted murder.

So I was in this shithole a couple more weeks, and one day they, came and got me and told me I was on my way to the Big House.

Chapter 90

I was transported from Lexington to LaGrange with one other inmate in a cop car. Cop had his wife, or girlfriend, with him. If not "Secret Lover." Anyhow this was like May. This kid told me he's served out in August, and I remember thinking, *You lucky fucker!* He was a big white kid.

The cop had the radio on, and the DJ went, "And right after the commercial break, Tears for Fears!"

I looked at the other inmate, and I went, "Watch. Next song is gonna be 'Shout, shout, let it all out.'"

When the commercials were over, and that song came on, the dude freaked out! "How'd you know that!" Gotta know your radio, jailbird!

Probably about forty-five minutes, an hour ride, we're there, the Big House, LaGrange Reformatory. We drove through the gate and got dropped off.

Getting processed, you got your hair cut off. I had long hippy, hair. A black dude was the barber, and when he gave me a crew cut, he apologized quietly, softly.

He said, "I am so sorry, brah." That made me feel pretty goddamn good! I mean, I was scared as fuck going to prison!

And here's a black dude feeling bad because he cut a white boy's hair off! Don't get me wrong, prison sucks. I was only there about a month till I got transferred to a county jail, Rowan County Detention Center, as they all started going by back then. But I had no bad experiences in prison. Again, I didn't do any talking to anybody in there when I got put in a wing. Probably a hundred beds, single, not bunk. Just a big long dorm room. You had a locker at the foot of your bed with a combination lock on it.

First day I got there, I had a shitload of guys ask me if I needed anything. All those two-for-ones, now-you-owe-him, blow-job-for-cigarette stories were running through my head, and I refused everything offered!

This one white dude from Indiana, Steve Something, he just kept talking and talking and talking to me. He asked me what I did, and I told him the truth. He said he had served ten years at Eddyville, was out a couple months, and caught a kidnapping-beating charge. Got ten flat.

This fucker was bald, about 5'10", 240, and looked like he'd lifted weights for ten years straight.

He offered me a pack of cigarettes, and I politely declined. He went, "Look, one for one. When we go to the store, just give me one back."

So I trusted him and took it. You could still smoke in prison but not inside. We had an hour a day to smoke.

If you got caught, it was automatic loss of good time. The trick was, smoke in the bathroom. If they caught you in there, they bitched at you and made you put it out. Caught you in the dorm, you did get written up. I never got caught. Then again, I always went in the bathroom and smoked!

Just like the school days!

The objective of prison, in my opinion, is to dehumanize, program, make certain you know you're a piece of shit and a loser, and if you get out, we'll see you again. I was already all those things before I went in, so I win.

Here is one funny thing I remember from prison: The toilets were right next to each other, so you may be one of four, five guys sitting there, taking a shit. You got so comfortable shitting around people you'd be reading the paper and go, "Goddamn! Read this!" And hand the paper to the guy shitting next to you!

Look, I'm not trying to make this sound like it ended up being okay. I mean, prison and jail suck, period. But if you're there, well, you are there. You are not getting out till they say so, period. End of the fucking line. The very end, period.

There was another guy who came in, his name was Steve also. He was from Breathitt County, Kentucky. This fucker was crazy. He said he never had a Social Security number, he came from a holler-criminal family. His bed was by mine, and when he was putting his shit up, he asked me what I was there for. I told him. He told me he was there for murder and got life. He swore he'd be out in a year. Said he'd been tried for murder seven times. He had evidence from the case he was in on.

When I asked him why he was in, he gave me a picture of a guy with his head blown fucking off, and he went, "Here's why I'm here, why you here?" He said, "I kept telling that fucker I was gonna kill him!" It was drugs, from what I can recall.

These two Steve's, neither quite normal, both liked each other, and they told me if anyone, *anyone*, fucked with me, let them know. As I said, I had no trouble in prison. Sure, couple guys fucked with me, but I showed it could be on right now, and *All Was Quiet on the Western Front.*

Chapter 91

I got to Rowan County Jail(pronounced *roun*, like round without the *D, roun*), and it was a shitty experience for a spell.

I had, like, three months, and this shit was done. I got there, and a day was taking a week for about the first month. I mean, this inbred fucker who thought he was runnin' shit called me out right away. I had to let him know I was just there to do my time.

This skinny fucker, nobody came to visit him, he never had money on his books; it was sad. I'd give him a pack of smokes, try to befriend him, and in no time, he thought I was his bitch. So we had words one day when he asked for a cigarette, and I said no. This dude was a pencil. I mean, 5'5", maybe a buck, ringin' wet. I would have snapped him in two. I wanted to.

We went out to this little cement pond with a basket and a fence over your head, all you see are four walls, clouds, and hopefully, some birds flying through the beautiful wonderful free sky for rec, and we started to have words again. Look, my entire mindset was this, *Seven months, twenty-one days, and I'm* done. *I do not wanna be here 7-22!*

These guards, these jailers? They are not there to protect you, I promise. I went in and said I should be moved, there's a real good chance there's gonna be some trouble in the violence department. These fuckers went, "This isn't a hotel! So what!" I was in a county cell, and they did move me to a state cell later that day.

I had a boat to sleep on in the pod dayroom because all the cells were full. I went to sleep as soon as I got in there. When I woke up, everyone was locked in their cell. I pulled a brown bag from under my boat, looking for a smoke, and I didn't recognize the bag by feel. I took it out, opened it up, and it was full of shit. I won a bag of shit! Here we go again!

When the guard came around doing his check, I asked him what I had to do to get thrown in the hole. He went, "Quit being stupid."

I was like, "Look, what can I do to you to get put in the hole?"

That caught his attention. I explained the bag of shit, showed it to him in the garbage, explained the getting fucked with, all I wanted to do was my seventy-eight days and get the fuck out of there! What can I do to be put in the hole?

He went, "Well, if it was medical…"

I went, "I have asthma, and I'm having trouble breathing. I think I need to go to the hole." He took me.

First day in there, I'd bet I was asked fifty times if I was ready to be moved back to civilization. My response was always no, thank you, though. Here's the thought process. *I have seventy-five days to do, and I can do it here, in peace and quiet, and read my books and think and sleep and not have to worry about getting fucked with and not have to worry a goddamn thing?* Fuck you! *I'm staying right here, jailer man!* The only downfall? No TV. Hey, fuck TV in its ass! It's 2019 right now, and I don't have cable, fire stick, nothin'. I have a TV that gets some shit, I guess. I had books.

I was a few days into solitary, and the only woman jailer in the place came in and went, "Ready to move?"

"No, ma'am."

"Look, I'm going to put you in Butch's cell"—he was the head trustee of the jail—"if anyone messes with you, I promise I'll put you back in here."

I again politely declined and told her I didn't believe her. She swore on God and everything, so I said, "Okay. But you promise to move me back to the hole if it goes awry!" I knew she was lying!

She took me to this cellblock, and she and a male guard opened the door, and the male guard went something like, "Listen up! This guy's here to do his time! Fuck with him, there's hell to pay!" Something along those lines. I lay down on my boat and went to sleep.

Chapter 92

Look, those last seventy, I think, two days, they were okay. I mean, everyone did their time, nobody fucked with anybody. Sure, there was trouble, a few fights. It's fucking jail!

Now here was my schedule those last couple months. I'd get up about eleven o'clock at night. This old dude and I would play Scrabble all night till breakfast. After that, if we didn't play more Scrabble, or I'd read a book till lunch and eat lunch. Every day, about two, I'd give this speech, "I don't want my dinner"—and someone would claim it—"please just make sure I'm up for breakfast in the morning." And I'd go to sleep.

Up at 11:00 p.m. again, repeat.

Now with Butch, the head trustee, he had some freedoms, and he had access to shit. Like one night, he gave me a hamburger made from store-bought ground beef. He said the guards brought it in, and he cooked it for them, and he brought a couple to us.

Every bite of that fucking hamburger, loaded with lettuce, tomato, pickle, onion, ketchup, mustard, mayonnaise, took my mind to amazing, beautiful, trippy, warm, kind places!

I was overthanking him, telling him he's God, you wanna fuck my old lady, all kinds of shit, and he went, in a real Kentucky accent, "Shut the hell up, man! You wanna help me with this?" And he showed me a joint. Later that night, we went in the bathroom and smoked that joint, him and me and another guy.

I didn't get high a lot in there, maybe three, four times, but it was nice when it presented itself.

Also Butch brought the leftover coffee in our pod on Saturdays, so I'd get wired as a three-year-old on Jeff Sang sandwiches.

Chapter 93

Now what? My mom was in Morehead to pick me up when I got released from jail. She took me to McShit, and I got some food, and we headed back to Garrison. I walked down to Steven Cooley's dilapidated trailer and told him I just got out of jail, could he get me high? He did. Smoked a couple joints with me, free of charge.

I remember, that first day out, Duke had a swing in the front yard. I sat in that fucker for about twelve, fourteen hours and drank coffee and smoked cigarettes. My mom would come out and go, "It's dark, it's cold, you ready to come in?"

"Nah. I'm good!" Everything was so vibrant, so fresh, so crisp.

I was thinking I was fucked. I had to register as a Ted Bundy sex offender for ten years. It wasn't bad. I worked from Cleveland to California, and when I tried to make a comeback, I stayed in San Antonio, all without having to change my residence.

First of all, when I was released from jail, I wasn't told dick about signing dick as a sex offender. About three years after I was released, I got a letter in the mail. So for seven years, I complied within the realm of the law.

After getting out of jail, I had no idea where I was gonna go.

The big town in Lewis County is Vanceburg. It has one stop-light in city limits, at old Route 10. Lewis County is a dry county, but you can buy booze in the county seat, Vanceburg. Actually to this day, you can fill your car, buy a rifle, pistol, shotgun, ammo for all, a case of beer, and a bottle of booze, all under one roof in Vanceburg. No shit. Pills at Police Chief Joe Billman's house.

Anyhow Duke's cousin is married to a guy who played in Artimus Pyle's APB band, and they live in the area, and he is crippled, and he opened a head shop-type deal in Vanceburg. No pipes, papers, nothin' like that. He bought amps, guitars, keyboards, shit like that, at retail price, then tried to sell it for what he paid for it.

Obviously I knew this dude wasn't too bright. He turned out to be a real sneaky snake piece of shit. Anyhow I'm hangin' out at his shop every day. We're smokin' weed, listenin' to tunes, talkin', gettin' pizza at Andy's next-door. I wasn't drinking at all. Tryin' to figure out what I was going to do.

Every day I'd see this woman across the railroad tracks, opposite side of the street, at this place called Victorian Rose Tea Room. It was a café antique store. And Robert, Vaughn, Hurf, he was a telemarketer, the hippy entrepreneur responded in a harsh manner, in his hillbilly way, "Don't you go fuckin' round with her! That's the president of the bank's wife! I got my house loan with him!"

I started going over there that day. I had to see what I couldn't have. I mean, aside from being your run-of-the-mill piece of shit, now I'm also a Ted Bundy! Who, at all, was going to want me, much less a banker's wife in a region where everybody was dirt poor, and there was no hope?

One evening, probably within the first few days of going over there, Joni leaned over the bar and kissed me. She was drinking white wine (she was *always* drinking white wine). We were sitting by each other at the bar, and she leaned over and kissed me.

I went, "What about Ben?"

She responded, "He might like the idea."

Look, the last thing I intended to do when starting this was not write a big long look-what-I-did-sexually bunch of bullshit. And I won't. I fucked a guy's wife—they were from Montana—while he taped it and made cowboy sounds. I fucked a lot of guy's wives, some knew, some didn't. I could'a fucked a teacher in high school, Ms. Ramsey; hell, half the basketball team did, including a kid who is now a principal, but she was ugly, and Greg Page had bigger tits than her, way bigger! I had lots of sex. Looking back, in a nutshell, I have had probably more sex than the average guy. I have no idea how many women I have had sex with. I don't care. I never had an STD, other than crabs. Caught the fuckers twice!

Anyhow as Joni was kissing me, Ben popped out of nowhere and went, "The next time that happens, I want it to be across the street!" (at their house). Their house faced the Main Street, Andy's Pizza was next to it, along the tracks on the small side street, then Vaughn's fake store. The tracks are right there, separating Ben and Joni's house from the main business district. Ben's bank, the Tea Room, and the *Lewis County Herald*, being basically it. Shaky Toll's Barber Shop. Can't forget Shaky!

We went over to their house and she and I had sex for, like, twelve hours. I mean, we'd take a break, and she'd drink wine, and I'd smoke weed, and we'd fuck again, again, and again. You get it. I'm not saying this necessarily in a disrespectful way, but Joni Pugh, to this day, is the biggest come-guzzling slut I have ever met. God bless her!

This went on for a few months. New Year's was coming up, and a guy in Vaughn the Gimp's band was going to take a Greyhound to see an old girlfriend from Maysville in Memphis, Tennessee. Joe Something was the dude's name.

I was like, "Brah, I got a truck." I had my Uncle Blink's 1986 Chevy S10. I drove him to Memphis and spent New Year's away from Joni and Ben. Joni did, however, give me money for the trip.

Again no smut log intended. However, five days and nights on Beale Street, I got laid three times.

Don't ask me how these, and other, strange sexual encounters have happened in my life, they just ended up happening.

I also did shrooms New Year's Eve and listened to live music till sunup.

Instead of taking 75 to, I think, 40, might be 44, I took the Bluegrass Parkway. It was shitty out and us in an S10. I picked a joint up to light it, and we were talking, and I just never lit the joint; I was just holding it. One of those forgot-about-it kinda deals. We were a good three hours into the trip.

It was late at night, I've always liked to travel at night, and we were near the Tennessee line, and out of nowhere, we started hydroplaning all over the goddamn place! I mean, I was tellin' Joe we're gonna wreck!

"Hold on! We're fucked!"

Then as I was turning the wheel back and forth, we just started going like nothing ever happened. I realized I had the joint in my hand, and we laughed and lit it.

Not long into smoking on that joint, we hit a massive traffic jam in the middle of the night, in the middle of nowhere! There had been a fatality wreck, and we were there a good two hours. Got through, stopped at a truck stop, hit the Tennessee State line, and the roads were bone-dry.

Chapter 94

Time was going on, and I was still not working. Ben Pugh hated my guts by spring. I mean, Joni spent the night with me on the floor of Vaughn's store and drank and sucked and drank and sucked on the night of his fiftieth birthday.

Now and then, she'd stop both and look at me and go, "It is Ben's fiftieth birthday! I should go home!" Then she went right back to sucking and begging for wine supplement.

He even called over there and told me, he went, "My wife is with you on my fiftieth birthday! Can't she come home?" I told him I was not keeping her there, which I wasn't.

Here's a question you have probably never been asked: have you ever gotten your dick sucked and fucked by another guy's wife, in their bed, in the middle of the night, the husband is hiding, spying, being a homosexual perv, and there's a knock at the door, state police, saying your son, Benji, is involved in a "strange" situation where Mr. Charlie has been shot and killed and the only two people there were Benji and Mr. Charlie? I have.

Rumor had it Benji shot Mr. Charlie because he thought Mr. Charlie was fucking his mom. Of course, this being a weekend, it took till Monday to sweep things up neatly and say Mr. Charlie shot himself. Benji was supposed to start the Maysville Kentucky Police Department that Monday. The only punishment he got for, in my opinion, murdering Mr. Charlie was not being allowed to be a cop. That's it. Daddy Ben moved him near Cincinnati. How come I'm Ted Bundy for grabbing a butt, but Benji Pugh is not a convicted murderer? He is a murderer, just not convicted. Sure do wish some-one would look into this case; a retard could see was murder.

His dad, Ben, was also a thief. I had a journal going in the Rose van, and he stole it when I got that DUI. Guess he thought I was writing about the perversions I was partaking in, and he didn't want anyone to read it.

I got a job in Cincinnati and ended up staying there a lot. I OD'ed in Cincinnati. Worked at a country club for about a year. Hey! Chef Jay! Hey, Sous Chef Goose!

The real-life bender from *Breakfast Club* was a line cook there. Long coat and all, refused rides. Had a long, long driveway. He ended up becoming an executive chef years later, I'd bet. Dude was amazing in a kitchen.

Just a little off-kilter.

When I lived in Cincinnati, I did not have a driver's license. I had lost it because of a DUI. Joni ended up giving me the Tea Room van to use while I didn't have a driver's license. It ended up being nine years, but I didn't use the van that long, nowhere near. I got a DUI in that van. Ben had called me and said if I didn't have it there that day, he was reporting it stolen. I was wasted drunk. Doing 90 mph all the way on the AA Highway. Got stopped on Herring Hill, just west of Vanceburg. They asked me to take a sobriety test. I asked them if it was really necessary.

I went to Cincinnati because that's where Joni was from. She'd come see me under the guise of visiting family. It's about two hours west of Vanceburg.

Chapter 95

The shit was hitting the fan with Ben. I mean, I was supposed to be his wife's sperm generator; she wasn't supposed to disobey the master for sperm boy! We were slipping away, getting hotel rooms in Lexington, having sex in the Tea Room van on the side of the road, at the Tea Room, without Ben there.

All the while, I felt miserable inside. This job I had, it wasn't a bad gig, as far as kitchens went. I had a title, sous chef. It equated to making sure the paperwork got done, all the orders were filled daily, and I had to work the line if we got busy because the GM was too cheap to have an adequate staff. I forgot his name. Nice guy. Just cheap. I know, I know. It's called bonuses!

We did a lot of parties, weddings, it was an easy gig. I got drunk every single day at this job. Six days a week, I did sixteen shots of something and beer washers throughout my shift. I know sixteen 'cause I'd give a bartender a sixteen-ounce cup for booze. I don't like ice, and I'd give him twelve jumbo shrimp.

I had this job about a year. I lost it in a good way. Now I had gotten a car and was driving without a license. On more than one occasion, I had gotten so drunk at work I couldn't drive. Not that I had safety in mind, or other people. I'd try to leave and realize, before I was out of the parking lot, I was too drunk to drive, so I'd go sleep in the men's locker room.

Members started finding me passed out in the locker room the next morning, and complaining. I was on the last chance at least four times. Finally Jay and Goose called me in the office and told me they couldn't go to bat for me anymore. I understood. This had to be '99. Not a bad year, considering the previous, eh?

Chapter 96

I went back to Lewis County and Rock Hill till 2000. I started fucking this girl, Brandi, who was married to Dale Gee, a state game warden who got convicted of swapping blood in a paternity test, trying to help a state trooper beat a case of having a baby with an underaged girl. So Brandi was married to Travis, cheating with Dale, divorced Travis, married Dale, and started fucking everybody!

These fuckers had a little baby too. It was a mess, and I stayed in it a few months! Dale Gee looked like, well, he resembled the kid on the bridge playing banjo in *Deliverance*. His mentality was the same.

In 2000, I decided I was "Going Out West" again. And I was gonna make a comeback. Terry Norris had lost his title, and First Fighter Squadron was nothing but a memory. Cowboy Joe had packed up shop and went to Vegas, so I was told.

Rudy Elias, the trainer, lied his fuckin' ass off to me! I drove from Kentucky to California, and nothing he told me was true. I stayed with a fighter of his, but I had to be up at, like, 4:00 a.m., when he went to work because he didn't trust me in his apartment alone. I left San Diego after about two weeks of this.

I called Tony Ayala Sr., in San Antonio, and he said, "Sure! C'mon over!" So I drove from San Diego to San Antonio to pursue the dead-end dream *again*.

Chapter 97

Now the day I left, I went to Mission Beach and drank and partied my balls off for a good long time! Well into the night! I stopped at a rest area not far from the Arizona State border and slept for a couple hours.

When I got up, it was still dark. I got on I-10, got off at the first exit, filled my 1987 ounce-coffee cup up, got a can of lip shit, got back on I-10 east, lit a joint, looked up, and saw a sign that said "Border Check One Mile."

I snubbed the joint, rolled the windows down to air the car out, and started praying to that nonlistening motherfucker I have talked about.

There were two lanes. A semi was in one, and the other one was open, so I went to it. When I did, the guard went, "STAY RIGHT THERE! DON'T MOVE!"

I knew they had me. How, cameras? I was scared six ways from fuckin' Sunday, Jack! I had about ten, fifteen joints rolled for the trip. I mean, it was a good 1,200 miles.

Did I forget to mention I had a suspended DUI driver's license? All I had was a Kentucky State ID card. I went from Lewis County, Kentucky, to San Diego, California, on a suspended DUI license and was headed to San Antonio, and it looked like we were done! Actually, I drove on a suspended DUI license for nine years. I got a DUI during this time, but it got mended down.

This guy went, "YOU PULL RIGHT OVER THERE, PAL!" And he pointed to a carport about a hundred yards away. As I was pulling over there, I ate every one of those joints at once and washed them down with coffee.

He came over and went, "Like to smoke pot, huh? Mind if I search your car?"

I told him I didn't. I had a 1988 Honda Accord hatchback. He's going under it with mirrors, knocking on it all over the place, asking questions. He never looked in the ashtray. Never opened it. Never checked the door where you can keep stuff, just looked for pounds. The hatchback was broken, and the back was packed full of garbage bags full of my stuff. He was trying to hold the back up and look and was having a real go of it!

I went, "Sir, there's a way to prop that up, want me to?"

He went, "Hurry up!" He was pissed!

They never once asked me for any kind of ID. Not once. Like a retard, I asked if I could use their restroom when they told me I could go! As soon as I got in it, I realized I should just piss my pants, and left.

Chapter 98

I trained with Papa Tony for about two months. I lived at the gym, the Zarzamora Street Gym. Did my roadwork at a park not far from the gym, every morning. Only white boy for miles!

I wasn't partying at all when I was there. I mean, I really wanted to fight again. I just knew I could.

After two months of training camp living, one day, after I sparred, Tony took my headgear off and went, "John Wayne"—he said I laughed like John Wayne, so he called me John Wayne—"I've known you since 1986. Emmanuel sent me a film of you in '84. You had the ability, at one time, to be a top-ten fighter. Every day has its sunset, my friend, your boxing career has had its. I can't get you any fights in good conscience." As I write that, those words still crush me inside.

I never told him, but I was always in pain. I was crushed. Even after two months of intense training, my body ached. So I headed back to Rock fuckin' Hill!

Chapter 99

I knew I couldn't stay here any length of time without ending up in jail again. I did get arrested for terroristic threatening, so Ben said I said I was going to kill him, so they got me. I couldn't be living in a scumbag, dead-end, nothing place and end up right back in prison 'cause I fucked the banker's wife.

When crooked ass Clayton G. "Buddy" Lykins, the county prosecutor (whose wife had been to Ben and Joni's for a "pizza party" or two), let me know he'd fuck me, I pled guilty to terroristic threatening. Part of the plea was to stay out of Vanceburg, don't fuck Joni, even if she came to my bedroom, and some other shit. None of it was hard.

I wrote a good long letter to the *Lewis County Herald*, which was next to the Tea Room and across the street from Ben's bank, explaining everything in detail what went on with the hierarchy in the county of Lewis, state of Kentucky. They didn't publish it.

Joe Billman was the chief of police forever in Vanceburg. He was also the ambulance driver. Rumor always had it he was a pedophile. I'd bet he is. He was also the biggest drug dealer in Lewis County. People have OD'ed and died at his house. Yet well, I'm Ted Bundy, according to the state of Kentucky. He's a chief of police in Kentucky.

How 'bout Deputy Pig Nut Toothless Weiner Stone? That's right, Deputy Pig Nut Toothless Weiner Stone! Fucker was an inbred sack of Charlie's monkey shit! Grew weed, dealt dope, broke in houses, typical cop from my experiences.

Weiner! Fucker was 5'4", toothless, weighed about eighty-one pounds (with all his military garb on, and trust me, GI Weiner was dressed and ready for war in them there hills), a deputy! Ever seen the movie *Walking Tall*, the original? That is Lewis County, Kentucky, as you read this.

How do you not laugh so fucking hard? You shit your pants when an inbred looking like this comes up to you and tries to be a badass in a girly, boyish, hill jack fucking accent, with no front teeth?

That Honey Boo Boo shit might be cute on TV. Try living with these inbreds!

Every time I saw the sheriff, Bill Lewis, he'd ask me if I was still drinking tea. Nah. Coffee. At the Tea Room.

They will arrest you, charge you with murder, convict you, and that's that. With no evidence, no nothin'. I promise.

Oh! Sure! Someone will end up dead, all right. You were probably in Briary Holler, fuckin' someone else's wife, while her husband was working out of state to put food on the table, and she gave her kids seventeen Benadryl to knock them out, and she made better beans and cornbread than your wife (who's at work at this time at the Quik Stop in Garrison), and you were gettin' some from this skank after you eat, before you fart, while a murder at the other end of the county is taking place.

Betty Joe isn't going to lie for you. I mean, and lose her security, free rent, place to take stray dick, have sex with him when he's home (which is okay with her, dick is dick). What about those seven kids?

Next thing you know, you're in jail for murder. They have witnesses, everything. Even the jury. You're a murderer, and all you did was get some coochie! On the other side of the county!

This shit goes on there, I promise.

Chapter 100

I have some fond memories of this mess. I mean, when I lived in Macon, I had a job for a minute at a place on Vineville Avenue, that's rollin' down Highway 41, boys and girls! Place wasn't far from the Big House (The Brothers' Big House, not the man's!). I used to drive right by it every day.

The guy who owned the restaurant, Tom, was a bad, bad liar. As bad as Sissy Pants and Gloria Jean (soap opera lyin' Susie slut's nickname). One night, he came in the kitchen and told me Chuck Levell had just left. He forgot to tell me when he came in to eat. It was a bullshit story. Tom knew I was a music guru.

Anyhow I'd stop by the Big House often and knock. I just did it one day. Who opened the door but Kirk West (tour manager for The Brothers), and he went, "Can I help you?" I told him I was a fan, could I come in and look?

He and his wife, Kerstin, lived there at the time. There was a room right inside the front door, to the left, full, I mean full, of memorabilia. The drum case from the *Live at the Fillmore East* album cover, letters to home when they were on the road, Duane's guitar, all kinds of shit.

When I'd stop, I'd read stuff over and over, asked Kirk a lot of questions. "Good old Sunday morning and bells are ringing everywhere." There's a church a block from the Big House with a big bell. Dickey's "Blue Sky." "Rollin' down Highway 41," Ramblin' Man.

Kirk ended up getting fired for dipping into the till, so the news stories read some years later. That's stealing, if you weren't hip to slang.

In December of 1997, when the shit hit the fan with me, this was what we had going on. We (Little Martha and I) had tickets to Frog Wings (Oteil Burbrige's band) at a club in Macon, Medesky, Martin, and Wood in Atlanta, and The Gregg Allman Band at the Macon Auditorium. First time Gregg had played Macon in years. I remember the date of that show, December 27, 1997. I was in jail, not jammin'. All these were within a week of one another.

Kirk gave us tickets because Little Martha helped him out with a website.

Hey, Little Martha, do you still have my Dickey and Jaimoe signed ticket stub from a show somewhere, sometime? Columbus, Ohio, I believe.

Chapter 101

So one of the things I did when I first got out of the joint, and had the Rose van, was venture right back to Macon, Georgia! I only spent about a week there before a place I was trying to get an apartment at said I had an FBI file and warrants in Georgia.

Lady was super nice about it! "I'm *so* sorry, sir! Says here you're an FBI file and warrants in Georgia for wrecking a car!"

There was this dude, Ken, that I got to know when I was there. He was a real little dude, 5'3", maybe a buck or two, had the Joe Dirt mullet. He was a big drinker, and he made origami art and sold it on the street to not get enough money to pay the rent on the apartment he had and was always getting eviction notices in. But he did get enough together to get drunk every day.

I stayed with Ken for this week. Saw David Alan Coe again, laid drunk that week.

One night, Ken and I were at Rose Hill. We were fucked up. We had been at the Johnston wall drinking, and we started our way back up to the entrance and his evict home. As we were passing Duane and Berry's, we noticed there was a chain-link fence around them.

Why, who would do something like that, Ken?

Why they put a fence around it (today it has about an eight-foot wrought iron gate around it), I'll never understand. I mean, not only was Rose Hill Cemetery a very popular place to hang out, Duane and Berry's gravesite was a supercool place.

People used to leave notes, poems, letters, matches, guitar picks, joints, roaches, rolling papers, all kinds of stuff, none of it harmful or bad. Met a guy there on Jerry's two-year death anniversary. We had a long deep conversation. There was never any litter.

Someone had torn that fence down. Looked like a two-drunk-guy job, I don't know.

Not sure if I've let you know, I have found cemeteries to be sanctuaries since I was a kid at Pinecrest. I've never been a desecrator of cemeteries. No litter, beer cans, nothin'! Fences don't belong around the dead bodies of saints, period. Heard Berry Oakly's sister did this. If she did, she's a fuckin' quack.

Chapter 102

In 1998, something happened I never gave much thought to till time showed up. One day, not long at all after I'd been sprung from jail, my mom brought home a cocker spaniel that was matted, shaking, scared, pissed on the floor, the whole ensemble!

She went, "some girl Sam"—my sister—"knows had this dog, and Sam took it and said you'd take care of her."

The story is, this dog, Sandy, as a pup, was raised by a girl who loved her to death and spoiled her rotten. Sandy was about eight, nine; this girl had to give her up for some reason. The girl she gave her to tied Sandy up outside and forgot about her for a couple years.

Sandy would sing "Bad to the Bone," no cue, no instruction, no nothin'! If it came on the radio, or you started singing it, she'd just start howlin' away! The longer the song, the higher-pitched the howl got! She was a huge three-chord George fan!

We got her cut and cleaned up, and that dog became my shadow. Couldn't piss, shit, leave, wake up, nothin' without that dog at my feet. She slept under the covers at my feet, even in the summer.

I got a job in Portsmouth, Ohio, telemarketing. If I wasn't at work, I was with that dog. No matter where I went.

Chapter 103

I'm aware none of this makes any sense. I'm not stupid. Maybe just a little punchy. In 2001, my sister bred her dog, another cocker, also named Sandy (coincidence), and she had two left that she couldn't get rid of, and she begged me to take one for a couple of weeks. Finally one day, she went, "Kip"—her inbred now-ex-husband—"is going to abandon them, take one!"

So she had one that looked exactly like a cow. Downfall was, he was a male. Still looked exactly like a cow with white fur and black blotches, and he was trippy! So I told her I'd take him. She went, "No! You have to take her! Someone else is taking him!" Got me!

That's how I got Sam. I never could come up with a name for her, and one day, I walked in the house, and my mom went, "Stop! Sam!"

I went, "Sam?"

She retorted, "You have to name her something! And Sam gave her to you!"

That dog lived fifteen and a half years.

My intention was, when Sandy died, she was getting old, probably thirteen or better, to get a German shepherd. I instead ended up with a pack of nonstop explosive energy that I was gonna beat to death for every second of those fifteen years!

Chapter 104

Sandy hated Sam with a passion! One day, I woke up on the floor, and Sandy wasn't at my feet. I immediately went looking all over the house for her. She was nowhere. Nobody was home. This was pre-cell phones for us. Anyhow I finally got ahold of my sister, and Duke was at her house. She said Sandy got hit by a car, and Duke buried her in the backyard.

I told her to tell Duke if he ever came home again, I was going to kill him and bury him in the backyard. After lots of convincing, Sam finally got me to believe my mom told Duke not to tell me; she wanted to, and she also told him to bury her.

One day, I had them both up at the cemetery on the hill by Duke's house, and I had Sam off the leash. She took off and would not listen at all! She left the cemetery and went in this backyard with kids playing before letting me leash her up! I wanted so bad to strangle her and beat her almost to death! Shouldn't hit dogs. Especially if you feel they need it, no shit. I tend to pull a Buddy on mine, explosive gonna dos.

What had me extra pissed was Sandy was following Sam, not listening to me either! That dog never disobeyed me ever!

Wasn't long after this, Sandy committed suicide. I tend to believe she woke up that day, went in the kitchen, and saw Sam in the pet taxi, said, "Fuck you, bitch!" Ate all the food in the bowls, drank all the water, went back in the bedroom I was in, on the floor, kissed me, asked Duke to let her out, and she waited till a car came before ending it all.

Sam ended up running out of the door one day, straight across the yard, into the road, and got run clean over by a red car doing about 40 mph. She came back in the yard and looked at me like, *What the fuck was* that? She was perfectly okay.

Not long after this, she was in that S10 with me and jumped out the window when I pulled in the driveway of Duke's; there's a steep hill. Again, that look!

I have dog stories. Sam drank coffee till she was about ten or eleven, then she gave it up. She liked to get high; again she gave it up in her older age, on her own. She drank beer. She was the most finicky dog on earth when it came to food. If you were eating a burger and fries, she wouldn't eat a fry as long as you still had burger. She'd grab it with her mouth and drop it on the floor! She'd have five, six fries lyin' there waitin' on that sliver of soy bean! When the meat was gone, she'd eat the fries. She learned this trick from Sassy, the German shepherd whom you haven't met yet.

Chapter 105

During this time, staying at Duke and my mom's, with these two dogs, calling people from San Antonio, Texas, while I was in Portsmouth, Ohio, asking them for money because the DPS (Department of Public Safety, what the cops are called in Texas) needed it really, really bad!

And getting scolded by the hillbilly supervisor for using the slang for wherever I was calling. He'd go, "*Quit* asking people in Massachusetts who has the best frap! Stop saying DPS in Texas! You'll get in trouble!"

I tried telling him I'd lived in all these places and spoke their language. He didn't believe me. He also didn't understand how I was always in the top-ten sales, and I didn't try at all.

Look, I hated this job. I read that script word for word. Sure. I empathized, read the script like a part, the entire time in my mind, I'd be going, "Please don't bite this bait, Mary, please, or, Joe, or any old fucker!" I did enough to keep my job.

I never did fit in in this region of the country. I tried. I mean, through the years, I'd met a couple to smoke weed with, and I had my share of times out with the good old boys here. But I never fit in at all. If you know me, you know I don't fit in anywhere.

Chapter 106

I lived in a dead-end place, I had a dead-end job, I had no hope, I had no nothin'!

During this time, I wasn't drinking. I mean, if I went on a little trip or stayed somewhere, I might get fucked up, but I wasn't drinking daily. Hell, looking back, in that almost year, I might have gotten drunk two times.

I had these dogs. I used to take them to the cemetery for hours, every day, or the school or the woods and just let them be dogs.

Sam was so easy to train. She played catch. She'd throw the ball back every time you threw it to her. I could take her anywhere without a leash. I mean anywhere, and that shithead dog would stay right by my side. Bud Man died on July 16, 2014. Sam died July 14, 2016. I think of both of them daily. Honestly I miss Sam more than Bud. The only thing Stinky Sam ever did to me was steal my sandwich off the counter and eat it.

Bud Man's ashes are on my dresser. Shithead Sam's are on Thelma's, next to Sassy.

I'm gonna be a pile of ashes someday. Who gives a fuck? Not me. "They ain't got what we got."

Chapter 107

So after being stuck on Rock Hill for about a year, I called a friend in Louisville, Kentucky, and asked him if I could go down and stay with him, get a job, and plot my next cross-country adventure. Mike said sure.

I had an apartment in his building in a couple of weeks and settled into a comfortable nonexistent existence.

The car I had broke down, so I had no transportation. I took the city bus everywhere, and I'd Greyhound it or hitch to my mom's to see her and Sam.

I wasn't in Louisville long at all, and I started my daily drinking again. Dying was always still there in the forefront of my mind.

Funny, when I look back at this, I held about the fourth job I had for quite a while. This place was a fuckin' circus.

I lived about five miles from work and had to bus it. That sucked because public transportation in Louisville is super slow in some neighborhoods. The neighborhoods who need them most. I lived in one of those need-them-most neighborhoods and worked in one of those yuppieville cool neighborhoods.

There was a skin-and-bones tiny frail bull dyke lesbian waitress, with a big, big mouth, at this place. There was a guy who worked there, who fits the description above, who thought he was a playboy, bookie, gangster, thug.

There was a dude who worked there like fifteen, seventeen years. He was a sous chef, Grit. He got hit by a car one day on the way to work, and they docked him a day's pay on his check.

The "chef" (I use that term so fucking loosely!) at this place was a sawed-off skinny midget named Francis (pronounced *Francees*), from France. I was told he had cost this dump a shitload of money in a sexual harassment lawsuit. That's why he still worked there, cheap labor.

Every day at work, he'd wait till a girl went in the restroom upstairs—every fucking day—and then he'd go in and act surprised if one of the girls caught him. He'd go, "I didn't know you were in here! I came to get a seat cover!"

I heard that story from every girl who worked there, even Bull Dyke. Hell, we all heard it!

Chapter 108

Let me let you in on a little secret. In my mind, I have done a pretty goddamn good job of holding this used, tattered, shit-stained rag known as my life together in alphabetic, numeric, blow-by-blow form.

In your mind, you're probably thinking, *How did I get this far into reading this? This makes no sense! This guy is a fuckin' quack!*

I'll just go ahead and agree with you and let you know this—I really don't give a fuck. Thank you.

Did you ever see the Grateful Dead? How about The Allman Brothers Band? What about Widespread Panic? Did you suffer repeated violent blows to the head and body throughout your entire childhood, well into adulthood? Did you ever have a dog for ten years, and that dog traded you in the split second she met someone else, only used you for shit when her new master wasn't around? Did your dad threaten to break your legs and put you in a wheelchair when you were ten because you didn't jogged?

Goddamn miracle I'm not a permanent on 4D!

Chapter 109

My drinking, at this time, grew increasingly routine. To this day, something I have never experienced is waking up with the shakes, needing a drink, waking up and having a drink first thing.

I woke up every day of my life going, "I am *not* doing that again tonight!" Feeling like death warmed over, running late for work. Say I had to be at work at 2:00 p.m. I'd get up about 1:30 p.m., 1:48 p.m. Of course, by midshift you gotta have a beer. Goddamn!

There are so many drunk stories. Honestly nothing to be proud of. A wasted talent and a wasted life. That's all. Still, "You ain't got what we got," bitch!

In one of the first 12 of 997 jobs I had in Louisville, Kentucky, I did something, I think to this day, rather unique.

I was working second shift and went in that morning at eleven o'clock to get my check. Paid on Thursdays every other week. After cashing my check, I figured I'd have a few cocktails before my shift.

I went to my favorite watering hole and started in on those few cocktails, and before you know it, it was time for work!

Needless to say, those drinks were going down extra smooth. It was pretty out, we had a pocket full of money, fuck, brah! What do we do? I walked to the pay phone at the corner, called my place of employment, and spewed this great spiel, I was in a car wreck. Nobody hurt, but I may be here a while.

Chef went, "How long you think you're gonna be there?"

I went, "Dude, I have no idea! Here's a cop, wanna ask him?"

I was told no, to get there *if* I could. I was still sitting at the same barstool that night when one of the front-of-the-house managers came in that bar that night after closing. She asked me if the wreck worked out okay.

Wow! More filth. Ah, never mind. Island Girl.

Chapter 110

Somewhere along the way, things changed in my drinking that I had no explanation for during this time. For one, whenever I'd get good and ripped, I'd always be able to sleep twelve, fourteen hours, wake up feeling like a champ.

I started going to sleep at five, six o'clock in the morning, and I'd wake up at 8:30 a.m., 9:00 a.m., and not be able to go back to sleep.

I would go three or four days with no sleep at all. No drugs, just alcohol. I went from a loud boisterous drunk to a quiet timid skeleton of a being. When I think back on this time in my life, one funny memory does stand out.

Bars closed at 4:00 a.m., so I was usually on my floor ready to pass out by 4:45 a.m., 5:00 a.m. Seems like every goddamn morning when I was lying there, trying to pass out, this commercial would come on and go, "Do you have an STD? Have you been with multiple partners? Yeah? You've been with their partners too. Do you always wear a condom? Do you ever wear a condom?"

Shit like that. I swear, this commercial was on a hundred times a morning before I'd pass out. It started fucking with me in a bad way. I mean, as that commercial would be playing, my mind would start flashing back to all the stinky I was with.

My mind would go, *Remember that fugly girl you used a baggie as a rubber with because you didn't have any? Remember how you lost the baggie and just kept on truckin? How 'bout all the girls who professed to never "do this" with someone they don't know? Think you're that special? Condoms? Condoms?*

I was a worry drinker and a problem drinker. I had problems every day, and I worried every day. I knew—I just *knew*—I had AIDS, and I was dying. So this was added to the list of problems and worries I drank daily over.

No. I never went and got tested. Are you fuckin' nuts? One morning, in a drunken stupor, while listening to *the* commercial, *the* message the Creator put there for me, I swore off sex forever till I died. Not that I was having any at this time anyhow.

Prayed about it and everything. Just asked my Creator to let me drink myself to death and not go to jail before I do so, and I was done being a whore, period. Pass out.

As they say, watch what you pray for!

Not sure how long it was, two, three years maybe. About three. I had this studio apartment on the third floor. I always had a job and was always getting a new one. I was never late on rent, and I laid as drunk as I could every night of my life.

The guy who owned the building was a retired police sergeant from the Louisville Police Department. Drug dealer on the first floor. Drug dealer on the second floor. Drunk on the third floor.

When I look back, I had a couple decent jobs during this stretch, a couple places you want to work at, I didn't see it at the time.

Drugs weren't a part of my life by now, other than booze and weed. And I didn't like to smoke weed very often by this time because it messed my drinking up. I couldn't drink enough without getting mind-fucked if I smoked weed.

I proceeded to go a good two, three years without having sex, without going to jail, and without drawing one sober breath. For some fucking reason, I lived.

Chapter 111

Somewhere along the way, I moved from one neighborhood to another so I could be closer to work. I went from Twenty-Fifth and Montgomery to Fourth and St. Catherine because I was working at 4th Street Live, a section they turned into a party spot/ retail shithole.

I had worked in a good three or four of the restaurants in no time. No problem. There were plenty of restaurants to go through, and it was only a ten-minute walk from home! And Freddie's Place was on the way home. A real drinker's bar.

One night, after work, I was standing outside the place, waiting on a guy I worked with to deliver me a bag of weed. It was a weekend, and I was pressed for time because another guy I worked with, Radar (looked *exactly* like Radar on *M*A*S*H*!), was coming over so we could do some serious drinking, and he was going to give me the intricate details of when he robbed a bank.

As I waited on this sack of nugs, these two women came by, and for some reason, they caught my attention.

Look, it was a weekend night, it was summer, there were lots of hot girls around. Looking back, meeting a girl wasn't even on my list. Hadn't been for a long time. Meeting a girl to fall in love with was never even on the fucking list. I am not a smart man, and I do not know what love is.

These ladies sat down at a table by me, and we started talking, and they asked me what I was doing. I told 'em I had just gotten off work and was waiting for a friend.

This fuckin' guy, Charlie was his name, was really fucking me because he already had the money for the weed, and he wasn't showing up. I was pissed because Radar had a bottle of moonshine, a good bottle, and I was going to miss the fun.

I was talkin' to these girls, and Charlie showed up. I got my weed, and one of the girls gave me her business card. I made it to St. Catherine, met Charlie, and we got drunk, and he told me how he got caught using dye pack money to buy crack after the robbery, and life went on.

Couple weeks later, I was cleaning my apartment. As I took the sheets off the foam I had on the floor as a mattress (only furniture I possessed), this business card fell out. "Oh yeah! Hottie in the little black skirt!"

I walked up to the pay phone and called her, thinking she'd never remember me. She did.

We ended up meeting and dating a few times, and she was not coming off the pussy, period. I went over to her house one night and drank a twelve-pack while I visited, and I couldn't figure out why she wouldn't have sex with me.

After seeing this girl a few times, she came over my apartment one morning when she got off work. She worked third shift for an alarm company, and my apartment was on her way home.

After about a month, that morning, she threw it on me. After we were done, I asked why it took so long, and she said, "First of all, I'm not a skank, slut. Second of all, I don't like having sex with drunks. I figured if I woke you up, you'd be sober."

That fucked with me! Either way, she was the first girl I had ever met and got to know a little bit, did things with before we had sex. At thirty-five years old, it was a weird fucking experience!

I tried not to drink around her, but well, *try* never did a goddamn thing. One night, she went out with me to a bar, and I embarrassed the living shit out of her. Tellin' a guy I worked with perverted shit, bein' real loud, typical me in action.

Seems like I stayed at her house that night, and she asked me to go home when I got up the next day.

I had moved back to the exact same apartment on Montgomery because she lived nearby.

She had a German shepherd, Sassy, and she let me bring Sam down and live at her house. So I got a woman I was falling in love with and had no idea how to accept, deal, handle it. Stinky Sam was a ten-minute walk from me, I was working, I was laying drunk, what's wrong with this picture?

Oh yeah, we'd been dating six, eight months, I spend the night, why can't I move in? "The short of it is, you drink too much."

One night, not long after the bar incident, I got ripped and went to Thelma's house to see Sam. We had been arguing that day, so I poured a drink on the anger and went to show her who was boss and got my dog.

She told me my mom had come and gotten Sam, she wasn't there, I wasn't welcome, leave! I almost had the storm door off its hinges when the cops showed up. I knew she was lying! She was stealing my dog!

I got arrested and charged with burglary and was looking at ten years back in prison. Thelma didn't press the charges, the cops did. She told me she was afraid of me. She said she thought I was gonna kill her that night.

I wasn't. I wanted to see Sam and cry and beg to stay the night!

I hired a lawyer that dealt in serious shit; a guy I was locked up with told me to call him. Alex Dathorne. I did. I pled basically to being a drunk piece of shit, from what I can remember.

Chapter 112

Now here we are, seven months into this relationship, and I just knew it was over. I mean, Thelma's told me how she was with a drunk for twenty-seven years, she's content being alone, maybe I should think about finding another woman to fall in love with.

Not like I hadn't heard this speech before. Funny, as she's saying this stuff and instead of my mind going down the I'll-show-this-bitch-what-drunk-*is* road, it started telling me things like, *Hey, asshole, maybe you should show her you can quit drinking and be a nice guy. Do that bit for a month or two.*

Throughout the years, wherever I would move to, or end up, I'd always immediately start going to meetings, dry out, and make a decision that this was going to be the start I was looking for. When I'd get a boxing trainer interested in me was when this, looking back, act would be played out.

That would last till I felt comfortable in my surroundings, and I had money coming in. Then what the hell? Let's have a drink!

This was different. I told her I was done drinking. She said she didn't care.

This was in 2005. We had met in July of '04. I had shown her something, just enough of something, to keep seeing me. Or she was just that stupid. Actually she has a big heart and doesn't like to hurt people's feelings.

So I make a decision to quit drinking, and I meant it. Around about some time in the first few days of laying off the booze, I spent the night at Thelma's house. She was sleeping, and I was lying on the bed, dealing with a case of the DTs.

Sam being there was the rationale for me wanting to stay over. Sleeping on the bed with her was because Sassy slept on the couch. Had nothing to do with me wanting to hold her! Which she didn't allow to happen!

Having been through them before and five rehabs, I knew what was going on. Looking back, I can't say I was scared. If anything, I was praying I died. Everything else in my life had always been a fuckin' circus, seeing faces flying around the bedroom wall, scream- ing out in silent desperation, and snakes and yellow and green bugs crawling on my body was really no big deal.

As I was going through this, I went out in the kitchen. Still saw the faces in the wall, but most of the bugs had left my body. Sassy and Sam both came in the kitchen with me. They knew something was wrong with me. I started smoking on some weed in the kitchen, and the faces in the wall subsided their circular motion along the wall and dissipated into thin air. Maybe they didn't dissipate. But things did slow down on the merry-go-round.

Those dogs sat at my feet and kept rubbing up against me.

Chapter 113

Look, this is multifaceted. I mean, Thelma is a big, big, big dog lover. When I met Sassy and immediately lay on the floor and let her lick and sniff me, I didn't know I was scoring brownie points. I got my German shepherd!

Sassy and Sam are probably the biggest, if not the only, reason Thelma never told me to hit the road, Jack!

After a couple months of dating, Thelma let me bring Sam down to stay at her house. There were times, I know, the only reason I was allowed over in the enclosed front porch was to see those dogs.

Tell ya what, this coming-off-booze thing is a drop kick in the nuts. The mental anguish, to me, was far worse than the coming of heroin withdrawals. With heroin, it was over in two weeks. With booze, the physical ailments were over in a short amount of time. The puking and shitting at the same time, shakes, sweats, runny nose, eyes, that shit was over in a couple of weeks as well.

The mental fuck, however, lasted a couple, few years. I'd say it continues to this very second.

Chapter 114

Why? How? Why not, when I was still young and had hope? If I could answer that, I wouldn't be writing this. There are a thousand ways to quit drinking. Just as there are a thousand ways to do anything.

I quit drinking in 2005 because I wanted to show Thelma I was really a good guy. I also know that you cannot quit drinking or doing drugs permanently unless your incentive is inner desire.

I figured I'd dry out and then be able to drink at my apartment on nights I didn't stay with her, occasionally. Hey, true thought process to the equation.

That didn't happen. This time, after twenty-one years of in and out of AA, trying to quit different ways, something was just different.

One day, not long after putting the bottle down, I started heading over to this guy's house I knew, and I didn't even know what the hell I was going over there for.

I was probably off booze a month or so when this transpired. I was a mess. Looking back, Thelma took care of three kids for a solid year, year and a half—Sassy, Sam, and me.

Anyhow I go over this guy's house, Rusty. He has a lot of drug abuse in his family; he used to be a druggie, his one kid is in prison, I mean, this guy's life was a mess. I had met him through a friend. He became a rock to lean on for me. He'd been off drugs for years, and that intrigued me.

I got to his house and knocked on the door. When he answered, he went, "Hey! What's up?"

I had no clue what to say, none! So I went, "When I was a kid, I was sexually abused!" And I started bawling like a baby.

He invited me in his house and went, "How old were you?" I told him six. He went, "What did you do wrong?"

What the fuck! I had never even conceived, not even at thirty-six years old, what happened to me was not my fault.

I mean, my dad going to blow his brains out was my fault. Valloyd Deed raping my mom was my fault. Us having to move all the time was my fault. My dad's drinking and whoring was my fault. Being Bud and Carol's kid was my fault. Every motherfucking thing wrong on earth was my fucking fault. So I had just always knew being molested was my fault. Had to be. I'm Bruce. A bad, bad kid. Chief Lonnie let me know that when I was five.

Here's exactly what I did. I worked the twelve steps of Alcoholics Anonymous. I'm not saying I went to meetings and sipped from the sober spring, met the Messiah, none of that shit.

I met another guy, not long after this, who had run crack houses, had hoes, been to the joint a couple times. Papa was a real player at one time, and he had had his shit together about eight, nine years when I met him.

Papa put me in his back pocket and carried me when I was too weak to walk. This was in '05

Chapter 115

That was almost fifteen years ago. Wow! Now what?

"Everybody's a dreamer. Everybody's a star. Everybody's in showbiz. It doesn't matter who you are." The brothers Davies, Ray Davies (pronounced Davis) and Dave Davies (pronounced Davees.) Yes. They are real brothers.

After being with Thelma for a few months, I did go get tested for diseases because I was tired of wearing a raincoat. Actually I got tested twice because I didn't believe the first results.

They both came back saying I didn't have any sexually transmitted diseases.

I'd have to say the first four years of not drinking were definitely the hardest.

Look, I started going to AA meetings when I was fifteen years old. This was 1985. Back then, I had guys there literally saying, "What the fuck you doin' here, a project for grade school? I spilled more on my tie than you've drank, ya bum!" Shit like that.

There were a couple few young people. By young, I mean early, midtwenties.

I was getting whisked off the AA meetings, then the gym, then it seemed things were normal for a brief time. Normal as in they were back to what they'd always been before the episodes of *Mary Hartman* played out in my life.

As I sit here, trying to relive all this used tampon so I can convey it to paper, yes, I still get angry. I still get upset. I still get a lot of things.

I know I had a dream last night because when I woke up this morning, I felt like I'd been somewhere, and I felt panicky. Like something happened last night, something not good.

All day today, from waking up through work, through going to see my mom to give her her medicine, the bath, dinner, the entire fucking day has been an I-ate-the-brown-acid kind of day.

It's not that I hate boxing. It's just, well, I hate fucking boxing, okay? You know how often I try to think about boxing, in any way, shape, or form? Never is the starting point.

Today you know what movies my mind were stuck on all day? National Silver Gloves, 1982, Peoria, Illinois. Enrique Sanchez stopped me in the first round. First time I'd ever been stopped. Was probably my twentieth, thirtieth fight.

No. It shouldn't have been stopped. Some fucktard named Frank from Akron, Ohio, was reffing, and this prick stopped every fight he ever reffed. Said he didn't want any kids getting hurt. He wasn't a referee long.

None of that shit is the point. Here's the point. You have any idea how many goddamn times I watched that fight in my head today? At least six hundred thousand times, easy.

I guess I said that to prove a point to myself unwittingly, unknowingly.

My mind has worked that way my entire life, for the most part. I'd say from five on. In a negative look-what-you-did, look-what-you-didn't-do, you-can't-do-that, you're-a-loser, you-shouldn't-even-try-that kinda way.

For twenty-eight years, I poured drinks, and I put dope on that mind to get it to think different things. It didn't work. I mean, it did work. Just not how it was supposed to.

Here's a question: if you ate a chocolate bar, and it made you puke, forget what happened for twelve hours, or two days, of your life, made you wreck a car, get in six fights, lose your watch, glasses, and car keys, call your mom collect in the middle of the night and call her bad names, and end up in jail, would you ever eat another chocolate bar as long as you lived?

I would. I did. I ate tons more of those fuckers for lots more years. Some things I learned about drinking, as far as I'm concerned is, for one, I cannot drink like a normal person.

I honestly knew by fifteen, I was a true alcoholic. Trying to recall that period in my mind, I had the thought, *So what, I like to drink.*

That mind I said I had absorbed shit. Same with AA and rehabs. I did learn things, in all those places, I still carry with me and use today.

All those years, I wanted to kill myself. Aside from knowing it would make so many people happy, looking back, I did have some hope and faith I absorbed without realizing it.

I remember seeing a story about a girl from Boston, on TV, who was homeless, and her parents were drug addicts with AIDS. She slept in hallways of places, alleys, anywhere she could.

That girl graduated number 1 in her class and went on to Harvard and graduated and became a real somebody from the pile of runny shit hand she was dealt from birth. I can't think of this girl's name, and she really doesn't care if I know it or not. I am a zero, nothing, never heard of to her. She is the most goddamn amazing person I have ever heard of, period. I don't care what her name is; she is a *hero*.

I was able to step out of my own pathetic mind when I saw this story long enough to suck some hope up, even though I didn't realize it at the time. I forget her name, but I think of that greatest fuckin' knockout of all time often when I feel like shit.

And yes, like now, I usually cry when I think of that girl. Because there is hope.

Chapter 116

Since I've quit drinking and tried to get my shit together, I do a lot of thinking. Not on purpose, but out of nowhere, shit will just pop in my head. Things I'd totally forgotten about.

Let me take you on a trip with me. We're in my mom's new 1989 Ford Tempo.

We pull out of Duke's driveway on Kinney Road and hit Route 10. We take Route 10 (a two-lane narrow road) east through Lewis and Greenup Counties, about a twenty-minute ride.

Cross the bridge into Portsmouth, Ohio, bear right onto Route 23 north. Three stoplights up on the left is the drive-through that always has the first six-pack of the trip for me.

On 23 north, you go through Scioto County, can't think of the counties these towns are in, but you go through Portsmouth, Waverly, pretty good chunk of road, then Chillicothe (second six-pack, sometimes). Then a few miles up the road, you go through the speed trap of South Bloomfield. Another ten, fifteen minutes, you hit 270–71 north.

Two hours' average trip.

Once on 71 north, it is always smooth sailing. We got tunes playing, our mind is living in some fantasy land bullshit, and we're drinking some beers.

On 71 north to exit 186, I believe, the Ashland exit. Get off, go right, about two, four miles, up the road, hang a left on Route 89. We're rippin' up 89, about seven miles, and go around the dangerous long snake curve, no problem. Here's where 89 meets Route 58.

We go four miles up the road on 58, and we're feeling super, super fucking good, hear me? So good we are working on that fourth six-pack. We get to 58 and 303, I think, the only stoplight in Sullivan, Ohio, and there is a detour.

We go right and follow the detour signs. We go left on a road, and we're cruisin' along at probably 55 mph, and a curve comes out of nowhere, and we go straight—straight into a telephone pole.

I came to and realized I was in a wreck, but I didn't think it was a bad one. As I sat there, I had recalled a wreck by a house we lived in on Middle Ridge Road, where after the guy wrecked, he tried to start his car, and it blew up because he was on a gas line. This happened on a curve also.

I remember thinking about that and saying to myself, "Try it! Try it!" I did. I tried to start the car, and all it did was turn over. No running engine, no explosion, nothin'!

I got out of the car and wondered what the fuck I was going to do now. I was covered in blood. A pickup truck stopped with a man and woman in it, and she immediately went, "You're drunk! We're calling the cops!"

I was pleading with this guy to talk some sense into her, and he went, "I'm calling too!" And they took off.

Thank God this was way pre-cell phones, thankfully. I was in the middle of nowhere, all kinds of shit were in my favor for getting out of this with no problem.

Don't misunderstand, we have a serious, serious situation here. We are drunk, we are covered in blood, we are in the middle of fucking nowhere, the cops are going to be looking for us, what do we do?

I walked this road to a country store and used the pay phone to call Uncle Jim and Aunt Sharon, who lived in Wellington, about twenty minutes up the road from Sullivan. I told them I was in a wreck, could they come get me? They had no idea where I was and told me I'd have to get where they knew where I was, and they'd come and get me.

I started walking these railroad tracks, thinking I was heading toward Route 58. It's late at night, I don't know, probably between two and four in the morning. I was right there where Sam and Aug were with Dan and Shirley when we were young, the rolling noth-ingness of Sullivan, Ohio, and its plentiful farmland and scenic landscape!

As I was walking on these tracks, I heard a car burning out and squealing and doing it over and over. I ran up the tracks to the road to see what was going on, and it was some dude laying rubber over and over.

I jumped in front of his car, and he stopped. I asked him if he'd give me a ride to Wellington. He said he had to stop by his girl-friend's first, and I had to give him gas money.

So he stopped, I gave him some money, and we were headed to Wellington. He asked me why I was covered in blood, and I honestly can't remember what I told him.

As he was taking me to Jim and Sharon's a Jerr-Dan passed us with my mom's car on it. I had him drop me off a little ways from their house, so he wouldn't know where I went.

They had moved from Amherst years ago and lived in a house right on that curve I saw that dead body in that car wreck when I was a little kid. I got there and figured I'd come up with good plan to work.

I had blood all over me. I mean, I looked like someone had bludgeoned me with a meat cleaver. I had an itty-bitty teeny-weeny cut on my arm, and it would not quit bleeding. That was it.

I told Uncle Jim I was going to report the car stolen. He said that was the dumbest thing I could do. He said, "Bruce, they'll know you were driving. You'll end up in more trouble. Ya gotta tell 'em the truth."

We went to the Wellington Police Station, and they had no report of my wreck. They told us to go to the sheriff. So we did. They sent us to a highway patrol post. "Ah! Yes! We handled that accident last night, this morning, in the middle of nowhere, where someone hit a telephone pole and broke it in two! Was that you, sir?"

Uncle Jim was doing most of the talking. You can determine what he said 'cause I don't know. Whole thing took very little time. This old cop told a young cop, he went, "This was a one-car acci-dent, no injuries. Easy stuff." And like that, that old cop left.

I signed some papers, and the young cop went, "I just have one question, why did you leave the scene?"

I responded, "I don't know. I must have been in shock."

Uncle Jim took me to the impound yard where the car was. I was under the impression I was going to be able to drive the car. Uncle Jim rounded the corner of the building the car was behind and saw it first, and before I saw it, he went, "You won't be driving this car anywhere!"

The car was broken in two, and it was a mangled mess. The only way we determined I could have gotten out of the car was a hole in the back window. I remember him saying we drove over a hundred miles that day.

Chapter 117

Hey, Martin Cove, you still alive? You see a movie here, brah? I mean, I haven't even gotten to the part where I found Jesus in a shoebox under my bed, and all is Utopia forever and ever yet!

I might have mentioned a Creator, a nonlistening motherfucker, somewhere in this jizz squirt of a life.

Since I had quit drinking and tried to like myself before I did end up killing myself, or end up in prison for life, I had come to choose there is a Creator, and He is not anything I have ever heard from some person or read in some book.

Here's some deep shit since I quit drinking. Maybe not, I don't know. Anyhow Bud Man was dying. He had COPD, asthma, high blood pressure, sugar, he had had a quadruple bypass, he was on cumin, oxygen, he had a lot of medical shit way wrong. He was eaten up with shit from Agent Orange that would leave blotches of discolored areas on his body, legs, arms, belly.

He was a fuckin' mess. Well, I hadn't had a drink for about six, seven years when he got pretty bad. I took him to the VA in Cleveland for his quadruple bypass surgery, and the night before his surgery, he said, "I am done with those fuckin' Marlboros when I get out of here, *done*!"

See, Bud smoked three packs of Marlboro reds consistently for as long as I can remember.

Well, I drove him from Cleveland to Huron, Ohio, where he lived, after the surgery, and we weren't even on I-90 from the hospital, and he went, "Hey! I need a pack of cigarettes."

I was like, "What the fuck is wrong with you, you sure?"

He said abso-fucking-lutely! Then I asked him if he wanted me to get him Marlboro Lights, and I thought his head was gonna explode when he yelled, "Fuck no! I don't want no goddamn Lights! I want motherfuckin' reds! Now ya got me sick, Bruce! Goddamnit! Just get the fuckin' cigarettes, will ya?"

See, when Bud got sick, real sick, I started going up there every weekend for the last year of his life. About a six, six-and-a-half-hour ride. And we talked.

Let me rephrase that—we talked as we communicated. We talked Becker. Lotta fuck yous, I'll still kick your fuckin' ass. One time, I said something to him that really struck a nerve, I mean really, can't recall what it was, but it had to do with him helping in a big, big way to fuck my boxing career in the ass.

The prick pulled his pistol from under his pillow and went, "I told you as long as this finger worked, you'd never be able to kick my ass, son! And I'm ready to fight!"

Something really stupid like that. All I did was tell him to fuck himself, and I went and sat at the dining room table.

He got off his oxygen and came over and lit a cigarette and said, "Bruce, I wasn't going to shoot you." And he started crying. I told him I wasn't stupid, and I knew he wasn't gonna shoot me. And I told him I forgive him. I knew I struck a nerve in his conscience. And trust me, that wasn't an easy Little Feat!

Honestly I do recall what that conversation was about. But it's none of your business.

We tried to talk every time I went up there. Over the course of 2013, Bud Man and I made amends, and we were cool when he died. I was even there.

Now here's an old prick dying. I mean, he looked dead long before he was. Fucker took a drugstore's stock of shit every day. It was pitiful.

He was living in a condo he bought off his piece of shit sperm donor, Valloyd Deed. And when that scumbag rapist died, his sisters, Susie Lyin' Sluts and Sally Valloyd Deed Becker Jr. Marty sent him a letter saying the lawyer told them they had to sell the condo.

None of it makes sense, and let me bottom line you. Bud Man, truth be known, fucked his rapist sperm donor to get the place, then my dad's scumbag plastic barriers of sissies, grotesquely overweight, spineless, gutless, plastic kid sisters fucked my dad.

I don't know about any agreements or anything when it came to that shithole. All I know is it ended up being Beckers fucking Beckers as only Beckers could, I promise.

Chapter 118

Bud and I talked. About a lot of shit. Talked about that time he wailed the fuck out of me at Pinecrest. He told me he really didn't remember doing it at the time, that he was in a blackout. I believed him.

Talked about the times he slapped the shit out of me when I came in drunk as a kid.

I was never a puker when I was a drinker. I mean sure, I did occasionally puke. But I was not a habitual puker. There are, however, way better puking stories than the one when I puked while Terry and Ruth Ann did the naughty, naughty at Billy's house when I was a kid.

Two of those puking stories involve a friend of mine. One involves the friend and an ass-beating from Bud. Chuck and I went out drinking. We went to Cleveland. He drove his, like, '76 Chevy Malibu classic with a 350.

We rode around downtown and drank a twelve-pack and drank on a bottle of whiskey. Neither one of us had any money at all, busted. But before we headed "Going Out West," back to Amherst, we went to Pat Joyce Tavern, across from the Bond Court Hotel and public hall on St. Clair, and tried to order a drink.

The bartender went, "You guys are too young to drink! You have to be twenty-one to drink liquor!" There was a law in Ohio at this time where nineteen-year-olds could drink beer if born before the grandfather clause, but not liquor.

The bartender went, "What, you guys from Chicago? Did you come to Cleveland to see the big-time wrastlin' across the street at public hall?"

Where this came from, I still don't know, but we said yes, and we said we were nineteen, and we thought we could drink beer in Ohio.

We each drank one Miller High Life and bailed without paying. Didn't run, didn't sneak, just took our drunk asses off the stools and walked right out the door and got in Chuck's car and left.

We're heading west on I-90 approaching 117th Street, and I started puking my guts out in the paper grocery bag we had the beer cans in. When I was done puking, I went to throw the bag out the window, doing sixty on an interstate, and that puke went all over me and the interior of Chuck's car.

I was supposed to stay at Chuck's, but I told him to take me home. Hell, it was kinda late, probably 1:00 a.m., 2:00 a.m., and even if Bud was home, he'd be sleeping on the couch with the TV so goddamn loud you could hear it at the high school! I'd just go up on my floor and crash.

As soon as I got the storm door open, I saw Bud's eyes get all wide, light up, show thirty different emotions in a tenth of a second, put his head back down on his pillow, and go, "Son, I think you better get your ass to bed, like, right fucking now!"

My immediate response was, "Fuck you, old man, I'm ready!"

Bud always told me when I thought I was ready, all I had to do was let him know. Well, I was ready, goddamn it!

He sat up on the couch and lit a cigarette and started, "Bruce, you don't know what you're fuckin' with, son! GET YOUR FUCKING ASS TO BED, NOW!"

Again. "Fuck you, old man, I'm ready!"

And I started walking toward him sitting on the couch, and I was getting ready to lay this motherfucker out and kill him fucking dead! He was still sitting on the couch when he grabbed my coat and threw me into the storm door, befalling my drunk ass.

I got up and went at him again, he had stood up, and the prick threw me into the door again! The third time, he grabbed my shirt and carried me by it to the dining room and sat me on a dining room chair so hard one of the legs broke. He started poking me in the chest (Bud was a poker, a *hard* poker), and he went, "I'm gonna talk, and you're gonna listen!"

He babbled for a few minutes, and I went upstairs to the sanctuary of the floor and albums, and slept.

We talked about all the fucked up shit he had me do from a young age that was not right. Before he died, he admitted to me, he realized he fucked up, that he had had three amazing kids who turned out to be fucked-up adults because of his actions.

I forgave Bud, I did. But I never forget. I even told him that to him on his deathbed. I told him he was lucky I came as often as I did, that if I was him, he wouldn't even have come once. I told that fucker every single solitary thing I could think of that he did to fucking terrorize me my entire childhood.

I told him I was sexually abused and scared to death to tell him back then, told him about his piece of shit sperm donor raping my mom, told him I knew he was dealing with Carmen behind my back, shit that didn't have anything to do with boxing, and that's why Graz was always breaking my balls. I also reminded that fucker of the one time I hit him with a solid right hand right in the fucking mouth.

I only did that because he was tellin' me shit like, "Don't be cryin', feelin' sorry for my ass! I can't wait to be dead!"

So I had to throw in the "Hey, remember that time I fucked you up with a Tommy Hearns right hand outside that bar in Portsmouth, Ohio?" Just to show him I didn't feel sorry for him because he was dying.

He retorted, "Yeah, remember how I didn't go down?"

See, Bud was on one of his never-ending get-rich-quick-schister motherfucker scams and, once again, had me involved in it.

This one had something to do with garbage bags—yes, garbage fucking bags. He had set up a meeting with some guy in Cincinnati, and he took me and Little Luke. Little Luke was about 6'8", 6'9", three-hundred whatever, and just big.

Little Luke was a cool dude. He was quiet. He was funny in a way. It's like, when he talked, he acted all serious and perceptive about whatever it was he was talking about. Then he'd look you in the eyes and go, "Do ya get it?"

No shit? Fuck yeah I got it! I can't say Little Luke was a leg breaker or a killer or a preacher or a cop or anything. I mean, from what I gathered, he was a truck driver. He never talked about trucking or being on any trucking trips or anything to do with trucking. But when he met people, he was always a truck driver.

We left Cleveland the day before this meeting in Cincinnati and went to Portsmouth, Ohio. Looking back, it was Bud wanting to be near Carol.

Anyhow Bud, Little Luke, and I got a hotel room and went to a bar and started drinking. This was one of about three times I ever drank with Bud. They all ended up like an episode of *Natural Disasters*.

I was drinking vodka and tonics, and Bud was drinking his rum and Cokes. I can't recall what Little Luke was drinking. He ended up getting up from the bar, away from Bud and me.

Here's probably the reason why. Bud Man and I were having words. To this day, I recall clear as a bell, sitting on my stool, minding my own business, drinking my drink, talking only silently to the voices in my head, watching the game of eight ball, patiently waiting my turn to run a rack or two, take these Cajuns for some free drinks, maybe some cash.

And Bud kept going, "Quit fucking with that guy."

I kept going, "What guy? There isn't even anyone here, fuck is wrong with you!"

No one was sitting by us at the bar, no one. He responded, "Quit fucking with the guy at the pool table!"

The pool table was a solid eight feet from us. I'd have had to yell over jukebox music, drunks yelling to fuck with the guy at the pool table!

He went, "You wanna go outside?"

We went outside, he started talking shit, and I cracked that fucker with a hard, hard right hand. Didn't sucker punch him. I said, "Hey, Bud"—not Dad—"fuck you!" And I cracked him.

He was dancing like a puppet on a string, doing the whipty whirl, I was fuckin' rocked, my mind was a swirl! And he came up to me, doing this crippled-man walk, and went, "Hey, Bruce, I didn't go down!"

He no sooner said that, and a Portsmouth cop came running across the street, yelling, "HEY! I SAW THAT! I SAW THAT!" 'Cause he was going to go down, I promise. I had that fucker on Queer Street.

Before the cop was on our side of the street, Bud went, "Hey! Hey! Mind your own business! This is a family disturbance." Cop just wanted to know how we were getting home. We told him cab. That was it.

Chapter 119

When I quit drinking the last time, I did things I had never done the previous twenty-one years of trying. I think voicing out loud I was sexually abused helped me clear all the other shit out.

I quit drinking in February of '05, and in November of '06 I saw fit to tie one on. Long time to go without a drink, if you're me. I drank a pint of liquor and a six-pack of beer and was puking sick in no time.

Didn't stop me from finishing every drop and drinking all the beer and lying on the kitchen floor 'cause I couldn't stand up, cussing, when I crawled to the Frigidaire, chile, and there was no more beer! I was looking at the ceiling, saying I knew I should'a bought a twelve-pack.

I was in bed for a week. I really did feel like I was gonna die. I lost my job, Thelma hated my guts, yes. Even the dogs were pissed at me.

It's through no fault of my own I quit drinking and realized I really didn't have to drink alcohol, or do dope, to exist, that I could learn to learn to like myself, learn to love myself.

This God, this Creator I have mentioned throughout my life, who I said was a nonlistener, well, I've always believed in a Creator. I was just always confused, as a lot of us are.

I have to say now, in my opinion, the greatest, hands down, book ever written on how to live a real, honest, happy, carefree, giving, open book, nothing to hide, meaningful thirst for life is *The Big Book* of Alcoholics Anonymous. Whether you're a drunk or not.

There is not one problem I have encountered in life I have not found the solution to in that book, to this very day.

Look, I said I was not a member of AA or any other anonymous group, and I'm not. I started going to AA meetings as an alcoholic at fifteen. As I said, wherever I went, I always went to meetings long enough to get a start, then I'd go back to drinking.

I have met every kind of fucking quack you can imagine, and then some, at AA meetings. When I was fifteen, there was a guy who had tried to kill himself going to meetings. He shot himself in the roof of his mouth. He'd go around asking people if they wanted to see it. Fuck yeah! I wanted to see! Can I touch it?

There was a guy in Jersey who said he was Frank Sinatra Jr. He'd sing Frank songs the entire time he was at the meeting. Had the hat, the look, everything.

I've had gay guys hit on me at meetings, I've had women hit on me at meetings. I came out of a meeting one time, and someone had smashed the entire driver's side of my car (I had parked next to a monster truck). I met a guy in San Diego, at an AA meeting, who tried to get me into porn movies. The only reason I didn't was because he kept saying, "Now you really have to protect yourself! They have this lube you can use, use *a lot!*"

Ultimately I never made a professional porno movie because I was afraid of AIDS. This was when porn still didn't wear food service gloves.

You ever get bored, nothing to do, find a meeting near you. You'll never be the same. Maybe not quite as entertaining as your local gym but a superclose second. Do both every day for ninety days.

Chapter 120

Here's a funny story. I was living in California and went back to Ohio to visit. The day before I left, couple pals of mine, Chuck and Doug, took me out. We started drinking early in the day. Plan was to "Sit around the shanty and put a good buzz on," go out to eat, and go to the Tribe game that evening.

We proceed to do the aforementioned, and as we are leaving the game, Chuck decided we needed to go The Flats and continue partying. Look, I was fucked up, but who am to say we should quit drinking?

We got to The Flats and went to Rum Runners. We were outside on the deck, place was packed. Doug bought us all a shot of tequila. As I did it, I told him if I puked, I was going to puke on him. So he bought another one for all of us.

Little bit of time went by, and I saw three girls sitting at a table. I swear, this is a true story. I sat down at the table with these girls, and within, I'd say, fifteen, twenty minutes, these girls were leaving with me.

The split millisecond they all said they'd go with me, my stomach said, *Hey, brah, we're gonna fuckin' puke down here soon!* I told the girls I had to use the restroom, and as soon as I stood up, I started going toward Doug and puking and hurling and vomiting like a real champ!

Over and over, *baugh! Bla! Spew!* Puking my guts out! The puke was going between the wood slats in the floor landing on everyone downstairs. People down there were all freaking out, wondering what that chunky shit was landing on them! It was a filet mignon, baker, and salad, people!

As Chuck and Doug were trying to whisk me down the steps and out of that place before someone realized it was me doing the puking and killing me, I just kept puking! Funny stuff.

Then at the end of the night, we went to a Bob's Big Boy on Brookpark Road and got a stripper to buy our breakfast.

Chuck reminds me of this story now and then. I try to forget it because I missed out on a lot of pussy on this night!

Chapter 121

Goddamn, dude! Stupid ignorant shit I've done. I've never been a dope dealer or a dope runner, but I have sold a little here and there, and I have moved some from one place to another on an occasion or two.

I took my cousin's boyfriend from Lorain to Columbus once, so we could score three pounds of pot at a good price.

This guy lived right on High Street, and right when we pulled up and parked on the one-way street across from his apartment, we could see him inside the UDF store getting arrested.

He had warrants, he said. Took JJ two, three days to bail this dude out. We stayed in this dude's apartment those couple days, and he had at least a hundred pounds of weed in a room, out in the open.

We did the right thing and didn't steal any, and we got him out of jail. We should'a fucked him, though, 'cause he did us on our three pounds by about six, eight ounces, from what I can remember.

I made that up, though. Because there were about eight, ten people who came down to buy weed, and not all of them drove.

Four or five wanted to stay a day or two longer, and I charged each one an ounce of weed for the trouble of taking them back.

Here's the gist of this story, just to show you how stupid people are. It's a two-hour ride, Columbus to Lorain. I was in an '84 Honda Accord, and I had four people in the back and one in the front. Every swinging dick in the car had at least a couple of pounds of pot on them, and they were wondering if they could light a joint when we got on 71. I wouldn't even drink till I got those fuckers out of my car!

Chapter 122

I really can't explain it, getting off booze. I mean, it really sucked for a good three, four years. I can look back and say that it sucked because, looking back, I was working through all the shit in my life I had put on a back burner. The shit I'd think about all those other times I'd quit drinking and start drinking over again, immediately.

I did a lot of reading; I did a lot of writing. I did a lot of seeking out people to get answers. I wrote Valloyd Deed that ten-page letter when I had been off booze a year or two. Still waiting to hear from that dead piece of shit. He was living proof someone could quit drinking, be a member of AA, and still be a scumbag piece of shit. That he was. A scumbag sack of shit.

A million ways to rationalize it. I mean, another way to say it is, I just wasn't done drinking. I was able to leave it alone when I had had enough.

I really don't care. I really don't. I mean, the reason doesn't matter to me. The greatest victory I have ever had in life is being able to leave booze alone for a quite a while now.

I have a life today. Demented and sad, but social.

When I reflect back, it is also sad the only thing I can say I ever really did is get off booze. Looking back, I really could'a been a somebody in life.

I mean, I am a somebody today. I actually care about myself. I love myself. What that transcends to is I care what happens to me. So I'm not going to do anything stupid to hurt myself or die or wind up in jail. It's just sad that's the only thing I've ever really accomplished in life. I myself am okay with that. The most important thing is, I, me, myself am my own judge. I do not need anyone's input on anything to do with my life when it comes to me being a winner or loser.

The only thing I have ever won at is being able to gain victory over myself, my demons. That's it. Again, I am okay with that.

Acceptance is the key ingredient to victory over one's self, in my opinion. Accepting shit and being okay with shit are two different things. The only way I was able to see this was when I was able to leave booze alone for a substantial amount of time.

Chapter 123

Look, for fourteen, fifteen years now, I have lived in one house, had sex with only one woman, don't drink alcohol, quit smoking reds, quit smoking altogether when I was diagnosed with that Chronic Ovulating Pulminary Disease, bullshit, and well, the getting-forty-jobs-a-year thing even subsided a few years ago.

I have questions today. I know we all do. Who gives a fuck, Brucey? I mean, I was born before my brother and sister. Bud and Carol didn't have them till after he got back from Nam. I've always wondered if all their health problems aren't related to Agent Orange and the other shit Bud got in his system over there. Especially Sam. And if they don't have a conscience because of the chemicals, or if they just have more Bud than Carolyn in their DNA.

My mom had Josef sometime in the '90s. I was happy she was able to have a kid and raise him under normal conditions. He was a great kid. Graduated school, never was a drinker or drug user. Got a job at the railroad.

When he met his now-wife, he turned his back on my mom. Here's a mess I'm only going to dance around the fringes of. Carol divorced Duke in the hills and remarried Bud. She moved back up to Northeast Ohio in the early 2000s.

Josef kept in touch with my mom while she was up there. I later found out he did so because she was paying his mortgage and redneck truck payment.

Carolyn has dementia, and I moved her down here with me so she wouldn't be alone.

I moved out of Thelma's house and got an apartment with my mom for a year, before I put her in an assisted living home. In that year, Sam, Aug, or Josef never called her, came to see her, nothin'. They still don't. They are all too busy. Really. Too busy in Lewis County, Kentucky, to help their mom three hours away.

The joke is on them.

See, when Aug met his skank hoe ex-wife, Gena, he traded his family in as well. They lived at my mom's and Duke's for about two years. When I'd be there, she'd get up about noon, eat, leave her mess, then take off till Aug got his lyin' thievin' ass back to the ranch.

I was never allowed to be around their daughter, Michalya, because I was a bad influence. Today Aug and Gena are many years divorced, their daughter is living with a drug dealer, squeezing babies out for him like a machine, so I'm told. Hilarious shit.

Sam graduated from college and became a respiratory therapist. Had a great job right out of school, couldn't wait to party like a rock star, lost the job, got one in a hillbilly county making a third of the money, lost that job, and is now living at Duke's on Rock Hill full-time, the last I heard.

It's my understanding Augie started drinking in his later years and is in and out of jail. That is definitely a Becker trait. And a thief. Aug has always made Elmer "Duke" Willis look like a rank amateur when it comes to stealing.

I hope all my siblings can get their shit together before they die.

Chapter 124

When I moved my mom down here, Josef was calling her when I'd be fortunate enough to work a day and telling her I was stealing her money.

Sam, she met Joey. Sam and I had developed a relationship before she met Joey. I mean, we talked on the phone literally every day for a good year, year and a half. Once she met Joey, the calls subsided. I'd call and leave message after message and got no call in return.

When we did talk, it was one of a short list of things. "I'm sick." "I have to work." "I have a headache." "I have a stomachache." Or my two favorites—"I'm going with Joey on a thousand-mile bike ride." Finally—"I can't. I'm going to a basketball game." Then back to "I'm sick.'

Sam was helping Joey pay his house off, all his bills, everything. Guess what? Joey up and fucking died one day, leaving Sam out of all the money she had invested in his house and motorcycle and everything. Joey's family got his house, his bike, all his shit.

Sam has Duke and her two kids. I wish her well the rest of her stay here on earth.

As I've told Sam and Josef (haven't talked to Aug in years and years), our mother's finances are an open book since she's lived down here with me. Of course, you have to take me to court to get a look-see at them. You will be sadly, grossly disappointed.

Chapter 125

I mentioned that nine-jobs-a-month thing coming to a standstill. From 1988 till 1994, I was able to hustle and live well. I mean, getting picked up at airports in limos, having dinner with celebrities, getting drunk with celebrities, being at all the big events, wine, women, and song for the taking, eating the best foods, drinking the best booze and wine, doing the best drugs with not a dime in our pockets!

To go from that to working a schmuck job is not an easy thing to do. I mean, off the top of my head, I could list a million fighters who made millions and are on the streets now, if not dead before their time. Why? Because we don't know how to live like you, normal fucking people, that's why. "You ain't got what we got."

I gotta say here, I have to steal a quote from Joe Louis, "I didn't end up in any of those factories either, Joe." Thanks, Mr. Joe Louis Barrow, for being a wonderful role model on how to be a human being with class, dignity, and character! Mr. Louis has been one of my heroes since I was probably seven, eight years old.

Joe got fucked by Uncle Sam, but hey, well, it was only Joe Louis. Not like it was someone important.

Hope you realize I'm joking because Mr. Louis saved our nation, on his own, that I am not joking about. Back when we had a nation.

I'm not going to babble about my expertise in a kitchen. Why? There is no expertise. That's why. I like to call myself adequate or functional (thanks, Rehab Chuck) in a kitchen.

There isn't any type of function, person, event, restaurant, diner I haven't worked in or cooked for. For a long time, I had a real passion for food, and it went straight to shit through the years because nobody working in food has that passion.

That's a deep question, really. I mean, on the other hand, you work in these places with these stuffy uptight yuppie jizz squirts that think they know something, and it's an endless war story about the heroic shit they've done in the kitchen. I might have PTSD because when retards do this, I want to mangle them. Really.

I burned out on the kitchen years before I walked out on my salaried position one day as asshole who runs this dump.

I'd been there a year and a half, I was working at least 80 hours a week; I averaged more like 90–100. I did have the occasional 110-hour week.

I'd love to tell you how wonderful the menu turned out, and how it made money and how exhilarated I was with my accomplishment. I would. But it would be bullshit.

Been about seven years ago now. I woke up exhausted. I mean, physically worn out. Had been a long month. I was in the process of working one of those 110-hour weeks, and we had a party this day.

I had spent fifteen hours the day before getting everything ready for the party. Had the ratatouille ready, had the mushroom leek and tarragon pasta ready, salads, desserts, everything was cooked off, panned up, and ready to go. All I had to do was bring everything up to temp.

When I got to work, I told the owner we needed to talk about some time off and a raise. I let her know I was running on fumes, without being an asshole.

Her immediate response was, "I own this place! If you don't like it, leave!"

Well now, let's see, what did I do? That party was going off in like two and a half hours. I went in the kitchen, where the guy I had helping me was getting stuff on the stove and in the oven to bring up to temp.

I took the pot of soup off the stove and threw it in the garbage. As I was taking the food out of the oven, he went, "What the hell are you doing!"

I responded, "She said this was her restaurant, if I didn't like it, leave. Well, I am leaving. And my food isn't going out for you to get credit for. By the way, tell your brother this job is available. I just quit."

To this day, I have no clue what they did for food at the pre-paid-for, predesignated-menu party. Also the guy who would come in and help me always let me know he graduated summa cum laude in his class at a culinary school, and his brother did too. And his brother would love my job.

As I was walking through the back of the place to my truck, the owner went, "Where do you think you're going?"

I told her it was her place, and I was going home. No idea what happened to the party. I heard some time later this place closed. Oh well.

Chapter 126

Restaurant business is so full of assholes, retards, drug addicts, drunks, perverts. Put it this way, if you feel abnormal in any way, shape, or form, apply for a job at your nearest fanciest restaurant, you'll fit right in! You don't even have to know anything about food service. And you never have to learn anything about it to move up to manager one day. If you wear enough brown lipstick. I promise.

I have a billion restaurant stories. I worked in a steak house that had an oven that got up to 1,500 degrees Fahrenheit. Place was small too. Only sat fifty-three people. Kitchen was a cubbyhole. Hot? This was Georgia hot.

I'd leave work, and it would be summertime, temperature would be in the eighties, and I'd have to turn the heater on in the car because I was freezing.

One thing I have never understood is how people do nothing but complain about how much they hate their job, then as soon as it's over, and you're drinkin' a cold one, what is the only topic of conversation? Yep, work! I have never been that guy and don't want to now. So I'll shut up about work.

I will say this. When I sat in my truck after walking out of that restaurant, the reality of what I did hit me hard! I mean, I have a girl, we have two house payments, cars, dogs, insurance, medicine, a serious coffee addiction, a pot addiction, now what the fuck am I going to do?

I thought hard about this on the twenty-minute ride home from work. Of course, when I got home, Thelma was working, so I did the only thing I could think of to do. I ordered a hot dog cart off the Internet and went golfing.

That's been some time ago now. Funny, how things turn out. I mean, when I let that salary go, I knew I'd get another one, but I didn't want to go to another kitchen. The flip side to that was, I can't learn a new trade at forty-three years old and make $9.50 an hour in doing so. Gotta go with what you know.

I will say this. I do okay. My bills get paid, I struggle. I get to be here for my mom because I am successful at what I do, I get to golf every day (before my mom came down, I did). I get to be here for Thelma if she needs me, I get to feed the homeless, I get to help people, in general. And I make money doing it.

No chef hovering over me being an asshole because he can't find any blow, or needs my help with something he doesn't know, no bitch waitresses demanding shit out of order, no shortage of sauces the day prep guy blew off so I have to make on the fly, no more drinking booze out of Styrofoam cups, none of this shit.

I stand on a corner, Eighth and Main, southeast side of the block, right across Eighth Street from Louisville Slugger Bat Factory and Museum, and sell all beef hot dogs, beef smoked sausages, Italian sausages, bratwurst, and one-third pound Angus beef burgers, bottles of soda, and bags of chips. Drink on a 987-ounce cup of coffee while I do it.

Chili, cheese, onions, jalapenos, sauerkraut, relish, ketchup, mustard, mayonnaise, barbecue sauce, an assortment of spicy mustards (about ten), lettuce, tomato, onion (raw or cooked), and celery salt.

There are usually about six homeless guys sitting on the benches located in the proximity of my cart, eating my food and drinking my sodas, and I usually have some kind of music playing. Jazzy, bluesy, hillbilly, gospel, depends on my mood.

Oh, that list of condiments, I forgot. I use one key ingredient that I find so very few others use. It is available to everyone who cooks food or not, most just choose to not put a splash of it in anything they make or do. I choose to. That one key ingredient is love. It makes a difference. I promise. Stop by and try one some time.

This whole big mess of a shit platter of a life has turned into that. I mention that nonlistening motherfucker, that Creator. Yeah. He put me on that corner with that stand. I see that today. I give thanks to Him for that today.

I thank Leonard Peltier in my prayers every day because he, a man I've never met, helped me get close to this Creator I knew nothing about. Being grateful is the biggest gift I will ever receive while here on earth. I was told to be grateful, and it would have positive results. So true.

Chapter 127

I've learned a lot since I quit drinking. My childhood was a walk in the park compared to lot of kids' childhoods.

I've come to realize my parents did the best they could with what they had. Which was nothing. Again, not making excuses. I mean, my dad was a very intelligent person, and he knew right from wrong. He chose to be a selfish greedy stingy prick all on his own.

Believe me, he knew everything before he died. My side of it.

I love my dad, I always did. I had empathy for him up till he died. But I also had hatred for him, in a sense, up till he died. After all, he was a Becker.

The Bud Man is dead, and he's a box of ashes on my dresser. I hope he's in a good place. A place where they have rum and loose women and no families to torture through his eternity of party bliss!

My mom has dementia, and I moved her down here with me about three, four years ago now. She's in an assisted living place and doing okay.

So goddamn funny, life is! Twenty years ago, if you'd have said I was taking care of my mom and not one of her other kids would help, not even call her, ever, people, anyone, everyone, would have said you were a fuckin' quack, and I paid you to say that!

Since I moved her in there, about two years ago now, I haven't missed one day of going to see her, not one. Sam, Aug, Josef, they haven't even called her one time in the three years she's lived here, not once. They are all too busy with boyfriends, girlfriends, partying, and making sure to stay on the top of the list in the Lewis County socialite little black book.

Josef can't get thousands off her anymore. Sam, well, she and my mom have had issues since Sam was born. I think it's one of those I-have-a-cunt things.

Aug, I heard he became an HVAC guy and got caught stealing an air conditioner from a house at night that he had installed that day. Other than being a thief—Aug has always been a thief—I heard he finally discovered liquor in his later years, and it treats him the same way it does all Beckers—jail, fights, car wrecks, and misery.

Way to go, Aug!

Aside from letting my mom make his redneck truck and house payments, Josef is a spineless heartless ball-less sack of coward shit. He married some holler rat who he won't speak a word till she tells what to say and how to say it.

It is my understanding he gave this skank inbred two kids so far. I say here and now, within ten years, she owns everything he has, including and especially the house, and has a new man by then.

I'd bet my sack right now, she has a case of the Joni Pugh's.

Anyhow I tried for years to let my family know I was here for them, and for years, they have let me know they aren't interested. Especially Sam. Oh well.

Chapter 128

I mentioned betting money. I've mentioned an uncle with a touch of the Brockton Jim's. My dad had it, Sally Valloyd Deed Becker Jr. Marty has it, Fat Susie Hammond is also afflicted by it, Valloyd Deed, the rapist Papaw, had it. It's called compulsive gambling. The entire Becker clan is touched by it. Some more than others.

Russ lost his bar, had guys looking to break his legs more than once, getting up there in the $20,000–$30,000 range of owing the book. At one point, Sally Valloyd Deed Jr. had to let Dot Head take her finances over because she and her husband, Charlie no-nuts Marty, had shot the wad, spent their fortune on lottery tickets. Gutless Turd Charlie and I-can-eat-more-than-a-barnyard-full-of-animals Susie lyin' Sluts had to file bankruptcy because they got so carried away with the lottery.

Do I, or did I ever, have a case of the Brockton Jim's? Let me tell you something. When you make enough money to buy a car, pay rent for a year, and drink single-malt scotch all night long, and all you have to do watch a basketball game, cover the spread? Would I be interested in something like this?

I am not a basketball fan. Haven't been since, like, the '70s. However, to this day, if I was going to bet on any kind of sporting event outside of the ponies, it would be pro basketball.

I haven't bet pro basketball in well over twenty years. More like twenty-five, as I think about it.

Let me set this up for you. I never used to bet the favorites, ever, and I never used to bet on teams or against teams that had a superstar player on their team. Just a rule of mine.

Well, it's around '93, '94, and Bud was living on the west side of Cleveland, and I was staying with him. He was making a decent living on the last scam he'd pull before he quit working.

This was an amazing setup. He lived right above his office, and there had to be fifteen bars within a five-block radius. These were all real drinker bars too.

Anyhow this job Bud had involved some pretty serious shit. I mean, I can't say I know any details, but I can say I know he had guys working with him with names like Cheeze, Mr. Z, Buzz, Rocco the Mop, and an assortment of other characters.

Cheeze got a check for being a union baker. He was a cool dude. He and I hung out a lot; he liked to drink, and he and Little Luke were pals. Must'a been that union thing.

When I went out drinking with these guys, it was just like in the movies. I mean, private tables, everyone wanting to say hi, people buying you drinks. Needless to say, nobody ever fucked with us. There was also Meat and Quido, union guys who ran with this group.

Anyhow I started booking through Cheeze. I got on a streak you wouldn't believe. I started out betting a hundred bucks a game. In no time, I turned that into a couple thousand.

I took that too and doubled it up in one night.

It got to where this had become my job. I mean, after laying out all night, I'd go in the Lorain Avenue Diner and eat breakfast and give that night's games a look in the *Plain Dealer* and pick my teams and go next-door and go upstairs and crash. Woke up, called Cheeze, placed my couple-thousand-dollars' worth of bets and went on about my day.

One day, Bud was sitting at his desk, and he called me in and went, "You're 23–2 your last 25 picks. You've made about $17,000 in the past two weeks."

Thanks, Bud, you fuck! That night, the Bulls were playing the Supersonics out west, late game. The Bulls were only giving four points. I went against my own rule and bet $5,000 on the Bulls.

I was watching this game, and the Bulls were covering the spread by one point with almost no time left. I just made an easy five large! Out of nowhere, Michael Jordan got in an argument with a referee and kicked the ball to the rafters, getting a technical. Sonics made the foul shot, foiled the spread, and lost the game by three, not four.

Cheeze came around to collect that Tuesday, and I didn't have it. I told him I needed some time to get it together, and he responded, "Have I ever told you I didn't have your winnings, you'd have to wait on them? That I needed time to get it together? No. I haven't. I can give you some time. I'll be back after my last stop. Be about an hour, you have it then?"

This was a bad situation. Honest. The end result was Cheeze's boss got 13 percent of the business my dad was operating, and I wasn't allowed to place bets with that organization anymore.

Once I lost the five, I tried to get it back tenfold quick. Didn't work that way.

From that day to this, something has been on my mind I'd like to get off right now. Michael Jordan, fuck you, you scumbag crybaby piece of shit! Fuck you! You're a crybaby bitch, Michael.

Tell ya what, Mike, wanna prove to me you aren't a scumbag plastic piece of shit like LeBron James? Let me win my money back off you. Simple as that.

I think it's only fair. I mean, I got guys who were gonna break my legs, all because you are a crybaby and a bitch because you didn't get your way, poor baby.

Play me in a game if pig, Mike. You chicken shit crybaby. I haven't played organized basketball since sixth grade, and I haven't even touched one in fifteen years, and I'll still smoke your crybaby ass on a basketball court playing pig, crybaby Mike.

Only stipulation being, I have to get *it* on you, you have to make me *A* horse's (apostrophe counts), cockhead. Whad'aya say, Mike? Too much of a chicken shit crybaby, aren't ya?

After I kick your ass in that game of pig, I say we play a round of golf for that $50,000 I now possess. Even up on the golf course, Mike, even fuckin' up, pal.

We can do this in front of the world, or we can do it in private. Either way, I'd take your money both times, crybaby Michael.

You, of all people, know how these fuckers operate. You are a compulsive gambler, yet you still acted like a fucktard kicking that ball. Glad my dad didn't get killed over it. Glad I was able to appease those guys, Mike.

Think I'm crazy, Mike? I am. And I'd fuck you up on the basketball court and the golf course. If you ever grow a set of balls and feel like being humiliated, I am not hard to find. Eighth and Main, right across Eighth Street from Louisville Slugger Bat Factory and Museum in Louisville, Kentucky. I'm there end of March till about the second week of November.

I don't expect to see you, though, Mike, 'cause you're a crybaby.

Hey, Mike, why not set it up at Valholla? I mean, I can't afford to play there as a layman. But I could kick your crybaby ass on that course as a layman and take your money, Mike. I got money to back my words, you crybaby Michael Jordan. You got pull, Mike! You could set it up, Mike! No? I know. Can't quit crying long enough to see the ball.

Kickin' a basketball like a girl in third grade on the playground because she's upset at the referee, poor girl! Mike, I had those fuckers, well, you know how they are, Mike, fuck!

I mean, five large was a lot of money to me back then, I mean *a lot*. I had a coke habit, a drink habit, a gambling habit, a booze addiction, I had a lot of shit going on, Mike, and it all involved money.

Hope I got your attention, Mike. Really.

Shouldn't go around sayin' shit ya don't mean, huh, Mike? I mean, those fuckers don't play, do they? You kickin' that ball all those years ago, do I still take it personal? Sure do. I'm not sayin' shit I don't mean either, Mike. I know better now.

You gonna get owned by me on the court and the course, or are you too much of a crybaby to play, lose against a has-been that never was, loser, bum, broken down, should'a never been like me? I got two large right now with my guy up at home, says you chicken shit out, out. I wish I had the five you cost me, then we'd be cool, sissy.

Chapter 129

I've yet to meet Michael Jordan in person. I've known people he has known. I just extended an invitation for him to reach out and touch base with me so we can do some things together. Hope he responds.

I have met lots of people you have heard of and seen on TV, for both good and bad things. To tell people, "Hey, I met so-and-so!" Or, "Dude, I got to see that plastic guy from TV!" Has never made sense to me.

I had 131 amateur fights, and I have zero trophies. I met a lot of people and did a lot of things, and I tell zero people. Why? It all boils down to, who really gives a flyin' fuck or monkey shit?

I did meet Sylvester Stallone, though. And I wanna talk about meeting that short midget, got-a-cock-in-my-mouth-can't-talk-retard, plagiarizin' piece of poo-poo.

I was about twelve, thirteen, and he was in on a promotional deal with the Giachetti brothers, who are from Cleveland. The promotional outfit was called Tiger Eye Promotions.

Word got out Sly was in town for some business, so one day, my dad took me to Giachetti's gym to work out, and who was there but Sly himself. As soon as I saw him, I went, "Wow! He's a midget!"

Some fucktard comes over to me and went, "Mr. Stallone doesn't like people talkin' about his height!"

He and Bud bumped chests for a minute, and we left. That has been my only meeting with Sly the midget Stallone.

Sure. He's been at a lot of big fights I've attended, parties I've been to, but I've never felt the need to go look down at him and say anything to him. I mean, he made his name by completely plagiarizing living shit out of Chuck Wepner. He's yet to make a movie that means anything.

Hey, Sly, you plagiarizing midget, if you ever need a writer who doesn't steal, uses his own imagination, call me, brah! I've been writing for years, original shit, Sly. Original shit. If I'm comparing my acting skills to yours, I am an Academy Award Winning actor.

Don't be stealing my real-life story and incorporating it into *Rambone 19* or *Rock Head 76* or anything either, Sly. Thanks in advance.

Chapter 130

Dear old Aunt Sally Valloyd Deed Becker Jr. Marty. I don't hate Valloyd Deed Jr. Honest, I don't. She is a plastic cunt, just like her sister. Sal, your kids are losers, period. I mean, I asked that sack of shit you called dad what he thought about Alison dating black guys, and he said he didn't care, she didn't have his last name.

No. Alison isn't a loser for dating black guys. She's a loser because she was raised by losers. Her ex-husband is a racist, just like Valloyd Deed was. I hear Alison was married to an airline pilot for roughly one week, and he found out she dated black guys before they met and he divorced her. Yep. After one week.

I hear your son Little Russ, who has a case of the Hammonds, a big fat blob of pure sissiness, pulls guns on people at stop signs because they looked at him, and he got scared. It's that sissy gene, Sal, it lies in your husband, Charlie no-nuts Marty. You and Sue Slut both married a male copyright of Dot Head Becker. Gutless, spineless, chicken shit sissies, period.

I was told your youngest dotting son, Ian, is trying to make it in the movie business from the confines of Mom and Dad's house in Amherst, the-movie-capital-of-the-world Ohio, in his late twenties. Someone he went to school with asked me if he ever came out of the closet. I told them I didn't know he was in one, we weren't a close family.

Sal, my all-time favorite story about you was when one of the times you were running around on Charlie, you got caught. Remember that?

Sally Valloyd Deed Jr. is getting some stray dick from some guy named John. She's bringin' him out to Russ's bar, that's how we knew. Here's how the entire town found out.

Sal the cunt and John were in a couples bowling league. Their team made it to the finals, and the finals were on a local cable TV station. Another true story. Of course, Charlie no-nuts stood by his man through this. Hey, Sal, you're a cunt. Remember calling your rapist dad to go over to your house and tell me why I was a fuck up, it was all my fault? I do. You cunt.

No. I don't hate you, Valloyd Deed Jr. You raised a sissy, an anorexic, retarded, liberal, cunt, and well, a closeter. I believe in karma, Sal Valloyd. I don't think it's done with you.

I mean, your kids steal too, Sal. Don't they? What about the money in Dot Head's account that disappeared the day she died, Sal Valloyd? Here's a question for you, Aunt Sal cunt Valloyd Jr., how fucking retarded are you, really? I mean, to join a couples-only bowling league with your fucking boyfriend is as smart as grabbing a woman on the ass! And you have an education!

Then you make the finals, and it's on fucking local cable? Worse than being the fortunate league winners, dumber than telling your pilot husband you date black guys, because he's racist like my Papaw, dumber than your fat sissy kid, thinking he's a worldly man, or even a man, you show up and bowl with your boyfriend while Sissy Charlie no-nuts is at the house dusting windows, doing laundry, and panicking he won't get done with his list of chores before you get home from bowling some frames and getting some real man cock.

Sally Valloyd Deed Becker Jr. Marty, that is funny, funny stuff! And you're more retarded than our cousin Lenny, who used to get high on model glue! Do you rape guys the way your dad did women? You are his spittin' image, Aunt Sal Val, thunder hips and all.

No, I don't hate you, Aunt Sal Val. Honest. Maybe I can come over and cook the family dinner one day soon, no?

Chapter 131

Well, there you have it. Not worth a shit, is it? I didn't think so. Hopes and dreams. Papa Tony Ayala Sr. used to talk a lot. He used to tell me story after story. He'd tell me, he'd go, "I fucked up. God gave me four aces, and I fucked them all up."

Again I absorbed a lot of what he said because I respected Papa Tony. Anyhow he told me once, a person with no dreams is dead. He said, if you don't have dreams you will die in no time.

I have dreams. One of those dreams is to take the money from Michael Jordan on the basketball court and golf course. C'mon, Mike, you crybaby. I got two large saying you'll chicken out.

I have more than that, but that's the one we'll concentrate on now because it's up to Mike.

I'd like to meet Jonathon Edwards and see if any of this shit I feel and see is real, and if so, how can I communicate with these people? These beings that tell me shit all the time, and I can't figure it out.

Yeah, Papa, I still have dreams. They get more fucked up and interesting every day. I wanna make a movie with two monkeys and a dog. Really. I do.

https://penzu.com/p/850f778fhttps://penzu.com/p/850f778f.

CHAPTER 132

I try not to reflect on my past too much. When I quit drinking, I really, really looked at my part in my life, and I looked objectively at others' parts concerning my life. I promise, I tried to be as fair, open-minded, and unbiased as possible.

I've dealt with everything and accepted everything. I've done my best to make amends to everyone I've wronged, all that.

Bret Dickinson, one of the Hidden Valley Gang, he's worked at Ford for the past twenty-seven years without knowing for a fact I stole his wallet that had eighty stones in it.

I did, Bret. After I got ahold of you on Facebook, I wanted to set a meeting up, and when I tried to reconnect with you, it said I couldn't. I'd have rather done it in person, which is what I wanted to do.

Anyhow, Bret, I'll try to look you up next time I'm in the area, and if you don't care to see me, tell the go-between who I should trust the money and lost wallet and interest to, please.

I know SalVal and no-nuts Mart were young and married. She was in nursing school to be a dyalisas star. Which to my understanding, she became excellent in her trade.

But I remember them being around. I remember them talking about all the shit going on between my mom and dad. I remember them saying it was horrible.

I get it. They were too busy to help, intervene, anything. I get it. Can't help someone who's mom my dad raped and took advantage of.

Susie and Sissy Pants, wow! You gotta understand, when I was young, I spent a lot of time with them, a lot.

All they did was talk about people while they ate. I'm not saying that to be mean, I'm being honest. They would tell me all the shit my mom and dad were doing that I didn't know about. They used to tell me my mom was no good. And me, a two, three, four-year-old kid.

I'm not making this up, none of this shit pile of my life. Nobody who has been in my life, my blood relatives, except Ma, ever tried to help me. Every one of them went against me.

The mindset I was in at sixteen, seventeen, I mean, I really could'a used some guidance. That was one thing I never had in life—guidance. The guidance I did have was wrong, all wrong.

I might have said something about knowing I wasn't having kids when I was five. I knew then. Had I had kids, they'd have been fucked up, just like Pops.

Here is a funny true story, told to me and countless others by the actors in this scene of sissyism.

Valloyd Deed and Dot Head Becker were living in South Jersey. This was late '70s, early '80s. Susie and Sissy Pants were living in the house on Dodge Drive.

This was like 1979, '80, Sissy Pants was laid off from the Ford plant, and he was working as a guard at the Lorain County Jail. He said one day, an inmate, a black guy, told him he knew where he lived, and he was gonna get 'em when he got out.

Not long after this, he and Susie loaded their little food compacter, Erin, into their truck. They headed out of Dodge Drive, onto Middle Ridge, up to the stop sign at Middle Ridge and Elyria Avenue, right there by the Legion.

There was a black guy on a bike—this is Amherst where the fire horn sounded at six o'clock to let the blacks know it was time to leave town, and it was super rare to see a black person in town—and Charlie said he got scared 'cause he thought it might have been the guy from the jail.

So instead of going where they were headed, they turned around and went back to 909 Dodge Drive, put the truck in the garage, and spent the evening in.

I know all about being scared. I know all about being scared to death. These are people who have told me my entire life shit that was false, not true, lies, period. They are so scared of a guy on a bike they cancel their plans and hide in their house. Charlie was an avid gun enthusiast, so I'm sure he took the family where he could "protect" them.

This is the DNA they passed down to their kids. I must say, my aunts' kids and my uncles' kids, they are all spitting images of their parents.

My parents' kids are spitting images of them.

When people get old, in my opinion, no matter what a piece of shit they were all through life, everyone gets sick, finds Jesus, and talks about all the good they did through life, all that good happy horse shit.

I say that's bullshit.

Look, I get people can change. For better or worse. Change means do things different. An example would be rapist Valloyd Deed coming to me when I was younger and saying something like, "I'm really sorry for what I did, and I'll do anything to show you I want to be a real grandfather."

I never heard anything like that. I never heard anything other than when I asked him if I could stay with them when my parents were divorcing.

Valloyd Deed said, "We're too sick, Bruce."

He was afraid I'd see he was still getting strange pussy and cheating on Dot Head and raping women if he had to. What else can I think, really? That he couldn't find the words to say sorry for raping my mom and threatening to kill me when I was young? So instead, we'll just make Bruce a bad guy, who does bad shit, and treat him like shit for all the shit I did? That's what happened.

About the Author

Under normal circumstances, an "About the Author" section would usually start out with all his or her accomplishments, awards, universities attended and graduated, wonderful wife or husband, beautiful, happy, healthy, kids, and the like.

This is not normal circumstances. The author has never completed or graduated anything. He has no kids, has never been married, and most certainly has never won any awards. Not by normal society's standards anyhow. He has survived. He is still here. That is his accomplishment in life.

Valloyd Bruce, as crazy and nuts as it was, is grateful for Bud and Carolyn being his parents. He loves them with all his heart and soul and would have no one different, if he could have.

He wishes with that same heart and soul that he could have a loving healthy relationship with his siblings and nieces and nephews, but he hasn't much hope in that, as of this writing.

He has done many things in life. He had an abundant amount of athletic ability as a kid. Ability to burn. And burn it he did. He fought amateur for a number of years, and pro a few years.

He also started drinking at an early age. From sexual abuse to alcoholism to violence to living with a preacher and his family to being strung out on dope in Southern California, the author has lived many different lives.

He is proud of none of them. The one thing he is proud of in life, the one and only thing, is he got off booze and drugs and started trying to grow up at thirty-six years old, after twenty-eight years of trying to feel better.

Aside from getting off booze and drugs, meeting his angel is the greatest day of his life. Without Thelma, Sissy Christian Valloyd Bruce Jr. would have been dead a while ago, no doubt. She is his rock and his foundation. She is also a constant reminder what an asshole idiot he really is. And she isn't shy about letting him know it either. He needs that.

Valloyd Bruce, in the end, found hope. He has no idea how or why. But he did.

He hopes you do too.

CPSIA information can be obtained
at www.ICGtesting.com
Printed in the USA
BVHW081052230223
659071BV00006B/134